Outer Coast Solo

A journey alone by sea kayak
along the west coast of Vancouver
Island.

Mike Laanela

Acknowledgements:

This book could not have been written without the hard work of the many historians, academics, writers, and journalists who came before me and whose accounts I have drawn deeply upon to create my own account of life on the west coast of Vancouver Island, British Columbia. I also owe an enormous debt of gratitude to everyone who read the manuscript along the way and offered feedback, and to my family for their support.

All images Copyright © 2015 Mike Laanela,
with the exception of the chart of Vancouver Island.

Published by Van Isle Press
576 Keith Rd, West Vancouver, V7T 1L7

Dedicated to everyone who has ever dreamed of going exploring, and everyone who has ever gone.

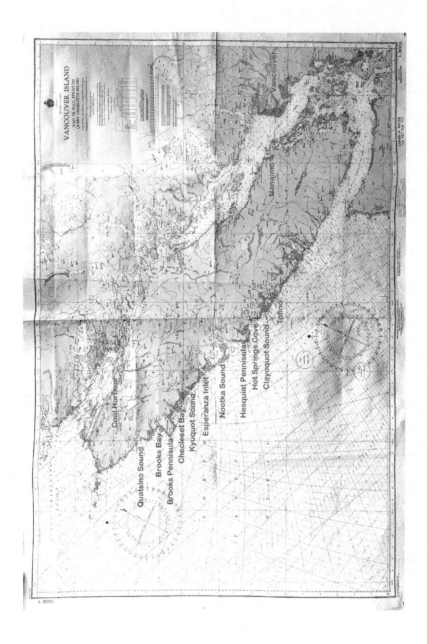

Table of Contents

Prologue

For months now I've been waking up in a cold sweat. Tossed beneath the waves, enveloped in a swirling of white-water, panic overtakes me as my breath runs out. I struggle in the churning sea to find the surface and roll up. I never make it. Instead I wake up with the fear still running inside me. Lying in the darkness, next to me I feel the warmth of Rose through the crumpled sheets and I ask myself why I would go. In the lonely darkness I find no answers. But what matters now is that I am committed to going.

As I lie watching the sunlight slowly bring in the day, my mind wanders over the many times I have left on other journeys. Coming and going has been the rhythm of my life, a never-ending washing in and out like the tides in the sea. In the fifteen years since I left home, this past year with Rose has been the first time I've lived a full year under one roof. My work as a travel writer and photographer has meant airports and bus terminals have become the liminal staging points of my life.

Although many might think of my job as some sort of quest for the exotic, or an unending searching for some elusive unknown, I've always looked at it as mapping new lands in my own self. I've always believed that travel teaches us not just of others, but most of all of oneself. When I am a stranger in new places, everything about me is exposed. But this trip is different. This time I'm going home to explore.

I am a storyteller and this is my tale.

1. Return to Clayoquot

"Excuse me Sir - can I take your tray?"

The Canadian accent of the flight attendant pulls me away from the window. I've been away from home long enough that it now seems exotic. Only a few hours have passed. Once again I am traveling alone. The seatbelt sign lights up and the pilot starts into the familiar landing routine on the intercom. I turn away from the distractions, back to the small window, and catch my first glimpse of Canada's West Coast in two years.

As the plane passes over Vancouver Island on approach to Vancouver my eyes strain for recognition in the landscape below, as if the shoreline should be intimately familiar to me. High above I can feel the swells rolling out of the pea green Pacific as they have since the mountains first rose from the sea. At the edge of the land the swells now rise and curl and break in white explosions on the dark line of the shore. This is the creviced coastline I've come home to explore.

My plan is a simple one – a three-week sea kayak trip down the isolated northwest coast of Vancouver Island. From the northern reaches of Quatsino Sound I'll make my way south to Tofino in Clayoquot Sound. It's a distance of about two hundred nautical miles along a coastline that is only sparsely populated and mostly unreachable by road. I have no certainty about my success alone on this trip. But I need that uncertainty now.

I used to guide kayak trips on this coast, but intentionally I've chosen this route that I've never paddled before. While my life of travelling may seem like an adventure of unbounded limits to those who meet me on a plane or a bus, to me it has become too routine. That certainty is killing me now. What I need now is to push up against the ordinary limits of my life to discover what lies beyond. In simple terms I need to know what I have in me. I'm not seeking escape, but a confrontation with those parts of myself that the everyday routines of life have made inaccessible to me.

The coastline disappears as the mountains of the Vancouver Island Range rise up to meet us. The snowcaps on the peaks cradle turquoise lakes. In the valleys the lush temperate rainforest is chequered with clear-cuts, scars from the logging industry that used to dominate this coast.

Past the mountains on the sheltered east coast I spot a lake in the suburban sprawl of Nanaimo, the small city where my parents still live. In the woods nearby I search for the roof of my family's house without any luck.

From the airport in Vancouver I cross to Vancouver Island by ferry, returning home on a route I have done countless times before. "How long are you staying?" says my mother as soon as I am in the door. I have not crossed my parent's doorstep in two years. "A couple weeks to get ready," I say. Already my mind is heading away, eager to begin with this journey. My father calls me the prodigal son.

***

The next day I pull my sea kayaking gear in the basement out of storage. Everything reeks with folded memories. I spread my tent out on the back lawn and peg it out. Tucked in the corners is sand from my last trip, now years ago. A paddling jacket unfurls with the story of the beach where it was found and the summer romance that brought me there. There are my two paddles - gifts from my former boss. My camp stove is corroded and pitted from the ever-present sea salt.

Spread across the basement floor everything looks like a costume and props cast aside at the end of a show. Since that last summer working as sea kayak guide out of Tofino on the island's west coast, I have been travelling almost non-stop. Looking at the gear that used to be the everyday accoutrements of my life I am reminded of the changes. Now in Australia I have made a new home, found a new love, and begun a life.

Under the porch of the house I evict the spiders from my sea kayak and pull her out beside my tent on the lawn. The two sit reunited in the sun like old friends eager for another journey together. My kayak's simple ivory coloured hull is scratched and chipped from years of hard use, but she just looks well seasoned to my eyes today. Several years ago I had her custom built with an extra layer of Kevlar on the bottom for extra insurance against collisions with rocky outer coast reefs. Even with the staff discount at the kayak shop, she still cost me twice what I'd ever paid for a car. Even then I was promising myself that one day I would do this trip. As I sit for a moment in the warm summer sun, surrounded by the familiar gear of my old life I ask myself why it took so long.

Some good friends have asked me to take them kayaking as a wedding present and I agree. A few days in my old stomping grounds will be a good shakedown trip to get me ready for my solo journey ahead. We drive across to the west coast for Tofino. This is where I used to guide kayak trips out into Clayoquot Sound, a land of temperate rainforest, deep narrow inlets, and long summers of fog. Guiding sea kayak tours was my summer job while in university, but even then it meant much more than that. Out on the water day after day, week after week, summer after summer, it was a simple way of defining who I was. My life has moved on since those simple days and I know already this journey will not take me back to them.

The town of Tofino is the same, although it has grown up a bit from the fishing village it once was. A new crop of garish signs line the road, tugging at the wallets of the tourists who flood in every summer. I take my friends Graham and Lorrie on a four-day trip up to Hot Springs Cove, a natural destination for a honeymooning couple. The weather is brilliant. They moon together while I entertain them with exaggerated stories of my guiding days. Graham and I have been on trips like this together before, but for Lorrie, a prairie girl, this world of tidal pools and bright white West Coast beaches, crisscrossed by the recent tracks of bears and deer is a new wonderland. It's a delight to watch her skipping down the beaches in the sun, discovering green anemones and limpets in the tide pools by the rocks. It reminds me of my own feelings of discovery when I was teaching myself to kayak. I think of Rose back in Sydney and wish for a minute she was here with us doing the same thing. But I know it was my decision to come on this trip alone, and ultimately that is what I need to do.

I have other concerns. It's been two years since I last paddled and it is obvious that I'm not nearly as fit as I was when I was guiding full-time. To keep the two honeymooners entertained I rehearse self-rescues and 'Eskimo rolls' in the warmer water of the bays, first on one side and then the other. Later I progress to more challenging tricks, pulling the spare paddle off my back deck underwater, reassembling the two piece while holding my breath, and then flipping myself to the surface, or rolling up with no paddle at all. Despite my enthusiasm, my old skills return slowly. Too frequently I tire or blow a roll and have to bail out to save myself. With each failure the cold awakenings, now alone at night, become more frequent. It is then that I can't escape the doubts that haunt me. Am I really ready for this? What is it that has driven me here?

At the hot springs, a wide fissure in the granite at the tip of Sharp Point we spend a whole day soaking, moving in the summer sun from the heat of the thermal pools to the tidal pools awash with sea creatures clinging to the rocks amongst the cold fingers of the sea. At sunset I pull out a wine bottle I had secretly stashed in the tip of my kayak out and we stay on past dark. When it is time to return to our camp by the government wharf, we realize we have no flashlight. So we have to walk back in the dark. It is quiet in the starlit woods. We feel our way along in the shadows, without even a sliver of moon, up and downstairs and along a full mile of rambling boardwalk. Somehow we make it to camp without any injuries. I tell myself I will need to be more foresightful if I wish to make it home safely on my next voyage down this coast.

Watching Graham and Lorrie together, I think of Rose and wish she had a part of me to touch and hold on to while I am here. When we get back to Tofino, I pick out a ring by a local native carver from a sparkling glass case. It is a silver band with a carving of a hummingbird inlaid in gold. The woman at the counter tells me it represents the healer, the bringer of joy and light. It feels right in the way that it reminds me of Rose. I check it for size on my smallest finger before she packs it safely in a little gold box.

Back in Nanaimo in the basement of my parents' house, the last of my preparations begin to engross me. I draw up equipment lists, repair gear, plan, buy and pack three weeks of food. Each item is fastidiously examined. Then checked. And then double-checked. Then assigned a place in one of almost a dozen waterproof bags. Each of these bags is then carefully packed, and then repacked, then fitted into particular space in the boat. Some items are discarded, others are replaced, but mostly it is a matter of recall and reuse

The evening before I go, I call Rose back in Sydney one last time. In the time delays of the long distance transmission we speak over each other and listen together in long pauses. She makes it clear she would rather have me home. I can't blame her for feeling this way. In the confusion I hear her say my name one last time as I hang up the phone

2. Coal Harbour

It's a day's journey up the Island Highway to Coal Harbour where I'll be launching. My father helps to tie the kayak to the van's roof. My mother and sister drive me north. As the highway enters the mountains, the houses and farms begin to fade, the human presence is reduced to a thin black artery. The smell of the forest, spruce, pine and Douglas fir tree, is intimately familiar to me, such a contrast to the pungent eucalyptus oils that hang in the air of the Blue Mountains west of Sydney where I have been rock climbing lately. Even the ocean smells different here.

My mother drives since I'm confused about which side of the road we should be on. As she does she runs over her list of concerns, "Why don't I have a radio, or some sort of beacon? Will just three flares really be enough?" In the valleys the clouds hang low, as if held up by the mountains themselves. "What about bears and my bags of food? Could I catch fish as I go?" At a lunch stop on the shores of a lake we all pull on jackets to cheat the wind while my sister pours a thermos of hot tea. "And if you twist an ankle or break an arm?" my mother continues. Like a worried customer on a guided trip, I placate her with set answers that seem like half-truths to me.

Later on the grey streets of Port Hardy, we park for dinner, fish and chips in a café by the quiet pier. As we sit waiting for our meal to arrive I watch the unexpectant faces of the locals passing on the street. For many years now the economy of this island, the logging and the fishing, has been dying. In the fish shop the smoky vapours of the deep fryer mingle with the reek of decline. The steady money that once fuelled this town is long gone. Those who stay here now can only see themselves as guardians of the past, it seems to me. I don't share their reluctance to move on.

The long summer evening lingers. From Port Hardy we turn west into the mountains again and roll toward the ocean on the outer coast. Finally just past the smart houses of the New Quatsino Indian Reserve, the town of Coal Harbour slips out of the trees. The ocean comes in here to meet us. Coal Harbour hides at the back of the narrow inlets of Quatsino Sound nearly twenty miles from the open Pacific as the crow flies. On the waterfront a large hangar sits shrouded in the cloak of its own rust. It was once a RCAF seaplane base in the war against Japan, and later a whaling station in the last years before the ban. It wasn't until the short-lived boom-times of the 1970s that the highway to the east coast was finally opened. Nothing much looks to have happened here since.

The yeasty smell of home baking greets us at the front door of our bed and breakfast. Chattering full speed, a pixie woman shows us to our rooms, every inch of wall space pasted with flea market kitsch. Cramped from the long day of driving, I step out alone for a walk through the overgrown streets. On the main street the tiny store shows no signs of life so I cross the empty pavement to the only café. From behind the Formica counter the lone occupant, an enormous waitress in a polyester dress, watches me swing open the door. Suspicious eyebrows rise over the scarlet cover of her paperback book. I glance up at the menu to appear busy. She returns to the romance in the yellowed pages.

Next to the columns of burgers and fries hangs a picture of Coal Harbour in greater days. A massive whale lies beneath the flensing blades on the town's pier, excoriated and eviscerated like rashes of bacon. The men stand proudly beside their killing work.

I'm eager to be away.

3. Departure

The next morning the clouds hang lower still on the steep slopes of the inlet. Down at the government dock a neglected fleet of fishing boats sits idle on slack lines. A floatplane thunders across the water breaking the silence, buzzing into the grey void somewhere beyond the end of the road. On the slippery rocks in front of the old whalers' pier, beside the lumps of rusted cables and broken pilings, I finally begin packing my kayak. The tide is rising as if to meet me. Like an eager puppy wanting to play, the cold water nibbles at my feet.

Out there on the water is where I want to be. Sea kayaking for me has always been about exploring my own limits. When I started to sea kayak, I had no one to go with and knew little of the sea. As a child on the beaches of Australia I had played in the Pacific. But at the age of four we had relocated and I spent most of the rest of my youth in Ontario. Like most Canadians, I knew all about lakes and canoes. But the sea? That was a world apart. Then, when I was fourteen we moved to Vancouver Island, and maybe something of my earliest memories were rekindled. Instantly I felt a desire to immerse myself in the sea. After university I bought a second-hand sea kayak from a newspaper ad and a couple books from the Mountain Equipment Co-op and began to plan my first trip.

The first book, entitled *Sea Kayaking – A manual for long distance touring*, by John Dowd was the de facto Bible of the sport, a book of sea crossings, drogue anchors for weathering hurricanes, and quasi-military rafting formations. Thumbing through, I got the misimpression that as long as I kept land in sight, I would be safe. The second book was an idyllic paddling guide to B.C.'s coast, by a peaceful-looking German couple, whose snapshots of island campsites and sunny paddling inspired an altogether different sort of image. I folded it open to Chapter One and using the two-tone map marked NOT FOR NAVIGATION I set off up North Vancouver's Indian Arm. The biggest danger on that trip was the wakes of the super-yachts to-ing and fro-ing from the mansions lining the densely settled shore.

By some miracle I survived my own self-apprenticeship to the sport. After that, many of my kayak explorations were solo affairs, ventures farther and farther a field, further away from people and closer and closer to myself. I still remember the fear of my first open crossing of Johnstone Strait on the east coast of the island late one September. Although today I would look at the distance as minor – just over a mile – on that cool fall morning, it was an entire ocean. In my tiny little boat, alone on the water a real terror held me all the way across. It was such a simple experience but that first solo crossing left me with an opening into myself, like a well that tapped a deep clear spring. Later, as I continued to travel and kayak, again and again, I returned to the well, alone, to quench the new thirst it had given me. It wasn't until I started working as a guide that I started paddling regularly with other people. In the company of other more experienced paddlers I learned practical lessons and was able to push rapidly to more challenging conditions. But I always came back to solo paddling. In solitude I found a way of reducing a situation to its most essential, a quality always missing in the chattering of a group. From it I gained a certain kind of knowledge, an intimate knowing of self that can only come from the rawness of experiences faced alone. What solo paddling offers might be best thought of as an ultimate sort of truth. It's one thing to believe that you can do something; it is quite another to know you have done it, you alone.

Now, in truth what has driven me here is nothing more than a single-minded need, to do something that lies beyond my ordinary boundaries. The risk is just as essential as the journey itself. I need the uncertainty. I need to push up against the ordinary boundaries of my life and break them open, or fail trying. I need to go to the bottom of myself to see clearly the barest parts of who I am.

Right now though as I pack I am happy. The routine is intimately familiar. At nineteen feet long, my boat holds nearly three times what I can carry on my back and I'm thankful for every inch of space. Years of packing and unpacking have taught me to load it a certain way. Although this trip will be longer and more committed than any other, my old routine still seems the best way. Behind my seat I stuff two old wine bladders filled with water. Up the bow I push my rolled up wetsuit, a small tarp for my kitchen, a down sleeping bag, one food bag bulging with two weeks' lunches and snacks, a cook set with two pots, a stove, two fuel bottles, a plastic thermal coffee mug (the UBC logo fading along with memories of early morning lectures) - all the odd bits of gear I might need during the day. Then I shift my attention to the stern and start working the pieces of my overnight camp down the back hatch - a sleeping pad, then my tent, two more large bags of food with breakfasts and dinners, a case of camera gear, and a large pack full of fleecy thermal clothes. Everything is carefully balanced not to upset the trim of the boat.

My mother and sister wait patiently as I finish, slightly amazed to see the huge pile of yellow bags reduced to almost nothing. Finally on top I nestle my bag of voices, a small stack of journals, histories and stories of others who have come before me to this coast. There are two anthropologists, a missionary, several explorers and one hereditary chief. It's an arbitrary selection. Of the stack of books gleaned from second-hand stores, only the lightweight paperbacks have been allowed to accompany me on this trip. Many other hardcovers remain back on my shelves. The selection also is biased by history. The native people of this coast were not often published until the cultural revival in the 1970s, when some of the elders recorded what remained of their oral histories. The majority of their stories either passed unrecorded on paper, inaccessible to outsiders like me, or were recorded by outsiders, a practice that inevitably compromises the authenticity of their voices.

With everything secure, I seal the hatch lids closed and snap the straps across. Just one small yellow bag remains. It holds the odds and ends like a few snack bars, a spare compass and whistle, and sunglasses and sunscreen (so hopeful!) that I might need while afloat. Plus the little gold box with a ring. This yellow bag is the one thing I'll be able to take with me if I lose the kayak and have to swim. Next I pull on my neoprene spray-skirt and my life jacket. Its pockets are also carefully packed with the barest essentials for survival on the coast – waterproofed lighters, fish hooks, flares and energy bars, even a plastic orange tube shelter. Then, there is nothing left to do but say goodbye and trade hugs.

My mother looks on stoically as I drag my kayak a few feet out into the deeper water. Standing on the shoreline, they wave and snap photos as I push off. I drift a hundred metres out and then stop and turn to watch them retreat to the van and climb the hill out of town. Then I turn my eyes back past the houses to the forest rising at the edge of town. I dip my paddle and pull my first real strokes.

Finally, I am away.

4. Quatsino Narrows

My kayak skates across the icy reflections of the clouds, an arrowhead of ripples spilling off the bow. So close to the water, there is a feeling of movement so slippery and intimate that I can almost feel the water's cold caress on my hull. The familiar push-pull effort of the double-ended paddle forces a surging warmth through my blood that runs out to the tips of my chilled fingers. For a moment I'm connected to the start of every journey I've ever made. This point of departure contains a thrill only travellers can know. Now nobody knows how this story will unfold.

Across the harbour the town slips away and the forest of Sitka spruce, Douglas fir, hemlock, and cedar crowds the shore. Drooping boughs laced with Spanish moss shroud a cliff face from which sea-caves bleed a visceral darkness into the sea. Despite the fact that it's a midsummer day, there is a chilly dampness in the air. For a while I just listen to the drip and slice of my paddle blades. But just beneath the beating rhythm of my own anxious breath there is a quiet rumbling I can't pin down. Is some Leviathan in motion beneath this placid plane?

Ahead on the surface of the water I spot a small grey feather. Rainwater has collected in the hollow of its curve. In the ripples off my bow it bobs like a boat. As I float past it, I pluck it from the water and turn it over in my hand. It's a great blue heron's feather. Distant cousins of storks, herons have always been a favourite of mine. Their long fragile legs and ungainly wings belie their graceful presence. Standing still along the water's edge, tiny prey swim by their feet. Then in a blur they strike. Patience and timing are the essence of the heron's success. They are also the twin virtues of sea kayaking that I will need to survive on my trip down this coast. I take this chance find as an omen and lodge the feather in the seam of my cap, tucked close above my right ear. Perhaps it might guide me on my way.

Another guide of a more empirical nature sits folded and encased in plastic on my deck. Labelled 3679 Quatsino Sound, it is one of six charts representing the coast that I will rely on for the trip. Inside the thick black borders are the tawny abstractions of land. Although I'm navigating on water, it's by the topographical curves that rise up into mountains that I will keep my bearings. Accompanying the land is the whiteness of the sea. Blue hydrographic squiggles claim to reveal the secrets beneath me. From the codex of soundings and fathoms I can read the water, and make estimations of conditions ahead. In some places where the land meets the sea are a few thin green smudges. These mark the intertidal zones, the nether regions that appear and disappear between each wash of the tides. These are the beaches and creek mouths where I will make my camps.

These charts are more than just physical maps though. Charting of this coast was initially a predilection of the Europeans. In 1774 the Spanish naval officer Juan Perez first passed along these shores. Along the whole coast of the island he approached land only once, in search of water, but never stepped ashore. Others soon followed, including the famous navigators of the Age of Exploration such as Captain Cook, the European first to land in 1777. Captain Vancouver followed in 1792 and made the first chart of the island that was to take his name. But it wasn't until 1862, that Captain Richards of the Royal Navy first accurately charted the interior of Quatsino Sound, deflowering the mysteries of its passages with the nub of a surveyor's pen.

My own chart is dated June 14, 1991. It's not the product of one mind or the collective memory of a people, but of aerial surveys, computers and digital imagery. Despite its physical accuracy, it still raises as many questions as answers. The place names in English, Spanish, French, Kwakwala and Nuu-chah-nulth, all speak of a deeper history that the simple mapping cannot reveal. The scattered symbols of Indian reserves, abandoned villages, churches, old fish canneries, are all fragments of stories now rarely told. As one who considers myself both a visitor and at home on this coast, their stories are fascinating to me. Who were these people who lived on this land and fished in this sea? What fears or desires drove them to leave home and why did they come to this place? Did they only pass through, or did they make a commitment to stay?

***

Some beery voices interrupt my reverie. A boat of sport fishermen putters past, trolling above the bottom one hundred and sixty metres below for some action. Not wanting to be disturbed I skirt the shoreline to keep well out of their way. A few minutes later the sound of their engine fades behind me and the other rumbling, now clearly audible, rises up in its place. It's louder and more menacing than before. Checking my chart, I realize it must be the churning waters of the Quatsino Narrows.

I squint my eyes. On the surface of the water, about a mile ahead, I can see a bubbling white line. On my chart I measure the distance with the width of my thumb and confirm my guess of a mile. The Quatsino Narrows is a tidal rapid, a saltwater version of a white-water river. Two nautical miles long, and only a couple hundred meters wide, with each changing of the tides it boils up in a mess of whirlpools and fierce upwellings. Everything flowing in or out of the inner sections of the Sound, all the water, fish, seals, fishing boats, kayaks and stray logs - everything has to pass through this narrow slot. Right now though, the churning white-water I can see in the distance tells me the tide is still against me, flooding in from the ocean, a river filling an inland sea. Knowing it will be impossible to battle upstream for some time, I head for a tiny bay, already thinking of lunch.

***

At the tail-end of the rapids, the swirling currents spin out onto the quiet inlet like tops set loose on a polished floor. A wispy Scotch mist hangs on the hilltops, weaving through the branches of the tallest Sitka spruce. Close by a seal splashes after salmon that have already arrived in the inlet for the late summer spawning. The seal spots me on the shore, also eating alone. Curious of the newcomer, it bobs along in a back-eddy full of flotsam - a tangle of bull kelp, broken branches and a bright yellow motor oil bottle.

An eaglet's rough cry echoes across from the far side of the channel. Like fresh surveyor's pegs, the parents' white heads are easy to spot against the backdrop of green smudges. They call back with clean trills, scales that corkscrew in the air. Now after months of feeding the eaglet is fat in the nest. The parents have grown skinny themselves feeding it with salmon caught on the wing. It is time for the young bird to feed on its own.

Teasing and coaxing, the parents entice the fledgling to fly. I watch it step up to the edge of the nest, well above the canopy of the surrounding trees, and I am reminded of one of Emily Carr's paintings. It flaps once. Then again, nearly falling off balance. Then it pushes off into the open air with a sudden leap, wings wide as if grasping the air. All the way to the ground, it thrashes and bangs off branches and trunks, before disappearing into the undergrowth with a crack.

For some time only silence follows the parents' calls. Finally, a rustling of mottled brown wings in the foliage heralds the fledgling's re-emergence. Bursting from the cover, it flaps to a low branch, beginning an erratic trip branch by branch up to the safety of the nest.

While I eat my lunch and watch the show, I keep an eye on the rapids for any signs of changes. I'm waiting for slack tide, the short window of still water when the current reverses. In the case on my deck along with my chart is a laminated tide table. It is a grid of dates, times and heights that tell me when science says the tides are going to change. I was counting on a change early in the afternoon to let me through the narrows. But the swirling water in front of me obviously does not agree. These tide tables are only accurate in one place and for this chart that's Tofino, still about 200 nautical miles away. My estimation about the narrows was very hopeful at best. The laws of hydrodynamics, and particularly tidal rapids, are inexplicably complex. Anyone who travels on the sea, particularly with a small craft like mine, soon learns that progress depends not on schedules and desires, but on chance and circumstance. It takes what sailors call 'local knowledge' to get around on this coast.

Down at the water's edge my kayak shifts. The rising water begins to lift it and I wander down to pull it up a few feet more. It seems the tide will not be turning for some time and there is nothing to do but wait, so I tie the bowline to a tree on the shore.

Unable to proceed, I concede to the strength of the greater forces and lie down on the pebbles for a rest.

***

Cold starbursts on my face wake me before long. A light rain is falling, leaving chiaroscuro dots on the pebbles. I get up to stretch and consider my options. In the narrows the current is still running against me, so I look around for a makeshift shelter from the approaching shower. A tangle of huckleberry and salal bushes guards the entrance to the forest behind me. I push through and pass through a crowded vestry of deciduous alder trees, before emerging out to the open forest of an old Sitka grove. Beside me, a trunk as stout as a stone column rises from its broad base of roots. Far above the branches intertwine in an organic configuration of arches. A green pane of needles and leaves diffuse the light from the sky. Pillows of velvety moss that almost glow with lushness sit in the crooks of the branches while diaphanous Spanish moss dangles from their tips. I lean up against a punky red stump and let the fecund richness infuse me.

Back when I was guiding I used to walk the tourists through the boardwalk on Meares Island, showing them the complex systems of the temperate rainforest, as dense and vibrant as any in the world. Those who live here just as often call the west coast the wet coast, because of the ridiculous amount of rain that pours from the heavens all year. It's the first stop for the big winter storms that blow in off the northern Pacific Ocean. Up to ten meters of rain each year falls in some valleys, creating some of the thickest rainforest in the world. Just like a tropical rainforest, the column of life stretches from the bugs and fungi in the thin soil, up the tree trunks past the birds nesting in the hollows, to the colonies of tiny voles inhabiting the green platforms of foliage where the trees meet the open sky.

The thick ground cover makes it difficult for me to push very far back into the woods, so after poking around a while I head back toward the beach. At the edge of the alder stand, I hear a hollow thud under my feet. A fallen tree has pulled up the earth with its roots. Looking down I spot some tiny white flecks in the rich black soil that has been exposed. I realize I'm standing on the grounds of an abandoned native village.

The white flecks are tiny shards of clamshells, evidence of shellfish harvests long past. Together with the black soil I can tell it's a midden, an archaeological term for a traditional native refuse pile. Before the changes that came with the arrival of the Europeans, the first people of the coast lived in semi-permanent villages. They shifted with the changing seasons to regular camps to harvest the widely scattered resources in their territory. At the villages, anything that no longer had any use was simply thrown into heaps outside of the houses, some times intentionally piled against the outside walls to stop drafts from blowing in. Since most of their possessions were made of natural materials, the refuse piles would compost into this rich black soil. But not everything decomposed.

My sister once worked as an archaeologist in Clayoquot Sound, documenting First Nations occupation and use of the coast for the Nuu-chah-nulth Tribal Council. After two seasons in the field she told me that almost every beach and bay had middens of some size, with thousands scattered through out their territory. While some were just food harvesting sites, other middens might reveal a story of a village that once stood there told in fragments of bone, shell, wood and, in rare cases, chipped or carved stone.

Looking around at the size of the alder trees I make a hasty estimation that the site has been unoccupied for at least fifty or a hundred years or even more. Alders are always the first trees to reoccupy a site when humans have left. Quick growing, their roots nourish the soil, returning nitrogen for other trees that follow. Somewhere in the records of the Royal Navy surveyors and the

Federal Indian Agents I might be able to look up the time the colonists first noticed the desertion of the village, but in most cases the abandonment of the villages was a slow and undocumented process.

Dating the arrival of the first people is an even more difficult challenge. Despite years of digging in the black pits, archaeologists have yet to reach any consensus about how or even when they believe the first people reached the island's west coast. The two main theories in archaeological circles are for a coastal migration from the north by a maritime people, or settlement by inlanders pushing out through the great river valleys of the mainland coast. The two schools of thought have their own camps of supporters. So far, neither side has unearthed evidence to conclusively prove their view.

Archaeologists do agree that the first people probably arrived on the coast some time after the glaciers began to retreat about thirteen thousand years ago (although some theories suggest their arrival before). Back then the sea levels were much lower. After the ice melted the sea rose up well above current levels, flooding the land for a millennium or two before it settled down to today's level about six thousand years ago. In this way almost all of the evidence of any earlier indigenous inhabitation was submerged beneath the waves. So the archaeological record can only tell a story that begins in the middle. Amongst the rocks and pebbles on six beaches here in Quatsino Sound archaeologists have found the earliest evidence of humans on the island's west coast - chipped stone tools estimated to be at least five thousand years old.

But archaeology is just one way of understanding the origins of people. A third theory of origins lies in the native oral traditions. The various groups on this coast were so isolated that each had its own origin stories, but most features some version of the exploits of various God-like creatures called the Transformers who took the form of animals, giants or natural features. In one book Quatsino Chief James Wallas recounts the creation of the land and islands by 'the Transformer with a two-headed serpent for a belt'. This transformer and his brother first stepped ashore on the northern tip of the island. He left his brother there and walked down the coast creating mountains and islands as he went, drawing on his serpent-garment for strength. Once finished he returned to the north, awoke his sleeping brother, bequeathed him the island and departed.

It's worth noting there are no large snakes on the island. But equally curious is that all the native cultures on the coast have oral histories of at least one great flood that pushed them up to live in the mountain tops before they came back down with the sea. Those could be memories of the tsunamis that sometimes hit the coast, or maybe of a time when the sea itself rose higher.

***

I walk back out to the beach and the rain and check my chart. The 'I.R.' marking meaning 'Indian Reserve' that I missed is clearly visible inside the dashed line. It forms a rough rectangle around the beach, like a fence. Whose identity did this line serve to delineate I wonder – those inside it's small boundaries or those who drew it? The distinction between native and non-native or white and non-white is still one of the most politically significant divisions on the coast. This patch of land strategically located beside the entrance to the narrows, the land now belongs to the Quatsino Band. They are the modern amalgamation of the original four tribes that once inhabited the sound. Their nineteen reserves were allotted by the federally appointed Indian Commissioner O'Reilly in 1886 - a grand total of 346 hectares for the people who once owned the whole of Quatsino Sound.

The name Quatsino is a European label, a derivative of the original Kwakwala word "Koskimo", which has been translated as 'people of the north country', 'the downstream people', or 'people who lived on the other side of the island'. They all seem to be various nuances of 'them over there'. Which is what the Quatsino were – very possibly the most isolated population on the entire island. Historically, the band is part of what European ethnographers named the Kwakiutl linguistic group, a fierce people by most early accounts of Europeans. They controlled the northern entrance to the northern entrance busy native trading route that ran up the protected waters of the Inside Passage between the mainland and the Vancouver Island. 'Kwakiutl' is also a European name, another derivative that means, among other things, 'smoke of the world.' In an act of self-definition, the people have since swapped the spelling and pronunciation, at least in ethnographic circles, for Kwakwaka'wakw, a word from the original Kwakwala language. It is a name I suspect only a handful of very dedicated non-natives will ever learn to pronounce correctly. Native languages on the coast are an unapproachable minefield of guttural utterances for non-native tongues.

On the beach the light drizzle soon turns to a beating rain, pulling the clouds down with it. I pull out my poncho and retreat to the sanctuary of my boat. In the cramped cockpit my legs slip into place. The boat rocks comfortably as I push off backwards, out into the moving water midstream. Although the current is still running against me, the worst of its wild strength is gone. Once again the waterway has become my free route of passage. It is on the water, not the land, that I feel in my place here. Behind me a loon, a bird of calm waters, calls out a long goodbye.

5. Old Quatsino

The narrow channel is about two miles long with a sharp right turn at the far end. Knowing the current will be strongest out in the middle, I stick close to the rocky shore. There is no danger to my light boat in these easy conditions. I use an old kayaker's trick to make headway against the current, catching free rides on the swirling back-eddies that spin off the rocky points and playfully pull me along. Still, I have to work hard to keep my boat on a straight course. It's a bit like fighting the wrong way up an escalator through a crowd – progress is slow and hard won. Out in the main flow a fishing boat slowly passes me, the old diesel engine throbbing steadily against the current, a loose steel cable in the spreaders clanging like a dinner bell. Through the small window in the wheelhouse the captain waves from the wheel. I suspect neither of us would prefer the other's seat.

An old friend of mine in Tofino, a salty offshore veteran who did the maintenance around the kayak shop, couldn't live without half a dozen boats for all the threads of his life. Decked out in rubber gloves, gas mask and bug-eyed from the fumes of fibre-glassing on a hot summer day, he would lecture me that boat design was all about compromise. No one boat could be everything because each improvement stole from its other strengths. Make it wider for stability and storage and you took away speed and handling in rough seas. Make it longer for speed and you reduced manoeuvrability. Add a curve along the length of the keel, known as rocker, to improve turning and you lost straight tracking, valuable against crosswinds or in rough seas. In the end, to understand any watercraft you needed to know the purpose and in some cases even the person it was designed for.

My own boat, chosen after two years of deliberation, is a modern Kevlar craft, loosely based on the original Aleutian native hunting design, but with some modern improvements. Slim and long for outer coast touring, at three times my own height, she is only a hand-span wider than my hips at the cockpit. This lean shape makes her fast in the water. The deep V shape of the bow makes her seaworthy cutting through surf and waves. Underneath me she rounds instead of flattening for responsive balance in rough seas. Fully loaded I can confidently run her in through heavy surf to land on a beach. But she doesn't touch bottom in ankle deep water.

The equipment onboard is a homage to simplicity. My chair is a simple foam pad in the centre cockpit, with a backrest for long days. Two pedals at my feet are linked by wires to the rudder. Another string allows me to retract it up onto the deck. It's a common mistake to assume rudders on kayaks are meant primarily for turning. The real use is to keep the boat on a straight course while paddling in strong crosswinds. For steering and manoeuvring I leave my rudder up most of the time and rely instead on sweep strokes and special sculls and braces.

In breaking waves anything not lashed down securely becomes a liability, so just the essentials remain on deck. Lashed behind me within arm's reach is my spare paddle in two pieces and a plastic hand pump called "Thirsty" - my best friend after a capsize. On the foredeck the only gear is the bowline and the two essential tools of coastal navigation - the plastic chart case and a compass. The bulbous compass is an offshore yachting style that rolls with the waves. It is permanently mounted on the deck where I can read it in rough seas.

As guides we used to spend hours debating the merits of different kayak designs, dreaming up fantasy boats, while fiercely deriding each other's preferences. Even amongst professionals working side by side, no one boat was considered superior by any majority. Our individual affinity for a certain boat designs was borderline obsessive about details, a state of mind that could only come from living from a kayak for several months of each year. To a certain extent our boats were extensions of ourselves. In the end though, as seaworthy as I believe her to be, this boat, like any other, is only as safe as the crew she sets to sea with. The most important choices are the ones made while at sea.

***

By the time I get through the channel the fishing boat is long gone and I've worked up a sweat for the first time today. It feels good to be underway once again. Already I'm feeling more at home in my boat. The familiar effort of paddling relaxes me. Up ahead the main passage of Quatsino Sound opens up and somewhere out of sight ahead the open ocean awaits.

Hugging the shoreline I round a corner into a sheltered bay. A large clearing faces the ocean. The tell-tale black earth of a midden, flecked with the familiar white shells, oozes from cuts in the embankment below the clearing. It is at least eight feet deep. A quick look at my chart confirms it's another Indian Reserve, the old village of Quatsino, once the largest in the Sound. Now just two houses, one yellow, empty but sound, and another grey and abandoned, fight off a wave of blackberry bushes that is cresting at their front doors. Nearby a white picket fence pokes through shoulder high grass. Amongst the fence posts, native carvings of killer whales stand on poles, sharp outlines in strong red, white and black. They are wooden headstones. Another white sign says in clear block letters: 'IR No trespassing." Once a village, this clearing has become a graveyard for the elderly who still wish to return.

As I glide past I hear voices coming from behind me inside the picket fence. Three stocky men appear in raincoats. They fall silent and walk toward the houses before stopping and gathering around something on the ground I can't see. Without exchanging a word they cover it over with a tarp. Curious, I wave but get no response. I'm not invisible here, the only boat on the water.

Not wanting to disturb them in their private task, I paddle on past the government wharf where only one small boat is tied up. A small islet guards the other end of the village, creating a quiet cove. As my kayak drifts out across the still water I scare a shy river otter away from its fishing, sending it scurrying up the bank on four tiny legs. Four herons perched high in some cedar trees are also startled. They take flight with a chorus of loud squawking. The harshness of their voices echoes across the silent cove.

This village is Old Quatsino, but was once called Hwates, and Quattishe, depending on how far back in history I read. Archaeologists sifting through the layers of the black earth documented four thousand years of human habitation here in this village. In the last days of the 19th century it was here that the remnant clans of the four tribes that once lived scattered throughout Quatsino Sound gathered to make one last stand against the white man's diseases and settlements spreading across their land.

It may never be possible to determine with any accuracy how many people once inhabited all of Quatsino Sound. Estimates of the pre-contact population vary widely from two thousand to several thousand. But soon after the arrival of the Europeans the population began dropping rapidly. According to the first recorded survey, by 1840 the population was only 1150. Less than fifty years later only 176 native people remained. Their numbers decimated, they retreated to this village. By 1929 the population reached its nadir at 46.

Much of this tragic story passed unrecorded in the white man's records. The largest documented drop in the population of Quatsino Sound - when eighty percent of the population died - was during a time of enormous social and economic disruption. The chiefs were wealthy from the fur trade, but the diseases the passing traders brought remained long after they had left.

To this day the events of that time are only half revealed through incomplete memoirs of explorers, traders, and native elders, or heard through oral histories in the many communities of both whites and natives that still dot the coast. These echoes are now several generations old and are open to widely varying interpretations. The 'truth' of what brought about the near extinction of a people is difficult to pin down.

The story is much the same as the rest of North America; only the dates are a bit later here due to the area's isolation. Pre-contact estimates of the entire population of the west coast of Vancouver Island range from ten to thirty thousand, but will always remain nearly impossible to verify. We do know the population fell from eight thousand in 1835, to sixteen hundred by 1929. That's an eighty percent decline in 100 years. Officially the current government calls that history 'difficult', which seems to still hold less than the truth.

The reasons for this deserve more than a summary answer. Warfare, alcohol, migration away and new diseases have been blamed traditionally as the responsible culprits. This is a version of history that seems to absolve whites of most of the blame, while finding plenty of faults in the natives' supposed 'bad choices'. Other explanations take a more coldly rationalist approach, saying the native people were simply overwhelmed by wave of more technologically advanced migrants. Other more radical voices say the invading Europeans were responsible for a near genocide, and have spent years hiding from the blame. In this debate 'truth' and 'history' are relative terms.

At the same time that native people were dying, they were forcibly removed from their land. In 1912 McKenna-McBride Reserve Commission offered a token opportunity for them to voice their concerns about the injustice of the situation. Dr J.A.J McKenna was a representative of the federal government, while Sir Richard McBride was the Premier of British Columbia. At the hearings in Fort Rupert, Chief Tsudaike of the Nackwacto band from Blunden Harbour expressed his view of the dispossession:

"I ask for the return of my country to me, and that the reserves be no more. It is not only just now that I came into possession of the country. It has always been mine from the beginning of time. There was a time when there was no white man in the country, and in those times I had full possession of all the county. What has been done to me with my country would be the other way – I would have measured pieces off for the white man, instead of the white man measuring off pieces for me. The one that has been selling my country has never been here – they have never seen it, and they have no right to sell it to the white men."

Modern events are not so difficult to uncover. In the early 1970s, despite the four horsemen of isolation, alcohol, missionary schools and unemployment, the population was finally growing again and the culture was undergoing a foggy revival. Government officials at the Department of Indian Affairs persuaded the Quatsino people to move to an inland reserve. A freshly surveyed reserve called New Quatsino on the new road by Coal Harbour promised jobs, better schools and health-care. Relocated from their ancestral home, for the first time in at least five thousand years the first people of Quatsino no longer lived by the sea.

I can't help wonder what this sort of change would bring to a people. My years of travelling from the deserts of Mexico to the islands of Indonesia have convinced me that the place we live and call home defines how we see ourselves. Our experiences in a place form our identities. And when we travel those identities are carried with us like a map of our souls that determine our perceptions of every new place. Our identity colours our perception of every new place. Even for a nomad like myself it is important to think someplace as home, to have touchstone or reference by which I can interpret the world. A large part of this journey is to come to grips with what this coastline means to me.

The herons circle around only to land in the same spot, bouncing on the springy cedar branches in their ungainly fashion. I am startled by voices behind me. I turn and look back. The three men lean against the bright red railings of the government wharf oblivious to the rain, casually talking as they watch me. What do they want? I wave. After a pause, one waves gently in return. For a moment I consider turning back, but unable to read their mood and already feeling ill at ease, I turn and paddle on. How can a few summers of my life compare with the depth of this burial land?

The collision of our worlds has affected all of our identities. Perhaps their connections with this place have anchored their identities or perhaps they too are a drift on this sea. On these matters I can only speak and think for myself. And I have come here seeking answers that lie so deeply within me, I expect that should I find them, that they will either build or destroy the constructed identity that is me.

6. New Quatsino

Just past the boundaries of the reserve, the shoreline turns into Hecate Cove. Tucked between the shoreline and an islet floats a ramshackle collection of buildings. They bob just a few inches above the water on a raft of giant logs, tethered by a web of ropes to trees on the shoreline and anchors beneath. A tiny glass greenhouse and two tinier sheds prop up a teetering shack. All are painted the deep red and white of schoolbook barns. In the greenhouse a few weedy plants press against the glass. A large loft window shows the finery of a feminine touch, feathers and beads. I paddle around curious to meet the occupants. But a small padlock on the door tells me no one is home. Perhaps it is the home of some fisher-folk who prefer a life at sea.

The sky is clearing. Further along on the far side of the bend is the other Quatsino, the white counterpart to the native village it faces. The warmth of the sun and lushness of the surrounding wilderness make it feel like a renegade outpost of Eden. The village is just a strip of a couple dozen houses along the shoreline. A few private docks have fishing boats tied up. Gangways of rough cedar lead up to old houses. Several have picket fences and stunted orchards out front. A big boat shed dominates the shoreline, while a two-room schoolhouse sits alone at the end of the cove. Just one road runs through the village. The only way in or out is by sea.

I paddle along the foreshore. Not a figure stirs. Strangers would be few in these parts. I imagine eyes peering back from behind the lace curtains. Then, past the red rails of the government wharf, I'm hailed by a stranger who already knows my name.

"Mike – that you Mike?"

I twist round in my seat to look back at the voice. Who can know in this place where I barely know myself? Fifty yards back on a wharf is a man standing beside a sailboat. I don't recognize him. Puzzled, I dig my paddle in backwards and back up to meet him. When I reach the wharf we look at each other without recognition. Tall and lanky in paint-splattered jeans, he pushes his hands deeper into his pockets as if trying to hide his embarrassment. It turns out he's mistaken me for the only other kayaker he knows, also someone called Mike. But unravelling the strange coincidence forces us to make introductions of a sort.

"Tim", he says with a reluctant handshake. With the ken of a seaman he takes in the length of my boat.

Those who don't paddle themselves generally treat kayakers as interesting curiosities. So in a way my boat is like a floating conversation piece, albeit an oversized sort. When Tim asks where I'm heading I'm reluctant to tell him at first. My instinct has been to keep my plans to myself since most people will instantly take me for some sort of fool for wanting to paddle alone down this coast. But he is obviously a sailor himself, someone well worth plying for local knowledge. He can identify with my desire to go to sea. So I tell him of my plans to paddle down the coast.

He nods in agreement when I mention my concerns about paddling around the Brooks Peninsula, a mountainous peninsula that juts out down the coast that is home to the area's worst weather conditions. He's never been around the Brooks himself except as crew on a commercial fishing boat. They always kept well offshore he says somewhat sagely.

I shift the conversation back to him and the village. It's his turn to be reticent. "Not much happens anymore in Quastino," he says after a pause and a glance around the empty harbour, "although sometimes it gets busy in the summer. Not busy like Coal Harbour or Port Hardy, but busy all the same. Sometimes we'll get a half dozen kayakers or sailboats come through in one day." I nod as if this is a possible version of busy.

With a bit of prodding he tells me how he came to Quatsino in the late 1970s to work at the sawmill and raise his young son. It was a good place. There was work then, and he was glad to leave the manic city behind. It wasn't meant to be a permanent stop. He started building a sailboat that he dreamt would one day take him to Tahiti and the rest of the South Pacific. But he always found some reason to stay on. Once though he motored to Vancouver to have the masts installed on his boat, but apart from that he rarely got away. Then the mill closed, years ago. His boy, now 28 was long gone to the city. It has been fifteen years since the village had a store. His sailboat, broad at the beam, well built for offshore sailing, sat beside us tugged on the heavy lines in the gentle current. Now he doubted he'd ever get away.

I ask Tim about the native village. He takes a moment before he replies. "I wasn't here then, but the old timers always say it was good. It meant there was enough kids for the school. Everyone was the same really. The natives lived over there on their land, but everyone worked together. You had to. But I can understand why they moved. It was for the kids really. To give them a chance to grow up somewhere they could go to high school and have things to do. The whole village had a real problem with alcohol before they moved. It's the same over here too. You know how it is when you have nothing to do. These long winters here, eh? Now you sometimes hear stories about the old ones wanting to come back, about how good it was back then. I guess they miss it. Maybe it's just nostalgia though, eh?"

I think of the graveyard and the men I saw just an hour ago, but I don't mention them. It is impossible for us to even guess who they believe themselves to be. Tim mutters something about having to go. So I ask him a last question about shelter down the coast. He mentions a few bays used by fishing boats during storms but the information is of little use to me. Kayakers and fishers make for different refuges when the seas turn against them. Then just before he turns to go he mentions something that catches my ear – a tiny cove he's never visited, but heard of from his friend Mike. He calls it Kayakers Haven, and it's right at the tip of the Brooks

7. Pamphlet Cove

A s a guide, I prided myself on my ability to pull up a fish from the deep for the evening diner menu. It was part of my role to be both a protector and provider in the wilderness for the clients of the company. A quick glance at the chart today and I can see a perfect spot to drop a line to jig for rockfish. At a rocky point at the edge of town I stop to try my luck once again.

From inside my cockpit I retrieve an old bicycle water bottle wrapped with fishing line. I pop off the lid and pull out a bright yellow and red spinner called a 'Buzz-bomb'. It is already tied to the line so I just need to drop it over the side. The line unfurls in cascading curls for a few seconds as the spinner heads to the bottom. When I feel it hit I pull it up a foot or two and start yanking. Within seconds I feel a tug and start winding it in. A spiny rockfish, about a foot long, flips half-heartedly on the end of the line.

I pick it up from the water, pull out my fishing knife and stick the blade through its skull to stop it from flipping. Then I inset the sharp tip in its anus, slice it up to the belly and gut it on the deck of my kayak, but not before the spiny dorsal fin stabs me in revenge. Then with the fish safely stowed under the bungee cords on my deck, I set a course for Drake Island where Tim mentioned I'd find camping in the oddly named Pamphlet Cove.

Leaving the village, a light south-westerly wind blows in from the mouth of the inlet still some ten miles distant. It pushes up a small chop that sets a rocking motion through my boat. It's the first blow on the trip, a visitor from the open coast. I pull down my rudder and bear off the wind onto a diagonal course. As I cut across the short waves, the distance between them grows until it is reaches the length of my boat. Right there I lock on to the course and slip into a rhythm. I pull up the on-coming wave with one stroke and down the backside with the other. My feet work the rudder to keep me on course. The familiar energy of the sea and the wind is reaffirming. For a brief time, in this boat, on this water, feels unquestionably like a place I am meant to be.

Out west by the open sea, long wispy clouds like mares-tails are brushed across the sharp blue sky. To the south though, a darker bank of clouds hangs over the mountains to which I'm heading. I try to make sense of this pattern to get a hint about what sort of weather might be on the way. But it's tricky in this new landscape.

Back in Clayoquot Sound I knew what cloud over which mountains meant a storm was sure to blow. I knew where to watch for gusts in the inlets, and what channels were bad in which winds. But this territory is new and all patterns here are still unfamiliar to me. From a copy of the standard issue Marine Weather Hazards Manual I've cribbed whatever notes I could find on Quatsino

Sound and the rest of the route on to the chart with red pen. But it's advice aimed at larger more sea-worthy craft than mine. The best information I can hope for will come from other kayakers along the way.

It's late in the day. The far island looks desolate compared with the village I'm putting behind me. As I paddle I'm overtaken by an unexpected apprehension. It is unsettling here out on the open water of the wide inlet. That creeping loneliness that usually stalks me alone in the dark has now found me in daylight. To distract myself I decide to practice paddling on a bearing, a navigational drill that will require my concentration and distract me from this apprehension. I mark a point directly off my bow on the far shore and read off a bearing of 190 degrees on my compass. Now the trick is to estimate the drift from the current and the wind and alter my bearing just enough to counter their effects and keep my course arrow straight. For the rest of the crossing I keep my eyes fixed on the lone island ahead. The currents here are tricky though. I'm unable to measure my success.

***

That evening in camp I fry up the fish and try to make myself at home on the grassy hummock in the centre of a muddy cove. As the tide retreats a crust of yellow algae settles like a blanket across the mud. The smell of the cooking fish lingers with a dank stagnancy in the air. After dinner I hunt around for a tree to cache my food. In the woods nearby I notice a big patch of old alders. It's another sign of an old settlement of some sort.

According to the journals of Major George Nicholson, an old-time magistrate from south down the coast, the first white man to settle in Quatsino Sound was Ned Frigon, a French-Canadian fur trader. Following the collapse of the east coast fur trade, in 1849 Frigon set from his Quebec home out in search of a new frontier. He decided to head west, but since no overland route across the continent existed, like many he headed south to Panama. There he crossed the overland trail and joined the stream of migrants heading north for the gold rush in California. Without luck in the goldfields he decided to push on to the edge of the frontier and caught a ship north from San Francisco to the Hudson's Bay trading post in Victoria on the south end of the island.

At that time the future capital of British Columbia was little more than a fortified stockade surrounded by Indian traders who arrived every summer with canoe loads of furs to trade for muskets, flour and alcohol. In 1821 a merger with the North West Trading Company granted the Hudson's Bay Company a trade monopoly over the entire West Coast of North America, north of the Columbia River. Already, busy supply lines and shipping routes were established up the Island's east coast. While the Company's Royal Charter granted in 1687 by King Charles authorized its use of force, law and order on the treacherous west coast of Vancouver Island was another matter. Even the Royal Navy, still just a fleet of fourteen ships for the entire Pacific Squadron, was unwilling to send ships up the coastline already known as the graveyard of the Pacific. After the loss of the trading schooner *Eagle* in 1852 on an uncharted reef in Clayoquot Sound, and then its plunder by the natives, the company prudently left all adventuring on the coast to privateers.

Frigon was one such privateer. When he arrived in the 1850's only four other whites lived on Vancouver Island's west coast. Frigon knew the fur trade and smelled opportunity where others would not go. There was little doubt in his mind where he should be. He chartered a schooner to sail him and his supplies, along with some lumber, up to the uncharted Quatsino to establish his own trading post. On aptly named Hope Island he built his first post. Not long afterwards he met the love of his life, a local Quatsino woman whom he renamed Lucy.

Of course, a lone interloper in Quatsino territory did not go unchallenged. According to accounts that survive, one night not long after Frigon arrived, Lucy heard of a plan to attack the post. She warned Frigon and he loaded the entire stock of six muskets, and together they spent the night barricaded inside the post. That night the attackers arrived to find the windows and doors boarded up and called off the attack. The next morning Frigon asked a native friend to carry a message over the mountains to the Fort Rupert trading post near present-day Port Hardy for some help defending the post. It took a month but eventually the HMS *Devastation*, a modern paddle steamer, finally arrived to lay down the new law.

It was the Steam Age. The revolution of coal-fired power was sweeping through the industrial world. New manoeuvrable gunships were reassigned to the Royal Navy's Pacific Squadron after the end of the Crimean War. In the dangerous waters they were able to negotiate the difficult entrances to the many inlets that had held gunships under sail at bay. To the surprise of the natives of Quatsino the Royal Navy commander paid a visit, threatening to lay each village low with cannon fire and incendiary charges if any harm was to come to Frigon and Lucy or their tiny trading post. Ninety years after Cook first reached the coast, British law had come Quatsino Sound. The Quatsino people were no longer sovereign over their ancestral land. Still, British rule was far from absolute. It was some time before Frigon felt safe to travel without an armed escort anywhere in the sound.

While the new developments must have been more than troublesome for the Quatsino chiefs, the future looked up for whites in Quatsino Sound. In 1881 a coalmine was opened and Coal Harbour was established. Grand plans were floated in the capital of the new province of British Columbia for faraway Quatsino. Colonial planners proposed using it as the terminal port for trans-Pacific liners and the terminus of the Grand Trunk Pacific Railway. Already stouthearted Danish settlers were taking up land to the north at Cape Scott that promised fine farming.

A group of Scandinavian settlers from North Dakota lead by two brothers, Fredrick and Chris Nordstrom, soon caught wind of the new frontier. The year was 1894. Together they chartered the steamship *Mischief* in Victoria to carry them up to the sound. At Coal Harbour they found the coal mine already abandoned and wintered in the empty cabins. With the arrival of spring they moved to the present site of the village and Chris returned to Victoria to obtain a Colony Charter. Within a year they had cleared the land and put up houses. With the arrival of their women and children the settlement blossomed into a village of thirty people.

Frigon, or 'Frenchie' as he was called, moved his trading post closer to the settlers and opened up a combination store, hotel and saloon. In the years that followed the settlers opened several mines in the area, but the seaport and railway never arrived. Always cut off by land from the rest of the country, and frequently trapped in the inlet due to the ferocious winter storms, the community survived by mining, fishing, and logging, even selling fruit from their orchards to the occasional steamships that started to call.

Lucy for her part, also became know in far off Victoria because like many Quatsino women, she had skull shape that anthropologists later described as 'sugar loaf' in shape. According to some early accounts head binding of infants was common on this part of the coast, although there is little real evidence to back up the idea. Nevertheless the practice was described in detail in the journals of Commander R. C Mayne, a surveyor on the coast, published in London about the time of Frigon's arrival:

> *"In appearance the Indians of Vancouver Island have the common facial characteristics of low foreheads, high check bones and large mouths. They all have their heads flattened more or less; some tribes, however, cultivate this peculiarity more than others. The process of flattening the heads is effected while they are infants, and is very disgusting. I once made a woman uncover a baby's head,*

*and it's squashed elongated appearance nearly made me
sick. By far the most flattened heads belong to the tribe of
Quatsino Indians, living at the northwest end of the island.
Those who have only seen the tribes of the east side of the
island may be inclined to think of the sketch of this girl
exaggerated, but it was really drawn by measurement, and
she was found to have 18 inches of solid flesh from her
eyes to the top of her head. It does not appear that the
process at all interferes with their intellectual
capacities..."* [1]

Years later Frigon and Long Headed Lucy, as she came to be
known, took up a homestead further up the inlet. Stories differ on
how they lived out their last days. In one, Lucy stayed with Frigon
until his death at the age of ninety-two. In another Lucy died
around the time of the 'first war' but not before the Provincial
Archives offered Frigon on thousand dollars for her skull. Despite
the obvious indignity of the proposal, Frigon insisted the payment
be in advance. The government man refused and when Lucy died
Frigon buried her "according to custom" standing up in a hollow
tree, and refused to tell anyone which.

Looking around the lagoon I wonder if it was Frigon's old post.
Perhaps Lucy is still standing upright in a nearby tree. It's not
unusual for locals to have entirely different names for the places
they know, and I can't find the two islands, Hope and Schoss that
they were known to inhabit anywhere on the chart. But on older
charts I find this island labelled Limestone Island while the natives
called it Mae'lela, simply meaning lying lengthwise into inlet. It
seems a likely spot though. It's got the only anchorage - however
slimy - of any island for miles around.

***

---

[1] Four years in British Columbia and Vancouver Island. Richard Charles
Mayne (1867) Reprinted 1967 SR Publishers Ltd. P277

Outer Coast Solo

In the last light of the evening I throw a line over a branch and pull my food up the tree, not really high enough to stop a bear, but enough trouble to keep out small creatures. It is growing dark and it will have to do. Then with a bite of chocolate and a mug of hibiscus tea to rehydrate, I sit down by the water. The lights of the village across the water come on. It has been a long day and this is my first night out. The solitude unsettles me.

As darkness falls, my twitchiness turns to other concerns. Nothing draws a bear into camp more than the smell of fish. My mind fills with images of hungry black bears with every snap in the woods. I know that snow still remains on the high mountains slopes where the berries usually grow at the end of the summer, and I imagine the bears might well be short of food. Years of trouble-free camping on the coast are forgotten. Rational thinking is overruled. Did I hang my food high enough? What if the smell of cooked fish still lingers on me? As darkness falls on my first night out, I strip naked far from my camp, hang my fishy-smelling clothes in a tree and retreat to the sanctuary of my nylon tent.

8. Mahatta Creek

No bears maul me during the night. Instead I wake up from a dream that leaves me far more unsettled. Floating in my kayak on shoreline at night, I can't see enough to land my boat. I know somewhere Rose is waiting for me. My eyes search for the flames of our campfire, but they have gone out. I'm stranded alone on the water.

Awake, I try to slip into my morning routine and shake off the loneliness I am left with. Instead I think of her back in Sydney and imagine what she might be doing. It would be the end of her day. She might be cooking dinner alone in our kitchen. It's as if I can feel her reaching out to me across the ocean I have put between us. I put water on my stove for tea. Searching for a lighter in the yellow bag I come across the gold box and the ring. I pull it out and turn it over in my hand as I wait for the water to boil. Looking at the pattern of the hummingbird, I can't help but wonder if I am who she believes me to be. No answer is forthcoming this morning. After a cold bowl of granola, I pack up and launch from the muddy beach, keen to desert the troubling post.

Cutting out of the cove I eye up the situation on the inlet. The morning air is still. My plan for the day is opportune. The tide is falling, seemingly offering a free ride out. I aim to make the most of the pleasurable conditions. As Drake Island falls away behind, the inlet spreads out before me. An open passage ten miles long leads toward the sea. I fall into a rhythm and for a couple hours enjoy a hard paddle, humming stupid ditties to myself to keep time. The splashes of water feel like cold fingers on my skin.

***

A patchwork of clear-cuts rises up the slopes of the inlet. In an hour I pass three active logging sites. The rumble of industry echoes across the water. Massive A-frames are noisily yarding logs down the slopes to the beaches. Logging operations are a common sight all over the coast. For at least a hundred and twenty years they have been felling the forests. After a couple hours of paddling I stop as the tide turns and stretch my legs on a pebble beach. A family of sea otters, the first I've seen in my life despite years of paddling on the coast, passes down the middle of the channel, splashing and playing as they go. Eager to keep my pace up, I wolf down a quick snack and push on for the Koskimo Islands.

A wide bay opens up on the south shore and I cut across it to make time. Boat traffic down the inlet picks up as the morning wears on - mostly sport fishermen on their way in. Between their fast passes the rumbling of a diesel generator keeps the silence at bay. Just before the islands I can see a large building floating on the water, surrounded by circular fences. As I approach I see the silver flashes of salmon leaping in the pens. Rock music is echoing from the nearby floating bunkhouse.

A man in a herring skiff – a type of flat-bottomed aluminum boat that passes as the pickup truck of the West Coast – is tending a giant funnel-shaped machine. The machine is firing a stream of pellets through the air into a nearby pen. I coast up alongside. After a minute or two he looks up, startled to see me there. Bearded and rough looking in jeans and a tattered sweater, he waves me over and shuts down the machine. Glad for the relative quiet I pull my kayak up to the skiff.

"Where'd you come from?" he asks. He speaks in a mild German accent. I tell him.

"Oh, so you're not a tourist, are you?" It seems to make a difference to him. He sits down amongst the debris in the skiff and pulls out a pouch of tobacco to roll a smoke in the sun. Curious of kayaks, he wants to know of my experiences, so I talk for a while. Then I ask him how he got here.

"I came over from German twenty years ago," he says, "I was living in Victoria until five years ago. 'Where the hell was Quatsino?' was the first thing I asked when I got this job. But now I love it up here, working outdoors everyday. My town back in Germany, it was an industrial hell. The last salmon was seen in our streams in the 1700s. Compared to that, Quatsino's brand new."

"And these fish," I ask, "Where are they from?"

They're Atlantics he says, five net pens with eighty thousand fish each. Fish farming is no 'Ma and Pa' operation anymore he tells me. The company that owns this farm is Norwegian - they just bought fourteen more on the coast at about a million dollars each. The industry got a bad reputation because there used to be a lot of slack operators, he says, but these days you can't do that anymore.

These days the industry still draws heavy criticism from environmentalists. Many would describe this operation as an industrial hell as well. Politics here in British Columbia are tri-polar. The three main forces are: industry, organized labour, and the environmentally sympathetic urban middle class. An unlikely alliance of Labour and Industry tend to unite on just one thing - opposing the environmental lobby. Looking at the nearest pen I can barely see a few feet into the water it's so thick with fish. They jump wildly, back flipping, rocketing, and even colliding in the air. Eighty thousand fish per pen, times five pens is four hundred thousand fish, all carnivores, cramped together in the space of a couple acres. Environmentalists claim the artificially dense concentrations of non-native salmon are a threat to already beleaguered local species. They incubate disease, release massive levels of fecal pollution, and are fed on an unsustainable diet of herring pellets, antibiotics and red food colouring Number Five

"Why do they jump?" I say

"Cause they are happy," says Dave. He is happy. Like most fish farmers he is happy to have a job. On the West Coast these days fish-farming work is one of the few remaining year round jobs. Because of this, it's quickly becoming one of the coast's major employers. The money is good. Much of these fish will end up in the United States or Japan, prized for the delicately marbling of fat in the flesh. For those who don't care what goes into it, there is no finer fish. Many foreign chef prize farm fish because the flesh is so much more tender that lean wild salmon. But at the last salmon farmers banquet in Tofino, friends have told me few of the workers would touch the plates of farm fish. Salmon and other fish are the only farmed carnivores in our diets. The concentration of dioxins from feeding on herring, which are also carnivores, is said to be dangerously high. But there is no reason to assume you escape the dioxins by eating wild fish. Their food at sea is the same. Antibiotics and food colouring are another matter.

We talk about this for a while and then Dave concludes, "Anyway, with the way logging has destroyed the spawning streams and how the wild stocks are being fished out, we'll just have farm salmon to eat soon anyway, eh?"

***

It seems fitting that wild salmon are jumping at the mouth of Mahatta Creek when I arrive. The name means 'having sockeye salmon' in the Quatsino dialect [2]. By their size and the time of year, I guess they are springs (or tyees or kings as the Americans call them), the largest of the four wild species of salmon on the coast. After four or five years swimming giant circles round the currents of the northern Pacific Ocean, these wild salmon have returned for the annual spawning run up the creek where they hatched. In a few weeks or even days when the autumn rains flood the creek, they'll push up the shallow stretches and rapids to the gravel beds to spawn. While some people prefer the lean meat of small Coho and Sockeye, personally I think nothing barbeques quite as well a big fat wild spring.

I check my chart and can see that the large clearing on the eastern shore is an Indian reserve. Already alders are growing up through the berry bushes, like oversized weeds. As I paddle across the creek mouth my kayak scrapes across a shallow line of rocks. Peering down I can see it's the remaining outline of a fish weir, a simple trap for catching salmon with the falling tide.

When the first people arrived on the coast they lived primarily on land resources. In the layers of the middens archaeologists have uncovered the gradual process of adaptation as food and materials from the land was replaced by maritime resources. In one of the first technological adaptations, bone and shell replaced chipped stone. The real transformation though, was nearly three and half thousand years ago when smoked salmon was invented. The people living by the salmon streams discovered they could lay away large amounts of protein and oil rich food for the long winters, by cleaning the fish and hanging it in the rafters of their smoky long houses. It was enough to prevent famine most winters. Suddenly two thousand years ago there was a population boom.

---

[2] BC Place Names (1997)

Villages sprang up, settlements became denser and new social stratifications developed.

The West Coast cultural type is the name archaeologists use to identify the cultures of the native people from Alaska to Washington State. It still is characterized by a system of hereditary ranks. Chiefs, nobles, warriors, commoners, and slaves, and ritualists all had distinct rights and obligations. Contrary to the popular notions that native people held all property in common, most of the resources, including salmon streams, clam beds, sea lion rookeries, offshore halibut banks, and even drifting dead whales were the property of the chiefs.

With increased populations and competition for the limited resources came the seemingly inevitable human scourge of war. Local histories record that this salmon stream was once in the territory of the Hoyalas, a large tribe that occupied most of the inland waters of the sound. According to some native accounts, the Hoyalas were wiped out by disease. According to other histories, it was a series of attacks by the outer coast Koskimo, just before contact with Europeans that finished them off.

On the west coast the foggy late summer months were known as the warring season. It may have been that after a particularly hard summer a flotilla of war canoes carrying the warriors of the Koskimo tribe set out for Quatsino. If they came through the mouth of the sound from their home on the north coast of the island, they may have made a treaty with the Giopino and the Quatsino, the two tribes that controlled the mouth of the sound, in order to pass through. Perhaps as allies they were offered shelter in the villages that night. After all, in the dark of night, your enemy is my enemy to.

On the West Coast there was little ritual in combat. Honour was measured by head counts and slaves taken. To maximize surprise the warriors would attack at night. A few scouts would slip into the village to silence any dogs and anyone unfortunate enough to be out. With the houses surrounded front and back, on signal the warriors would storm in en mass. The strategy was to catch the enemy warriors sleeping and crush their skulls with stone axes. Even when guns were available the natives were said to prefer close hand-to-hand combat. Afterwards, if all went well the houses would be torched and the women and children would be taken as slaves. Back home the heads of the enemy would be impaled on posts for bragging rights. If practiced successfully, warfare was an enterprising undertaking. Great chiefs became greater by capturing more salmon streams and maintaining a workforce of commoners and slaves to bring in the harvest.

More often than not though, a first attack would result in a partial success with the attackers retreating with a few heads and hopefully some captured booty and slaves. Victory often required a longer campaign of war. And of course there were other allied villages to worry about. Archaeological surveys have revealed the remains of a rough fort once built here. It suggests the Koskimo may have used it as a base for attacks on other villages further up the inlet. Nobody knows how long it took, perhaps a month, perhaps several years, but eventually the Koskimo took control of the inside salmon streams of the sound. But tribal lines were constantly shifting on the coast. A hundred years later, the Newetti, another outer coast tribe that occupied the space the Koskimo vacated when they left the outside, would raid this inside inlet and nearly do the same thing to the Koskimo.

***

These days nobody lives at Mahatta Creek, despite the blood once shed for it. The only things moving are myself and the salmon that now jump unmolested. Government regulations keep recreational and commercial fishermen outside of this section of the sound, but perhaps the Quatsino still return to this creek for their food fishery. The rising tide has flooded the creek right up to the edge of its banks. I take advantage of the high water to paddle up into the forest. Along the banks slender trees, protected all their lives from the winds of the open inlet, drip elegant veils of moss and lichen. Half a mile back a little cataract stops me.

I squirm out of my kayak on to a smooth rock, and carefully manoeuvre my boat up so I can open my back hatch. I flip open the heavy seals on my camera case and switch lenses. Then I raise the camera to my eye to frame the picture. Something seems wrong. I look up at the forest and realize the thin line of trees hides a clear-cut behind. This West Coast Eden I thought I had found is little more than a veiled illusion. The forest and most likely the spawning beds of the salmon further up stream are no more.

9. Treasure Hunters

A s I return to the mouth of the creek a skiff buzzes in from the direction of the fish farm and lands on the beach in front of the Indian Reserve. A man and a woman with a shovel step ashore and walk up the embankment to the old village grounds. After watching them wander around for a few minutes scrapping at the soil I decide to paddle over.

The woman, young and blond in jeans and designer label T-shirt spots me and waves. The man, wearing hip waders and dark sunglasses looks up from his scraping and shouts hello.

"Are you the guy paddling to Tofino?" he asks.

"How did you know?" I say. I'm beginning to be surprised by the number of people who seem to recognize me around here. So much for my plan to travel alone.

"I work with Dave at the fish farm."

"What are you looking for?"

"Supposedly you can find old trade beads, old bottles and stuff here."

"Lots of history here, it's an old village," I reply. I consider mentioning the inappropriateness of digging for treasure on someone else's land, particularly an old village site. Before I do though, it becomes obvious they only have a superficial interest in scratching at the dirt. They give up and we talk for a few minutes about kayaking and the coast. They are city folks. He travels up from Victoria for the work, while she is just visiting for the weekend.

"I've worked here three years, just around the corner, but this is the first time I've ever come up this creek," he admits. I take my leave, still contemplating this admission of disinterest and cross to the far side of the creek. On a grey stone beach I clean and cook a green-fleshed fish I caught earlier for lunch. A light westerly wind has blown up. The weather forecast I overheard on the fish farm radio was calling for moderate to strong wind in the afternoon. As I cook my lunch I see the treasure hunters abandon their search to motor up the creek.

Treasure hunting was once a competitive business on the coast. While the first Europeans to reach these shores paid scant regard to the crafts and artwork of the natives, by the 1870s local Indian agents and traders had already begun buying up 'curios and relics' for sale in Victoria shops. It was the summer of 1881 when Adrian Jacobson, a young Norwegian arrived on the coast. His lucrative commission with the Royal Museum in Berlin was "to undertake an expedition of several years' duration to the Northwest Coast of America in order to obtain ethnological specimens."

Jacobsen's was the first of the large-scale museum expeditions to reach the island. Financed by wealthy 'gilded capitalists' of the Industrial revolution, the new museums of New York, Chicago, Washington, London and Berlin were assembling collections for the new fields of ethnology. Ambitious curators placed orders with professional collectors who roamed the world. The West Coast as far north as the Arctic Circle was soon flooded with collectors. They scrambled to buy (and in some cases steal and extort) anything to fill the rail cars bound for the display cases of the east. They paid U.S. dollars on the decks of their boats, for weapons, masks, carved feast bowls, canoes, the older the better. At first it was a quick way for the natives to clear out the rafters of junk that was nearly falling to pieces anyway. In today's terms it might be considered a cultural theft, but it was in those far off museum cases that almost all the artefacts of the transitional period that survive today were preserved. Most valuable of all were the totem poles. In most villages the owners refused to sell them, but the carvers soon began taking commissions. Soon the fistfuls of American dollars launched a renaissance in native carving that continues to this day.

Jacobsen was well suited to the rough life of a collector. Raised on the deck of his father's fishing boat on the seas north of the Arctic Circle, he was a self-educated man with incredible faith in his own abilities. Already a seasoned collector with two seasons in Greenland and Labrador, he was not daunted by the many challenges of collecting on the coast. Arriving by steamer from San Francisco, he spent a few days in Victoria, pilfering nearby native graveyards before catching the Grappler up the east coast of the Island to the Hudson's Bay Company post at Fort Rupert, near present day Port Hardy.

He stopped only briefly on his first visit, long enough to meet Frank Hunt, the commander of the post before setting off to northerly Queen Charlotte Islands. Upon his return a couple weeks later he hired Frank Hunt's half-native sons, George and William as guides, along with a small sloop named *Mystery* to explore the surrounding coast. After a week in the eastern Kwakiutl villages, he decided to "undertake a strenuous walking trip through the primeval forest ...in order to visit the villages of Koskimo and Quatsino on the west coast."

Like most Europeans, Jacobson was drawn to the most unusual distinctions in the cultures he encountered. The sensational and shocking dominated the popular European conceptions of native people, fostering impressions of savagery and 'otherness'. His own journal of the trip later published in Germany records these words:

> *"The inhabitants of ... the almost unknown west coast of Vancouver Island are some of the wildest and robust specimens of mankind know today. Practices of the ancient past, like murder, cannibalism and other have been kept under control by the British gunboats.... Now the 'good old days' are over when they could kill slaves and prisoners of war and eat them without hindrance, but they have found another way, one might say more horrible to gain their ends. Nowadays before their great feast they eat the bodies of the dead; and not just those of recent origin, but some that have been dead for one or two years."*

On that first visit Jacobsen spent a mere two weeks amongst the Kwakiutl collecting – enough to make him the leading expert on the culture in academic circles. A colleague named Hagenbeck was taken by this description of an Indian still living uncorrupted by European influences. The following year Jacobsen returned with a second commission. This time the commission was for live specimens. It was still the age of exploration, and European audiences delighted in meeting the exotic people inhabiting their expanding empires. Jacobson had already run two commercially successful ethnic expositions with Hagenbeck, once bringing Eskimos from Greenland and on another occasion Laplanders from Norway. Now he had his eye on the farthest reaches of the Pacific, which by this time had been under European influence -- but not control -- for nearly a century. Getting the first natives back to Europe would be a certain coup.

Jacobson returned to Fort Rupert that fall. He hired the Hunt brothers and their father's boat once again and the trio set off around the rough seas of Cape Scott in search of some willing 'Long-heads'. In the Koskimo Village, after some initial trading he convinced the son of a local chief named Wachas, along with his wife and two others to travel to Europe. But the entire family fell sick on the stormy trip back to Fort Rupert in the small boat and the Koskimo villagers' enthusiasm for travel so far from home began to waver. To make matters worse, the Fort Rupert Indians, long-time enemies of the Koskimo, played on their fears, telling them that the voyage round Cape Horn would take them nine months. Jacobson pointed out that they would be travelling by the new railway overland, but to no avail. One night the Quatsino family slipped down the overland trail home leaving Jacobsen empty-handed. Meanwhile back in Victoria, a letter awaited him from Hagenbeck. Some mysterious disease was being blamed for the death of his five Fuegians from Patagonia all in one week. Depressed by the whole affair, for the time being, Hagenbeck lost interest in ethnic expositions.

Undeterred, Jacobsen returned in 1885 with his own brother Fillip, once more in search of live specimens. This time with the two Hunt brothers they recruited eleven Kwakiutls, including two long-headed women (one was the wife of William Hunt) to travel to Europe. But again they were thwarted, this time by, an English missionary who had since taken up residence at Fort Rupert. The Reverend Alfred J. Hall was against the maltreatment of his newly claimed flock, and when Fillip and George went off to do some more collecting, Hall played up the fears of the Indians and like the previous group, they slipped back down the Quatsino trail home.

Undeterred yet again, in a display of Nordic stubbornness, Jacobson and his brother Fillip signed on a passing group of Bella

Coola. The clan was a northern branch of the Kwakiutl, on their way south to the pick hops in the fields of Washington for the summer. The troop soon departed for Berlin. While the brothers had failed to secure any 'long-heads' for the trip, they hoped they had another ace up their sleeve. Amongst the Bella Coola were initiates of the secret Hamatsa society, the reputed cannibals of the West Coast.

The Bella Coola quickly adapted to the demands of the European tour. Their evening performance was an abbreviated version of the secret winter ceremonies. They had spent two thousand years developing their show, and their skills as ingenious illusionists rivalled the best in Europe at the time. The lead star was Pooh-pooh, "a rather attractive young cannibal" as the German press described him. He performed enrobed in a dance clock with carved wooden skulls -- eight in all -- rumoured to represent the eight times he had eaten flesh. The climax of each evening performance was a fiery sensation in which Pooh-pooh, half delirious from dancing stepped into a wooden box and was carried into the fire. As one observer recorded, "After a time, it went up in flames among the cracking and glowing fire. What a strange sight! In the shimmering glow a charred head and skeleton. As the astonished crowd stared at the spectacle, with a sudden yell the shaman reappeared and almost as quickly vanished into the dark"

For their part the troupe adapted remarkably quickly to German food and clothes. The troupe played up on their "savage mystic" showing off bite scars on their chest or arms, leading one Hotelier to joke he needed two new kitchen boys everyday just to keep them fed. They picked up the language, made friends amongst the ladies (as they said back then) and ended up staying two years. But despite the sensational pyrotechnics, as a commercial endeavour the show failed. It was ironic but nobody had ever seen a native from the West Coast before. Familiar only with stereotypes based on Plains Indians, the Bella Coola didn't look red enough to be real

Indians to the suspicious European audiences. They had the wrong noses, didn't wear buckskins and had little skill with a bow and arrow. It was proof enough to convince at least one reporter they were Japanese or Chinese in disguise.

Yet, the living specimens were greeted with considerable interest by the academic world. Several German scholars took careful measurements of their skull sizes for phrenological data. Another young scholar, an apt linguist named Franz Boas met with the group several times, taking careful notes on their language and customs. A physicist by training, Boas had a growing interest in the young sciences of ethnology and anthropology. Little did anyone suspect, that over the course of a lifetime his studies of the Kwakiutl would revolutionize scientific inquiry into the origins of humankind. But before Boas's ground-breaking work could begin, he had to meet one other man, a cultural informant who lived with one foot in each world. That man was George Hunt, Jacobson's Kwakiutl guide.

***

The weather looks likes it's turning for the worst, so I unfurl my chart on some dry stones. Using the thin red cord from my hand compass, I measure out the distance to the small fishing village of Winter Harbour. It's the last human settlement I'll be passing up for over a week. It's about eight miles away with few options along the rocky shore for shelter. Not too far - about two or three hours depending on winds and tide, but it's not the distance that worries me. It's the exposure in crossing the mouth of the sound, open to the Pacific and the bad weather that seems to be brewing. I know I'm not yet fit enough to be pushing myself on long days. After deliberating for a while, I reluctantly concede to myself that it would be silly to try and elect to make camp in the cramped cove. Tomorrow I'll bypass the village to make time down the coast.

Outer Coast Solo

I content myself with a boggy patch of grass, suspecting I am evicting a deer from its usual bed. Even thought it's summer, I'm bundled in long pants and a fleecy thermal jacket. My blood has already gone partially Australia it would seem. My one concern is drinking water. In my kayak is a two-day supply I collected up the creek today. But clear-cutting has left it too brackish and silty for anything but cooking. Stirring my pasta, I break my only spoon. After dinner I set my tent in the woods and bed down before dark.

I fall asleep with thoughts of home, not sure anymore that I know where mine is.

10. Rowley Reefs

In the morning I awake several times before sunrise. At the first hint of light in the woods I emerge from my tent for a stretch. Beyond the shadows of the forest, low clouds hold a calm over the inlet. The only thing stirring is a salmon, slapping the water at the mouth of the creek. Anxious to make the most of the conditions, I wolf down a bowl of cold granola using my fork. From the bow of my boat I retrieve my motley collection of neoprene.

I strip down on the rocks and for the first time on this trip, I pull on the vestments of outer coast paddling. My skin prickles up into goose bumps in the morning air. The sleeveless 'farmer John' style wetsuit is cold and damp. Next comes my warmest thermal shirt, then a river-kayaker's dry-top, and some neoprene booties. Finally I stuff a skullcap and gloves within reach inside my cockpit. Initially it feels claustrophobic to be binding myself up in the rubber-wear, but the familiar struggle of shimmying into everything soon warms me up.

I pack my kayak and check it from bow to stern, pulling the rudder lines to see they are free, inspecting for fraying, and tightening down the gear on deck. About four miles from here I'll be leaving the shelter of the inlet for the outside. Along the open coast the conditions will be far less forgiving. This wooded shoreline where the forest grows right to the waterline as if it were a lake or a river, will give way to storm-pounded cliffs. Beaches and other safe landing sites will be fewer and farther in between. For here on in, I'll be truly on my own.

While I've practiced my self-rescues and rolls in everything from swimming pools to forty-knot winds and breaking surf, everything that is practice is always less than real. I know the true danger is always unexpected. Tired and overtaken by an unexpected gale, capsizing, or 'dumping' as kayakers call it, could easily be deadly. Even if I manage to roll up or re-enter my boat, whatever knocked me over is still going to be around when I come up. Without a wetsuit I would be lucky to last twenty minutes in this water before becoming hypothermic. Even with one on I wouldn't last more than a few hours I suspect. Once that deep chill sets in, coordination and clear thinking soon fade away. Eventually, I'd slip into a cold slumber as the sea raged around me.

There's an old saying that sums up the essence of seamanship most succinctly. It was told to me by an experienced guide at a training workshop. "When you start kayaking, you don't know what you don't know". That summer the whole sea kayaking industry was reeling from the first fatal accident involving paying clients the summer before in the Queen Charlotte Islands. It was a wake-up call for many small operators. Unaware of the sea's unpredictable energy, the biggest danger most novice kayakers face is their own ignorance. They simply cannot see the danger they are in until it is too late. "Then, you know what you know," went the saying, meaning, you gain some skills and some confidence, but are still unaware of the sea's treacherous nature. "But finally, after many years, you learn the most valuable lessons of all - you know what you don't know." That lesson is the hardest one to learn, because it can't come from a book, or a workshop with an instructor. It can only come from time spent on the sea. Only then do you truly understand your own limitations.

***

Under the cloak of the clouds the water is dead calm as I push off. Despite my long sleep, the kayak, or rather my own body, feels sluggish as I steer out across the glassy surface. The first two days of hard paddling have caught up with me now and I feel like I am fighting an incoming tide. My goal for the day is to reach the forbidding sounding Restless Bight by this afternoon, a distance of about eight to ten miles, depending on where I can get ashore. I try to shrug off the chill in the air with the rhythm of long stokes, working out the kinks in my back as I stretch out on the open water. The first leg of the morning soon passes under the wing-beat of my paddle. Just over an hour later I edge round Cliffe Point at the mouth of the inlet.

At the edge of the Pacific Ocean, I finally stop to catch my breath. The horizon is lost in a distant haze without colour. Between the sky and the water I can make no distinction. Beyond the Gillet Islets that guard the entrance, only a hungry grey void sits before me. This is a moment I've been dreaming of, a moment that has awakened me countless times in the dark of night since I set my mind to this trip. From here on I will be heading away from people, from towns and phones, from contact with perhaps anyone for at least the next week. Ahead lie rocky shorelines, surf pounded beaches, hidden reefs, and the majestic isolation of the Brooks Peninsula.

In the days of sail this coast was known as the graveyard of the Pacific. In 1864 the Royal Navy published the first Vancouver Island Pilots Guides, a sort of handbook for navigators on unfamiliar coastlines. Using the newly published charts of Captain Plumper, it offered the following advice to early navigators arriving on the west coast of the island. The first step was to get one's bearings; the second was to avoid the dangers of the coast:

"When first making the land, an unbroken range of mountains will be seen, on a nearer approach it appears thickly wooded, and apparently fertile, intersected with many deep openings and valleys which in most cases are some of the islets. The coast is generally low and rocky, but rises immediately and hidden dangers, especially near the entrances of the sounds and exercise of great caution and vigilance will be necessary on the part of the navigator to avoid them even with the present Admiralty charts.

"On no occasion, therefore, except where otherwise stated in the following pages, should a stranger attempt to enter any of the harbours or anchorages during night or thick weather, but rather keep a good offing until circumstances are favourable, and when about to make the coast, it cannot be too strongly impressed on the mariner to take every opportunity of ascertaining his vessel's position by astronomical observations, as fogs and thick weather come on very suddenly at all times of the year, more especially in summer and autumn months.

"The west coast is very thinly populated, highest estimates of the native population not exceeding 4,000 [sic] dividing into a number of small tribes. As a rule they are harmless and inoffensive, though in a few cases the

crews of vessels wrecked on their coasts have been plundered and ill treated."

As I sit contemplating my own journey, a sport fishing boat comes buzzing in through from outside. A minute later, a second, then a third. I push further round the point and my view of the shore opens up and I see first ten, then twenty, and finally about thirty of the small boats patrolling the line of cliffs to the south. Prevented from fishing the inside of the sound by government regulations, they hope to catch the spring salmon as they arrive from the open sea.

I turn south toward my destination, still a few weeks away. The stench of engine exhaust creeps along over the water. Most of the boats are trolling slower than I paddle, their deep lines pulling spinners and flashers in the darkness below. Some locals, about five of them, are piled into an old water-ski boat. About three inches of freeboard keep them afloat. Short of seats, one sits up on the outboard like it's a throne, his belly draped over his belt. A smaller dirty two-stroke trolling engine smokes along beside him. Between swigs of beer they cast suspicious glances at my kayak. It seems early to be drinking

"Catching any?" calls out the king on the motor over the rim of his can.

"Not trying" I respond, "You?"

"Couple a' springs. How far you going anyway?"

"Tofino."

The King is silent while he considers the idea of paddling down the coast in a boat he wouldn't cross a lake in. Then, "You got yer wife in there to keep you warm?"

Further on I watch a pair of old-timers land a spring salmon almost as thick as my thigh.

"Nice size," I offer.

"Not like they used to be," says one, without looking up from the business of netting.

"Where you from?"

"Campbell River."

"Not much fishing there now."

He nods in agreement and then adds, "No, people are going farther and farther to find them. I guess this is the last of them."

In recent years salmon runs that have been over-fished for years are now apparently finished and no one seems to have any faith in the government's ability to manage a recovery. Instead of favouring conservation, the commercial fishermen and sports fishermen appear to be battling each other for the right to finish them off. Just like in the cod banks of the East, the salmon are being sacrificed for political ends.

"Soon we'll have nothing left but farm fish," I say, repeating the wisdom of yesterday. He shakes his head, as if to agree, but says nothing. Instead he picks up a wooden club and turns his attention to the fish banging in the bottom of his boat.

Beside me the shoreline rises up into a cliff, deep red in the overcast light. High above on the slopes are precariously perched trees. Past the fleet I make a quick stop for water at Harvey Cove, two miles down the open coast. The water tastes only marginally better than the Mahatta Creek. Looking at the contours of my chart I figure it's probably the same massive clear-cut stretching for miles across the hills. This is no wilderness. It's another rainforest watershed converted to an industrial drain. After a quick snack I push off, happy to forsake this place.

***

Out of the cove a southerly breeze is blowing up a small chop. I notice the tidal current is running faster against me. Even out here there is a cyclical current that pushes and pulls north and south along the coast. Ahead lies a tricky section of shallow reefs and small islets. I turn my attention to the chart. Crosses, stars, the numerals of soundings, kelp marks, reefs and tidal rapids are all jumbled together in a tight cluster on the paper. In rougher conditions it might be tricky to navigate, but for now it is an easy matter of staying alert. This is my first real navigational challenge of the trip. I'm lost in my own solitude charting the route when there is a loud splash behind me. I whip my head round only to see an empty ring of water. I wait and watch. Finally almost a minute later a juvenile male sea lion surfaces far behind me, obviously still taken aback himself. My stillness must have camouflaged my presence. He swims rapidly away, his sun-bleached head receding, two black saucer eyes fixed straight at me. Further along five grey dorsal fins arc through the black surface, less perturbed by my presence. This family of harbour porpoises pass so close that I could touch them with the tip of my paddle. The quiet puffs of their blowholes are not the only reminders of the bloodlines we share. Everyone has come to fatten on the rich flesh of the salmon. While the fishermen have captured the best territory at the entrance, these denizens of the black realm beneath my hull will have to do with second best. At least they face no government restrictions on heading inside. The cunning sea lions might even steal a fish off the fishers' lines.

At Rowley Reefs in the lee of some islets, I gain some welcome protection from the rising wind. As I thread my way through the rocks I spot three small shapes floating on the water. Even from a mile off, the rhythmic rise and fall of their paddles tells me they are kayakers. From a distance kayaks always appear to be moving too slowly. They would be comical in the landscape of mountains that disappear up into the clouds and an ocean that stretches off into forever, were it not for my own situation. Instead they are reminders of my own insignificance. As they near, I hail them and they turn to intersect my course. I can see they are three men, about forty or fifty years of age.

In the familiar manner of kayakers everywhere, we raft up alongside each other, reaching across each others' decks to grab lines and pull ourselves tightly together like sardines in a can.

While we all catch our breath we look each other up and down. From the worn accoutrements lashed to their decks, I can tell they are well prepared. I'm heartened at the chance to learn something of the route ahead from experienced paddlers.

"Where you coming from?" they ask. I tell them of my trip out from Coal Harbour. There is no point exchanging names.

"We've been on the outside of the Brooks for nine days," says one, his unshaven face bearing the proof. By their accents and the brands of their gear I can tell they are from the States.

"Did you go round?" I ask.

"No, and you?"

"Heading south...to Tofino."

"Really?"

"Well, trying to anyway. Any good campsites?"

"Yeah, we just came from a good one at Restless Bight, and there is another round the back of Lawn Point."

"How about round Cape Cook?" I ask. I'm still hoping for more information on Kayaker's Haven.

"Last time I was there was eighteen years ago. Can't really remember where you can land. You got a radio?"

"No."

A pause. I know they consider it foolish to be alone on this coast with no emergency communication. Then some advice, rather than a lesson, "Well, it's forecast to blow southeast thirty to forty knots for at least the next two days, but it was already Southeast at 4 AM this morning at Solander Island. You might want to start looking for shelter"

"Shit."

We exchange a few more pleasantries and then I push off. As predicted the wind continues to build, accompanied by a light rain. Taking at least some of their advice to heart, I head inside the islets. As I look out at the darkening horizon I take heart in my own decision not to bring a radio. I wouldn't have left camp this morning if I had heard that weather forecast. The knowledge would have effectively paralysed me. But the real reason I have chosen not to bring a radio, or a satellite locator beacon is more complex. In truth I am here to be truly alone. I want no fall-back plan, no emergency escape. I know that if I carry a radio, I am carrying a link, a support that will tie me and the decisions I make back to that which I want to escape. Just knowing I could make contact in a bad situation would alter how I would approach every situation. I would hedge my bets and takes risks that might count on that ever present net of support. I know if I am going to make this journey, I need make it on my own.

***

It appears that the clouds are just a passing squall blowing by farther out at sea, so I decide to drop a line in the shelter of some islets and try to catch a fish for lunch. It's an ideal spot but the rain and strong tide have put the fish off the bite. Unsuccessful, I paddle onward to a nameless beach facing north out of the weather and fry up a tuna and cheese sandwich for lunch. As a guide tuna-melts were my failsafe distraction for a soaking wet crew on a lunch stop. The smell of toasting bread, the warmth in the stomach, the feeling of satiation and comfort that only a hot meal can provide would lift anyone's spirit on the unfamiliar coast. Today it's just me that I am working the spell on, although for now it seems to be working. As I sip my tea, the rain worsens and in the downpour another kayaker passes, heading north towards the mouth of Quatsino Sound. His dim shape vanishes quickly into the grey void.

From the shelter of the beach the wind doesn't seem that strong, despite the rain. So I pack up and push off into the narrow channel between the reef and the shore. But once I'm back out on the open water it's obvious conditions are still deteriorating. Ahead the ocean is whipped with whitecaps. From the shelter of the rocks I can just see round into the entrance of Restless Bight, which is nothing more than a shallow rocky bay well deserving of its name. Waves are smashing on the reefs that guard the entrance. I stop and take a quick look at my chart. Six-pointed stars, marking partially submerged reefs, are scattered across the entrance like a minefield. Except for a break two miles to the south across the open water, there is no easy way through.

For five minutes, then ten, I toy with the idea of going, reluctant to admit I can't deal with the conditions. In truth I don't know if I can. I have no experience on my own in such a challenging situation. The wind continues to stiffen and foam starts to streak down the faces of the waves. In the end the shear foolishness of continuing is clear. I am looking dead straight at my own limitations. I pull my kayak round and retreat to my lunch stop to wait out the rising storm. With no real idea how long the blow is going to last, I haul my gear up the sandy beach, pick a sheltered spot amongst the driftwood logs, string my tarp off the trees, change out of the damp wetsuit in to dry clothing, try to shrug off the feelings of defeat, and turn my attention to getting warm.

***

Lighting a fire on a stormbound beach is more than a lifesaving skill. It's an affirmation for me – a near ritual action that restores my sense of belonging in this place. From my piles of gear scattered across the driftwood logs that make up the impromptu furniture of my camp, I dig out the three necessary tools – a rusty hatchet with a red fibreglass handle, bought for a hiking trip in the Queen Charlottes years ago, a Buck knife, found in a hotel room up in the B.C. Interior one summer while tree-planting, and a standard Bic lighter - I prefer the red ones, they just look luckier. (Matches are for fools on this coast.) In the beating rain I scour the piles of driftwood for broken pieces of cedar. With an armload, I settle down under my tarp and begin splitting it into kindling. The fragrant oils that protect the inner wood from penetrating dampness burst out as each piece snaps neatly under the blade of the hatchet. The exposed wood is bone dry and the musty smell soon wraps around me. Once I've split all the wood, I pick up a piece and start shaving paper-thin curls off a dry edge. Then I shape the shavings into a fist-sized bundle of tinder and crouch down on my knees to light my first fire of the trip.

I put my lighter to the tinder and spark a flame. The curls start to burn almost immediately. As the tiny flames licks up, I carefully lay more fuel across it. Like a starving chick it devours all I can feed it. I move to thicker pieces, until finally it grabs a hold of the larger ones and the sap starts to snap from the heat. A few more and I can lean back to relax for a minute, chaise-lounge style against a log and soak up the warmth. Staring out at the rain from the shelter of my tarp I feel an easy contentment come over me. There is little point in putting my tent up yet, it will just get wetter and dinner is still a few hours off. For the first time on the trip I have nothing to do. I am choosing the right course of patience and right timing. I have made the right decision for me. For the moment I'm happy just to let my mind clear and consider the journey ahead. Absentmindedly I pick up a cedar stick from my woodpile and begin carving its fine grain with the steel curve of my knife.

***

Long ago the natives discovered the excellence of the cedar tree's long smooth grain for carving. The natural oils of the wood act as a preservative in the damp climate. Two species of cedar grow on the coast – western red, the most common, and yellow, found at higher elevations. Traditionally, there were few parts of life on the coast where cedar was not an essential resource. During the winters the men of a village would be occupied carving and working the wood. Everything from totem poles to feasting bowls was shaped from the aromatic grain. The famous dugout canoes of the West Coast, capable of holding twenty people or more, are still carved whole from single trees. For roofing, large planks as wide as a man was tall were split from the side of living trees. The women also stripped the fibrous bark in the spring when it was soft. It was then scraped, soaked, pounded and aged until finally they could weave the soft fibres into watertight baskets, and capes. Warm winter blankets might be interwoven with mountain goat hair, acquired in trade from the mainland.

Beyond their practical connection to the cedars, the native people also professed an animistic connection with the trees. In their cosmology, all objects had a spirit, be it a rock or an eagle. Such was their reverence for the cedar, that before stripping bark or cutting into a tree, a prayer of forgiveness and permission was offered. By virtue perhaps of their sheer size and longevity cedars were believed to have particularly active spirits that might seek revenge if not properly appeased.

Cedar was also honoured for the healing properties in the living spirit of the tree. Shaman, both male and female, shaped the soft bark into spiritual poultices, and applied them to the ill to draw out sickness and curses from the body. The healer would rub the sick with a bundle of the soft shredded bark, and then divide it into four smaller pieces. These they secretly buried in the doorway of four houses. If the person who cast the curse crossed one of those thresholds then the curse would turn on them.

With the right prayers a tree might even be persuaded to act as an ally of sorts in spiritual matters. Hilary Stewart, a modern ethno-botanist recorded the following Kwakiutl prayer to a cedar. It was from a man seeking a cure for his sick wife:

> *"Look at me, I am to be pitied*
> *on account of my poor wife...*
> *sick for a long time*
> *with an ailing kidney.*
> *Please have mercy on her*

and, please, help each other with your powers,
and with your friend, acrid root of the spruce,
that my wife may get well.
Please Supernatural One,
You, Healing Woman,
You, Long Life Maker."

In a remarkable way, the respect the natives gave to cedar has returned directly to them in modern times. While most of their villages have disappeared, and their old hunting and gathering areas pre-empted by white surveyors, the old trees that stood there a hundred, or five hundred, or even a thousand years ago still stand today, and many still bear the axe marks and wounds of bark stripping and plank harvests. These trees are living evidence of aboriginal use of the land. Known as Culturally Modified Trees, or CMT's to trained archaeologists, they play a valuable part in documenting modern native land-claims.

***

Dinnertime finds me still under my tarp, stirring pasta on the fire with my new spoon. After dinner, I put up my tent and take a walk in the rain, picking up firewood for the evening ahead. The giant Sitka's that line the edge of the woods are still swaying in the rough wind. Back in camp, I brew up some herbal tea to keep rehydrating and pull off my rubber boots to dry my feet by the flames. From under the shelter of my tarp I watch the outline of the shoreline fade into darker and darker shades of grey, until finally night overtakes it all. For a few hours I sit alone with the flames

11. Stormbound

In the morning I wake to the sound of wind in the treetops. A steady rain is pelting the tent, so I roll over and try to fall back asleep. But a short time later a team of bikini-clad invaders arrive in a flashy boat. Bare female flesh flashes everywhere as they pitch a volleyball net in the breaking sun. Halfway through the excitement of the warm-up sets, I wake a second time, thoroughly disappointed by the sounds of wind and rain. I crawl out of the sanctuary of my tent, pull on my rain gear and rubber boots and trudge down the beach to the lookout. Down the coast, whitecaps cover the sea and the rocky offshore reefs are exploding. Visibility is barely half a mile in the driving rain. Looking up at the tops of the Sitkas swaying in the storm, it doesn't look like I'll be doing much of anything on the water today, least of all knocking a volleyball around.

I walk back to camp, picking up firewood as I go, wondering what Rose is doing back in Sydney and what I'm doing here? On the beach a flock of small sandpipers wings its way along in the shelter of the bay, each tiny body a perfect partner in the tight formation. Twenty or more, they weave through the air as a singularity. The white of their underbellies and wing feathers flashes like turn signals, giving the squadron a cat-like agility some that seems to require no leader.

Finally alone on the coast, as I have long sought to be, my plan now strikes me not as challenging but strangely antisocial. I puzzle over the roots of my own motivations as I carefully peel strips of tinder for my fire. What is this need to be alone and from what part of me does it come? Is it merely my ego at work, struggling to prove my worth and courage to my family and friends? Or is it some greater inner demon that I hope to confront on this coast, to slay my own doubts about myself? A few minutes later I touch the flame of my lighter to the curls, grateful for the warmth as I cup my hands around the flames. Superficially I might appear to be driven by my ego, but inwardly none of this feels that way to me. There is a searching here that I am doing, but even the question itself seems to be defying definition. The answer may as well be hidden in the flicker flames.

No clarity comes to me this morning though. The wood is damp and the fire smokes along for half an hour before I can boil water for tea. Over a long breakfast of porridge, I stare out at the grey void wondering what to do. I'm keyed up to paddle, but clearly the storm seems to be worsening and I know it might blow for days. I have food, water, heat and shelter and a boat to leave in any time. The paddle downwind back into the shelter of Quatsino would be an easy one. But I am pretty happy just to sit and wait out the storm. In the end, with few options, the morning takes care of itself. I shift my tent to a dryer spot beneath a stout cedar, tend the fire like a newborn babe whose comfort I have come to trust, read a bit, and stare out at the sea sipping endless cups of strong black tea.

West Coast rain is unique. Unlike tropical downpours, or Prairie thunderstorms that arrive with a diluvial opening of the heavens and depart minutes later with a final peal of thunder, it's far more persistent. Often it hangs round for days or weeks, or even months at a time, dimming the life force in everything. Rarely do firecracker arcs of lightening spark up the sky. Instead it descends like a blanket that cloaks entire mountains, pulling down the sky, and swallowing the horizon. All our familiar terrestrial markers are erased, often for days at a time. Caught in the midst of it all, the bearings by which we mark our place in the world are erased. The only option is to retreat to the inside.

For the Kwakiutl, the long storms of autumn and winter were a period of immensely social activity. With the harvest of summer safely laid up in the rafters of the clan houses, the important winter ceremonies could begin. With the arrival of the winter storms, the tribes would retreat to their most sheltered villages and welcome the new season of *Tsetseka* with a four-day festival. Everything from songs, music styles, dances and even proper names and identities were transformed. The hierarchy of the clan system was replaced with a new social order, one based on ritual identity. The winter ceremonies were controlled by the villages' secret societies, made up by selected initiates. In Kwakiutl cosmology, these ritual identities defined a person's real position in the much greater supernatural world.

Along with the winter ceremonies were the intertribal 'potlatches', a name taken from the Chinook trading language meaning 'giving'. The potlatches were lavish feasts lasting several days held to mark important events in the life of a chief and his family, like a puberty ritual for a daughter. Allies, enemies and extended family from hundreds of miles up and down the coast were invited to witness the important bestowing of hereditary titles and ranks. Although the Kwakiutl were matrilineal, power and authority rested firmly in the hands of the men. It was often transferred between families through the marriage of women, who brought a dowry of their father's crests, songs and dances to her new husband, or material wealth in the form of copper plates carved with crest, blankets or slaves. The new husband could not use the titles himself, but only acquired them for any sons or daughter his bride might bear. In return the bride's family had a right to demand a bride's price, repeatedly, much like rent. If he could not pay, he was shamed, and the bride could be remarried to a new suitor. For the noble women 'staying for nothing' was as shameful as a husband's inability to pay. Often chiefs' daughters would be remarried up to four times to give her maximum prestige.

It would be wrong to think native cultures on the coast were static before contact with the Europeans. Like all cultures they were continually evolving and reinventing themselves. Initially, the arrival of Europeans only complicated the Kwakiutl traditions. For the first hundred years after contact, the native cultures were stimulated through the newfound wealth from trade. White trade-goods, like blankets and muskets quickly took a central role in the exchange of gifts. Potlatching and winter ceremonies increased dramatically, leading to what some anthropologists call the golden age in West Coast culture. New metals and paints fuelled a rapid surge in elaborate mask making and totem pole carving and other artistic expression. But at the same time their populations were being decimated by diseases such a smallpox and influenza, and sterilizing venereal infections against which they had no natural defence.

By the 1870s, another force was working against the native people. The first wave of settlers who inevitably followed the explorers and traders began dictating new laws for the land. Unlike the first wave of traders, collectors, and navy officers who valued stable peaceful relations with the Indians, the new wave of settlers and miners were largely unsympathetic to any Indian concerns.

They wanted land and had little concern for what they considered to be only heathen superstitions. When the new colony of British Columbia passed into Confederation in 1871, the Indians also had a new identity thrust upon them. Without consent or treaty they were designated wards of the Federal Department of Indian Affairs, based several thousand miles away in Ottawa. It would not be until 1969 that Canada would finally admit the natives of this land were citizens of the new dominion that now controlled there lives and land and finally gave then the right to vote. To this day most native bands in British Colombia do not have treaties with the government that has taken over their lands. It is a continuing source of political tension in the politics of the province.

Along with settlement, large numbers of natives also joined the new wage economy spreading up the coast. Many took seasonal jobs in the numerous fish canneries that dotted the inlets, or signed on as hunters on sealing boats summering in the Bering Sea. The cash wages injected more wealth into their traditional society. Old harder ways of living were cast aside by the younger generations. Commoners with cash wages could now challenge the chiefs in potlatches, gaining titles and crests they previously could not afford. The result was a near revolution in internal social order of the Kwakiutl.

To European eyes the potlatch was often perceived only as an uncontrollable inflationary cycle of senseless giving. But to the natives it remained an important tradition that redistributed wealth and a cultural legacy. It ensured that elderly, to whom much was owed, would not languish in poverty, but collect on a lifetime of giving themselves. Most controversial of all was the role of women, who were traded amongst the old men without their consent, and the 'Squaw dance houses" that opened up on the outskirts of Victoria, a young city largely populated by single men. Church leaders were outraged, complaining that the avails of prostitution were used to pay for the gift giving of the potlatches. Finally in 1884, the government amended the Federal Indian Act to ban potlatches, shaman's societies, winter ceremonies and spirit dancing. It was intended to be the killing blow to a culture they believed was on the verge of extinction.

Then in 1886, this letter appeared on page six of the *Daily Colonist* newspaper in Victoria:

"TO THE EDITOR: - My name is Maquinna! I am the chief of the Nootkas and other tribes. My great-grandfather was also called Maquinna. He was the first chief in the country who saw white men. That is more that one hundred years ago. He was kind to the White men and gave them land to build and live on. By and by more white men came and ill treated our people and kidnapped them and carried them away on our vessels, and then the Nootkas became bad and retaliated and killed some white people. But it is a long time ago. I have always been kind to the white men.... And now I hear that the white chiefs want to persecute us and put us in jail and we do not know why.

"They say it is because we give feasts which the Chinook people call 'Potlatch.' That is not bad! That which we give away is our own! Dr. Powell, the Indian agent, one day also made a potlatch to all the Indian chiefs, and gave them a coat, and tobacco, and other things, and thereby we all knew that he was a chief; and so when I give a potlatch, they all learn that I am a chief. To put in prison people who steal and sell whiskey and cards to our young men; that is right. But do not put us in jail as long as we have not stolen the things which we give away to our Indian friends. Once I was in Victoria, and I saw a very large house; they told me it was a bank and that the white men place their money there to take care of, and that by-and-by they got it back, with interest. We are Indians, and we have no such bank; but when we have plenty of

money or blankets, we give them away to other chiefs and people, and by-and-by they return them, with interest, and our heart feels good. Our potlatch is our bank.

"I have given many times a potlatch, and I have more than two thousand dollars in the hands of Indian friends. They all will return it some time, and I will thus have the means to live when I cannot work any more. My uncle is blind and cannot work, and that is the way he now lives, and he buys food for his family when the Indians make a potlatch. I feel alarmed! I must give up the potlatch or else be put in jail. Is the Indian agent going to take care of me when I can no longer work? No, I know he will not. He does not support the old and poor now. He gets plenty of money to support his own family, but although it is all our money, he gives nothing to our old people, and so it will be with me when I get old and infirm. They say it is the will of the Queen. That is not true. The Queen knows nothing about our potlatch feasts. She must have been put up to make a law by people who know us. Why do they not kill me? I would rather be killed now than starve to death when I am an old man. Very well, Indian agents, collect the two thousand dollars I am out and I will save them till I am old and give no more potlatch!

"They say that sometimes we cover our hair with feathers and wear masks when we dance. Yes, but a white man told me one day that the white people have also sometimes masquerade balls and white women have feathers on their bonnets and the white chiefs give prizes for those who imitate best, birds or animals. And this is all good when white men do it but very bad when Indians do the same thing. The white chiefs should leave us alone as long as we leave the white men alone, they have their games and we have ours.

> *"I am sorry to hear the news about the potlatch, and that my friends of the North were put in jail. I sympathise with them; and I asked a white man to write this in order to ask all white men not to interfere with our customs as long as there is no sin or crime in them. The potlatch is not a pagan rite; the first Christians used to have their goods in common and as a consequence must have given 'potlatches' and now I am astonished that Christian persecute us and put us in jail for doing just as the first Christians.*
>
> *Maquinna, X (his mark)*
> *Chief of Nootka"*

***

As I toast up another sandwich for lunch on the fire, a sport fishing boat motors slips out of the shelter of the islands to the north and coasts into the bay. Reflectively I step back into the shelter of the overhanging branches and pull apart my fire to stop it from smoking. The boat turns and motors slowly into the secluded beach next to mine, the occupants unseen beneath the canvas dodger. They disappear between the rocks and I hear the engine cut off. Voices echo through the trees. Not wanting to be disturbed, I flip through my pile of books and pull out a dog-eared anthropological monograph and settle down by the remains of the fire to thumb through it.

Some time later the visitors, as they turn out to be, re-emerge from behind the rocks in their boat. They drift out into the bay without starting the engine. I wonder now, as they sit floating, if they have spotted my camp. I doubt it. I would much rather be left alone than have to deal with some guests. Then, without a sign, they power up. The boat curves out across the bay and disappears back into the islets, back toward the shelter of the Sound.

Curious what they were up to, I build up my fire to keep it going and head out across the rocks to the tiny cove where the visitors landed. I find a small A frame squat tucked in the edge of the woods and surrounded by a garden of discarded Budweiser and Miller cans and assorted empty forty-ounce whiskey bottles. The rough shack was likely built from driftwood split and chainsaw-milled on the beach. The steep roof is covered in a velvety mosaic of moss and lichen. I step up onto the small porch and peer in the glass pain window. It's Spartan, but not abandoned. Inside are a tin stove, a table and chairs made from driftwood, and a small loft for sleeping filled with a nest of old blankets -- the rudiments of life on the coast. I poke around for a while and eventually find a trail round the back leading off into the woods. With nothing better to do, I head off up the small hill.

It feels strange to be separated from the sea. Inside the woods there is a smell of dank fertility mixed with the fragrance of green sap. After about half a mile I pick up the sound of the surf again and I can see light peaking through the trees ahead. A stout cedar shingle outhouse appears on the trail and then another more solid looking green cabin just at the edge of the woods. I check the chimney but see no sign of smoke so I step up on the porch and peek in the windows. At a table by the window, playing cards lie in three hands, as if laid down moments ago. From the porch there is a sweeping view out across the Bight. The water is darkened by the gusting wind, while an endless advance of white caps smash themselves over the scattered reefs. The far shore, only a couple miles away, is lost in the thick mist of the rain.

Along the beach I spot a simple wooden ladder leaning against the thick trunk of a windblown tree. From a low branch a rope swing hangs out over the steep beach. I can't resist. Seizing the rope in one hand I climb up the ladder and lean back against the tree. Then with a big breath I step off and swing out. Twenty feet in the air, high over the beach I scream like a madman into the wind and rain, again and again. My exhilaration surprises me.

Afterwards walking back to my camp over the trail I realize that until now, a strange calmness had replaced the normal oscillation of my moods. Without people to share, my emotions have already started to flat-line. But I also notice a second more troubling change at work. Between the long stretches of flatness there are almost alien spikes of anxiety. The night sweats that stalked me alone in my dreams have now invaded my waking moments. When they strike, the feelings of impending danger are often so far out of tune with whatever I am doing, often something mundane, that they seem foolish. But I can't ignore them or brush them away. Through unknown channels in my mind they trigger a sudden physical constriction in my chest. They are too strong. I know what I fear, and I know more and more what I have come to face. I know now that it is going to take all of me and more to push through.

Back in camp I stoke up my fire. As I sit down to write in my journal for a while I startle a squirrel on a log behind me. Momentarily stunned by my arrival, she freezes, and I spot a wide-eyed pup clinging underneath to the fur of her belly. Perhaps I have camped too close to her hollow for her liking, or perhaps I disturbed her along the pathway. Then with a chattering, they disappear down the logs.

12. Raven's arrival

Later in the afternoon the sky looks as if it's clearing. I consider packing up. As I stand looking out at the sea I hear a strange croaking from the treetops. "Go" the voice seems to say. I walk further on the beach to investigate but see nothing, so I turn my attention back to the sea and its condition. It seems calm and the rain has lifted. I wonder if it will last. As I stand considering my options, a large coal-black bird drops from a high branch above my camp and swoops down toward the beach. Deftly it pulls its wings up into a stall, and steps to the ground just at the perimeter of my camp. Nearly as high as my knees, the large bird looks directly at me, cocks its head, and pauses, as if waiting for my next move. Ah, so it was you Trickster, I say almost out loud. One swart eye regards me for a moment. I wonder what it sees.

Ravens have a reputation for cunning. *Corvus corax*, as they are known in academic circles, is recognized as the most intelligent of all birds, surpassing even parrots in cleverness. Supremely adaptable, they are ubiquitous across the northern hemisphere, spreading their broad wings from the frozen tundra right around the Arctic Circle, down to the peaks of the Himalayas and Central America. Studies have proven them to be highly social, capable of sharing and working together as an extended family to raise the young. They work in teams to steal food from sled dogs, and cached food, and show off to each other by teasing wolves and foxes at a carcass. Even the great Roman naturalist, Pliny the Elder described their ingenuity 2400 years ago when he observed a raven fill a narrow vase with rocks to raise the water level so he could quench his thirst.

I've often seen them playing and rolling like fighter planes in the air, looping and diving for no apparent reason, other than just fun. They also have an incredible vocal ability, with some observers recording over 64 distinct calls. They can imitate a human voice or the calls of other birds. They are even known to identify themselves with personal calls, much like names within the tight family groups. But they also have a darker reputation to match their feathers.

As carrion feeders, stories of ravens often mirror human attitudes toward death. Throughout Europe, ravens were commonly associated with battles and plagues. Their dark outlines darkened the skies ahead of Viking raiders, harbingers of the death that was soon to follow. The Vikings revered the black scavengers and painted them on standards that were carried into battle. The English immortalized the battle bird in epic poems. In Beowulf, the ravens awaited battles as their good fortune; "Not at all shall the sound of the harp wake the warrior, but the black raven, eager for the doomed ones, as he shall say much to the eagle of what success he had at feeding, when he, with the wolf, plundered the corpses." A 'Ravenstone' was an executioner block, and the sight of the bird was a common warning for travellers that they were approaching gibbets at a crossroads. After the Great Fire of London in 1666, huge flocks of the black carrion eaters feasted ravenously on the corpses rotting throughout the charred city. In despair the citizens petitioned King Charles II to kill them off. But a soothsayer warned the king that if he did, a greater disaster would befall England and turn his palace to dust. So instead he passed a royal decree that six would be kept captive in the Tower of London, a practice that is continued to this day.

The raven is not just associated with death. Its powerful wings and clear intelligence bestowed upon it a reputation for prescience and farseeing, even control of the weather. Two ravens sat on the shoulder of Odin, the Norse god of war. Named Hugin, meaning thought and Munin, meaning memory, the sharp-eyed scouts alighted each dawn to reconnoitre the secrets of the earth, returning each evening at dusk with tales from the edges of the earth. Even now in Ireland, "Raven's knowledge" means to know and see all. Noah first sent a raven from the Arc while at sea to follow to land. But it did not return, perhaps because it found a corpse to feed on, prompting him to later send a dove. It's doubtful though the ravens would have been missed on the crowded Arc. According to Jewish folk tales they alone defied Noah's ban on mating in the cramped quarters.

It was in the New World though, where the Raven's reputation reached its zenith. The stories of Raven's deeds are linked to the dawn of humanity's appearance on the continent. Here he is revered as a Trickster and a God (much like Coyote in what is now the U.S. Southwest). From the Bering Sea, where humans first crossed the land bridge, his legend spreads like two fingers along the coasts. One trail of exploits is carried eastward along the shores of the Arctic right across to Greenland by the Inuit people. In their oral histories Raven created humans from rocks, along with a menagerie of other creatures for his own amusement. But when they proved too durable, he switched to making them from mere mortal dust. Always mischievous, he later made life harder for the people of the land by stopping the rivers from running uphill as well as down, and turning the rich fat that grew on trees to useless fungus.

Despite all his malevolent behaviour, North American's first peoples do not see Raven as evil. Indeed the Western concept of evil has little place in many of the traditional beliefs. Rather Raven is regarded with caution and amusement, a trickster who will use his cunning for his own ends. Sometimes he could even be of help. As the hunter's ally and informant, he is the one who is turned to for help when game is scarce. Right through the long arctic winters, the Raven lingers in the arctic, feeding on the carrion left by wolves, bears and the Inuit hunters. Amongst the Koyukon of Alaska, Raven is known to guide them toward game, calling ggaagga-ggaagga (animal-animal) as he flies overhead, tucking his wings and rolling to lead the hunters to the prey. As such, the popular folk hero is revered and never eaten.

The second line of myth stretches south along the West Coast. Here Raven is also widely known as the Trickster and the creator of life. The Haida tell how Raven opened the clamshell from which men first crawled out upon the earth. Later they say he gave humans fire, while the Tlingit say he created mosquitoes to plague the people.

To Western readers, accustomed to a narrative tradition in which stories are structured with a predictable progress from beginning, to rising action, to climax and finally to denouement, native stories might seem wandering and anecdotal. They often lack a formal moral conclusion, leaving the reader with feeling of uncomfortable ambiguity. These expectations say as much about our own culture as any other. One of my most favourite Raven tales is a good example of how different the styles can be. In this story the storyteller warns the people of Raven's untrustworthy nature without casting a Christian judgement on his actions. In this story about Raven, known in the local language as *Qo'ishinm'it*, the well-known trickster heads out fishing and comes back with an unusual catch. It was recorded by Frank Hunt in Mochawat, a Nootka Sound village to the south in 1916:

"Raven was one of the chiefs of the Mowach'ath tribe. One day he met his friend Black Bear. When they met, he said to Black Bear, 'Will you go out to fish for halibut, for we have no food to eat?

"Then Black Bear said, 'Yes I will go with you if you will promise to take good care of me.'

"Raven said, 'Why, what harm can I do to you? You are four times larger than I am. It is your place to take care of me, for you have greater strength than I have.'

"Bear replied, 'That is so. Let us be going now!'

"Raven told him to get his halibut fishing-line; and Bear went into his house to get his halibut fishing-line, and took it down to the beach. He also had a piece of octopus for bait, and he put it into Raven's canoe. Then he told his friend Raven that he was ready:

"'For,' said he, 'my paddle and my halibut fishing-line are in your canoe.'

"Raven took his halibut fishing-line and his paddle from the corner of his house and went down to the beach, where his canoe was. Then Bear went to the bow, and Raven sat in the stern. They paddled out to the mouth of Muchalat Inlet. Here Raven said to Bear, 'We are far enough out; I will let go the anchor; we will stay here anchored while we are fishing,' and he put the anchor overboard. After he had done this, he turned toward the stern of the canoe, away from the bow, for he did not want Bear to see him putting the bait on his halibut hook. Bear

took his halibut hook, put a piece of octopus on it, and fastened the hook to his line. Then he put the two hooks on the spruce-pole crosspiece, tied the stone sinker to the middle of the crosspiece and threw it over the side of the bow. Raven did the same to his line; only Bear did not see what he put on his hook for bait.

"As soon as Raven's hook reached the bottom, he got a bite, and hauled up his line. There was a large halibut on it. He took his hook out of the fish, and then threw the hook overboard again. Soon he has another bite, and he hauled up his line with another large halibut on it. He kept on doing this until the canoe was half full of fish. All this time poor Bear did not catch a single fish.

"Then Black Bear said to Raven, 'Friend, tell me how it is that I do not get a bite, and you have nearly filled the canoe with halibut? Will you not give me some bait to put on my hooks?'

"Raven laughed, saying, 'O friend! The bait that I put on my halibut hook I cannot give away; for after I have finished using it for bait, I shall have to take it from my hooks and put it where it belongs. You have the same thing on you. Why don't you take yours off and put it on your hook for bait?'

"Bear replied, 'What have you put on your hook for bait, that the halibut bite it so much?'

"And Raven said to him, 'If I were to tell you what I have done to myself, you would not do as I did.'

"But Bear said, 'O friend! I would do anything to myself rather than go home without getting one fish, and be laughed at by our friends.'

"Then Raven laughed, and said, 'I will tell, I have used my privates for bait. Therefore I am getting all the halibut to bite at my hook.'

"Then Bear asked him how he could take off his privates; and Raven said, 'I cut them off.'

Bear replied, 'Does it not hurt you when you cut them off?'

"But Raven said, 'I think it would hurt me more if my people should come to the beach and laugh at me because I came without any halibut. I think it best to stand the little pain of cutting off my privates rather than be laughed at by our people, for it would hurt my feelings enough to kill me.'

"While they were talking, a man came paddling out to them in a canoe. It was Cormorant. He anchored close to where Raven was fishing, and he could hear every word they were saying. After he had let down his anchor, he put some octopus bait on his hooks, and dropped the line overboard. While he was waiting for a bite, he heard Bear say, 'Come and cut my privates off; for I believe I could stand the pain for a short time better than being laughed at by our friends.'

"Raven said, 'Why can't you cut them off yourself as well as I can?'

"Bear inquired, 'After I have cut them off, how shall I put them on again?'

"Then Raven laughed while he was chewing gum [spruce sap], saying, 'Why, of course, I can put them on; for you see that I always chew this gum, and after I finish using my privates for bait, I gum them on; and when I want to use them again, I pull them off without any pain.'

"'Well' said Bear, 'come and cut them off, for you know how to do it.'

"Raven said, 'I will give you a chance to get some halibut, for I don't want our people to laugh at you until they kill you; it is better to stand a little pain now than to be killed slowly by shame;' and he took his large mussel-

shell knife from the stern of his canoe to where Bear was sitting. When he came up to him he said, 'Now, my friend, lie on your back, with your two legs as wide apart as you can get them, so that I can make a clean cut.'

"Then Bear lay on his back, as he was told; and just as Raven was taking hold of his friend's privates to cut them off, Bear asked if it wouldn't hurt when the cutting began. 'Well,' said Raven, 'you must be foolish to think that a cut from a knife won't hurt for a short time. When I cut my privates off, it hurt me, I know, but it is better to stand pain for a short time than to be laughed at by our people until dead.'

" 'Well,' said Bear, 'cut away, then!'

"Then Raven took hold of his friend's privates and cut them off as quick as he could. After he had cut them off, he said to Bear, 'Now go to sleep for a short time; then, when you wake up, you will feel well again:' and he went back to the stern of his canoe. He had not been sitting there long, when he saw bear give two kicks, and stretch out his body. Then Raven went to look at him and found his friend dead. Then he said to himself, 'Now I have my wish, for he was a fat man. I will go ashore and cook him and eat him before I go home.'

"Then he looked round, and saw Cormorant close to where he had been. He had heard everything he was saying to Bear before he killed him. So he hauled up his anchor. After he got it up, he paddled to where Cormorant was, and said to him, 'What are you doing here?'

"Cormorant said, 'I am halibut fishing, but I can not get a bite of any kind of fish.'

"All the time they were speaking to each other, Raven was wishing in his own mind for Cormorant to ask him for some of his gum; and they had not been speaking long, when Cormorant asked Raven what he was chewing.

"Cormorant said, 'Will you give me some of your gum, for I have been here so long that I want to drink some water, and where I am I can not get any water to drink; your gum will moisten my mouth.'

"Raven said to him, 'I can not give you any gum unless you will let me take it from my mouth and put it on your tongue, for I am not allowed to put it in your hands,' said he.

"The Cormorant said, 'Put some of it on my tongue!' and he put out his tongue as far as he could.

"Then Raven took some of the gum from his own mouth and put it on Cormorant's tongue. As soon as he had done so, however, he took hold of Cormorant's tongue, pulled it out, and threw it in the sea.

"Then Raven said, 'Now friend Cormorant, speak!'

"Cormorant tried to speak, but could not say a word.

"Then Raven said, 'Now I have punished you for trying to come to spy on me. Go home; but now you can not tell our people what I have done to my friend Bear;' and he went toward the shore of the small bay.

"Then he went ashore and made a fire. He put a stone on it; and while the stones were getting red-hot he went down to his canoe and took out his dead friend, carried him up the beach and laid him alongside the fire. After he had done this, he saw that the stones were red hot; he then took the fire away, went for grass and moss, and carried them to the heap of red-hot stones, then put Bear on top of it. Then he took the moss and covered him up to keep the steam in.

"After this he went to his fisherman's box and took all his spare halibut hooks out. When it was empty, he filled it from a little stream of water, and poured the water on the moss which covered the dead Bear. It had not been cooking long, when he uncovered it and saw that it was done. *Then he began to eat, and continued until he had eaten his friend up. After he had finished eating, he picked up all the bones that were left and hid them in the woods. Then he went home in his canoe.*

"When he drew near the point of Yokwat, he turned the heads of the six halibut toward the bow of his canoe, as though they had been caught by Bear. These were the largest six he had in the canoe; for all Indians, whenever they catch halibut, always put them in their canoes with the tails away from them and the heads toward them. After he had done this, he paddled until he came round the point, where the people of the village could see him. Then he began to cry as loud as he could to make the people of the village hear him; and this is what he said while crying:

"'I lost my beloved friend Bear while I was fishing halibut with him. He had caught six large halibut, and was hauling up the seventh one, when his leg became entangled in the line. While he was trying to club the fish, he missed his blow, and the large halibut went down and carried him down also, and I never saw him again.'

This he said as he was paddling. The Mowach'ath went down to the beach to meet him. At first they did not believe him. Some said, 'Oh, Raven killed our friend Bear and has eaten him up!' and some said, 'He has left him on some island to die.'

"As soon, however, as they saw the six large halibut headed toward the bow of the canoe, they said to one another, 'It must be true that he was pulled over by a large halibut, for we can see these six large halibut our poor friend Bear caught; and it is true that sometimes the line will get tangled round either our arms or legs and nearly pull us overboard.'

"While they were talking, Cormorant was trying to tell his friends the Mowach'ath that Raven had killed Bear;

but they could not understand him, for his tongue had been taken out by Raven so that he might not tell his friends of what he saw, and Raven told some of his friends to take their large halibut and give them to Bear's friends. So some were given to his wife, and Raven kept the rest; and that is why there are Ravens on Yokwat Island, but no bears.

***

As night starts to fall, by the light of the fire, I consider my situation. Progress has not nearly been what I've expected. It's the fourth day and I've scarcely done twenty miles. Making it all the way to Tofino is beginning to look like a rather unrealistic goal unless this weather breaks soon. But the storm shows no signs of letting up. In the falling darkness my loneliness catches up with me. Under the shelter of my tarp I stoke the fire and watch as the islands in the distance disappear into the deepening shades of grey. In the darkness the forest at my back seems more unfamiliar. Strange sounds emerge from everywhere. At the edge of my campfire, the woods are filled with flickering shadows of twisted branches and stumps, hideaways of malevolent spirits

13. Franz Boas

In September of 1886 Franz Boas, the young physicist turned American ethnographer from Berlin, strolled down a steamship gangway onto the muddy streets of Victoria. The rowdy provincial capital was the gateway to the new frontier for hundred of settlers, prospectors and missionaries heading up the coast. All summer long, migrants flooded in to resupply at the trading posts, catch rumours of good land and new utopias, which they would follow, by catching steamers farther up the coast. As one of the farthest outposts of the British Empire from London by sea or overland, it was still a place where refined European sensibilities often rubbed up against grosser pragmatic manners. Boas himself was the sort of man rarely seen in the newly constructed bar rooms and hotels of the capital of the young colony, a brilliant and wide-ranging scholar raised in the liberal intellectual atmosphere of Westphalian Jewish society. Only twenty-eight years old, he had already completed a doctorate in physics, a field of study he had quickly abandoned in order to move into the young science of ethnography.

This was his second field expedition. His first was a self-directed tour of the Arctic to study the Eskimos of Baffin Island and pursue his own radical theories that their physical development might be influenced by the environment they lived in. Back in Berlin, he was one of the first academics to take an interest in Jacobson's touring troupe of Bella Coola dancers. Gifted with languages, within a few days Boas picked up enough of the native tongue to converse with Pooh-pooh and the others without an interpreter. He wrote, "My fancy was struck by the flight of imagination exhibited in the works of art of the British Columbians as compared to the severe sobriety of the eastern Eskimos." Combing through Jacobson's rough notes, he caught a glimpse of the "wealth of though [which] lay hidden behind the grotesque masks and elaborately decorated utensils." But Boas was also frustrated by the academic conservatism of his native countrymen. Shortly afterwards he decided to forsake a promising teaching career in Germany for the broader prospects of the New World. In the wealthy liberal institutions of America new ideas were flourishing. It was there that he planned to make a name for himself in the emerging field of American Ethnography.

As soon as Boas arrived in Victoria he hurried to the Indian camps that sprung up every summer on the edge of the town. The population of the shanty towns swelled to two thousand by late summer as canoes full of men and women from as far away as Alaska arrived to trade, gamble, arrange marriages, announce potlatches and spend their wages. Amazed at the cultural diversity living under the rough roofs and tents, Boas wrote back naively, that he had found one of the last places in North America where native people could still be found living uninfluenced by whites. In one location he could learn the languages and stories of the Tlingit, Tsimshian, Haida, Bella Coola, Salish, Nootka and Kwakiutl – all the major language groups of the West Coast that remained undocumented. His gift for languages allowed him to quickly pick up Chinook, the trading language, and he soon 'discovered' a previously undocumented Salish language, Pentlatch, spoken only by a few families near Nanaimo. Everyday brought new surprises and the material threatened to overwhelm him. The young ethnologist was overcome with amazement by the unrecognized potential of Canada's West Coast.

Boa's main concern though was with myths and languages, which he believed would provide the necessary key to mapping the tribes. But he still had some financial realities to deal with. To pay for his trip out west he had convinced a wealthy uncle to loan him the necessary capital. To repay the debt, he intended to collect artefacts to sell to museums. But prices in the camps were too high already, so after a month of frantic research, in early October, he accompanied a Kwakiutl Indian on a steamer heading to the northern end of Vancouver Island.

His timing proved to be perfect. Arriving in Newitti, an island north of Fort Rupert, the local tribes were gathering for the first of the winter ceremonies. In the isolated village his presence was first met with the natives' usual suspicion. White visitors usually came either to trade or proselytise. But Boas persevered and his patient interest soon gained the natives' respect. On the fourth day he gave his own potlatch to pay for a dance he wanted to see. In return the chief praised him, gifting him the name *Heilsakuls*, meaning "He who says the right things". Overjoyed by his success, Boas stayed to attend eleven days of dances, potlatches and shamanistic healings, making him the first white man to record the details of the ceremonies. With good relations established, he spent one hundred dollars buying up the used ceremonial material, taking care to record the origins and stories associated with each piece.

Two years later Boas returned again to Victoria, this time for the distasteful work of digging up graves in the burial ground around Victoria to acquire skulls and bones. His sponsor for his second trip was the American Museum of Natural History in New York, and they instructed him to send back a large collection of skulls and bones. Phrenology was a new branch of science trying to explain the differences in human cultures by comparing the physical characteristics of races. Measuring the diameter of skulls was a central part of the work. It was a busy summer for Boas in the graveyards, but a recent smallpox plague ensured a plentiful supply of specimens. In a few short weeks he shipped back eighty-five skulls and fourteen skeletons, many eventually purchased from local traders, and then left with an order for more. Boas himself would eventually be the strongest critic of phrenology, using his own data to discredit its racist agenda. It would be just one of his many ground-breaking theories that would pit him against the most established anthropological scholars in America at the time.

But before he could do that, Boas had field studies to do. He already believed that the key to understanding human origins lay in the complex work of mapping languages and mythologies, not measuring skulls. With the distasteful grave robbing done he was anxious to return once more to the isolated villages, which he believed were far away from the corrupting influences of white society. He was desperate to depart in time for the start of the winter ceremonials. His urgency was fuelled by the boatloads of settlers and missionaries he saw departing everyday. He knew that they would forever change the native people they encountered. Already the anti-potlatch law was seriously disrupting the native traditions. Languages were disappearing, elaborate grammars were being lost, and even the distinctive physical features of the native people were dissolving through intermarriage. He wrote back to his sponsors, "After ten years it will be impossible in this region to obtain any reliable information regarding the customs of the Natives in pre-Christian times."

Boas was anxious to push farther north on this second trip to tribes he had not yet encountered. But his patrons, who now controlled the finances, instructed him to stay on Vancouver Island to fill in the gaps of his knowledge. Basic questions remained unanswered concerning the customs and territory of the Salish, Nootka, and Kwakiutl. So he caught a steamer up the island's west coast to Port Alberni. There he spent sixteen days amongst the Nootka, the name then given to the Nuu-chah-nulth, the Kwakiutl's southern neighbours. His initial assessment perhaps reflected the difficulties he had learning anything amongst the highly secretive people. He wrote, "The Nootka were remarkably uninteresting ...[and] without any trace of originality." Disappointed, he hired some Nuu-chah-nulth guides to lead him across the difficult trail across the island's interior mountains. On the east coast he caught a steamer north up to Fort Rupert.

Boas' style of collecting was later to become known as 'salvage anthropology' – attempting to reconstruct the prehistoric past by collecting and recording the fragmented memories and artefacts that remained. What Boas did not yet realize was the extent to which a hundred years of trading relations had already irreversibly altered the West Coast cultures. It was at this time that he began to develop his theories that would philosophically diverge from prevalent beliefs and to understand that human history was too complicated for any 'universal laws' to govern it. He could already see that contrary to the established beliefs of the era, Mankind was not moving from a state of savage wildness through identical stages to an inevitable goal of civilization.

The new empiricism that Boas promoted was based on evidence, not just theories, and was in radical contrast to prevalent orthodoxy of the inherently superior nature of European civilization. For Boas, the main aim of ethnology would eventually be to prove "that civilization was not something absolute, but that it is relative and that our ideas and conceptions are only true as far as our civilization goes." Perhaps because of his lifetime of exposure to different societies he realized that how humans perceived themselves and the world around them was, above all else, shaped by the societies in which they lived. What he saw in ethnography was also a way of connecting how the environment in which we lives shapes our culture and thus our identity. He hoped this would ultimately allow us greater knowledge of ourselves. He wrote, "Ethnology opens to us the possibility of judging our own culture objectively."[3]

Boas was to dedicate much of his career to collecting the materials, oral histories and myths of the West Coast, compiling a valuable record of the disappearing cultures. One culture though, always remained central to his work, the Kwakiutl. Over the course of his life he would ensure that its myths, histories, dances and songs were documented more thoroughly than any other on the coast, creating such a reserve of knowledge that in later years, the Kwakiutl would turn to the pages of his work to recall the lost traditions themselves. But before he could do that, he still had to earn the confidence of one man. That man was George Hunt.

***

In the morning I wake to clear skies. It looks good for paddling so I pack quickly, eat a cold breakfast and launch in less than an hour. Just before I push off I hear the raven croak again. Too late trickster, this time the decision is mine, I think. As I paddle out, the sea is delightfully calm and I slip out of the bay on the last of the southbound ebb tide. Soon, with my mood lightening, I am heading out the channel between the rocks where two days ago I had turned back.

By the time I reach the end of the narrow passage the outgoing tide is rapidly sweeping me out to the ocean swell. It's a bit windier on the open water and a small chop is beginning to brush the tops of a deep ocean swell. The difference between chop and swell is critical to kayakers. You can have windless day with a mirror smooth surface on the water, but the swell from a distant storm hundreds of miles away might be rolling in as long deep waves that don't break. Chop, on the other hand, is the smaller breaking waves blown up by local winds across the water.

As I paddle out to the open water the combined effects of the chop, swell, and current, plus the waves rebounding back off the rocky point put me on edge. My feet become tense on the pedals

---

[3] Cole, (1999) p 132

and my thighs instinctively tighten on the foam braces inside my tight cockpit. In the chaotic water it's impossible to predict the strength or direction of the next wave. The only solution is to paddle harder to get through it, using the strength of my strokes to keep my balance. The Quatsino had prayers for such moments. They called dangerous rocky points such as this *no 'mas*, meaning old man, and the simple prayer Boas recorded went like this:

> *"Look at me, old man! Let the weather made by you spare me, and pray, protect me that no evil may befall me while I am travelling on this sea, Old-man, that I may arrive at the place to which I am going."*

As I turn into Restless Bight looking for shelter I realize that I'm running head-on into a giant tidal back-eddy. Quickly I ferry across the choppy current to a kelp bed at the entrance to the shallow bay. As I reach it I notice the breeze is freshening and the clouds are starting to descend from the mountaintops. Although just an hour ago I was looking at clear skies, I'm not really surprised by the rapid change in the weather. On this coast I've seen flat seas become white with foam in minutes and with less warning. I know I need to make a decision fast. I grab a stalk of the kelp as thick as my wrist and pull it across my deck to stop me from drifting while I look at my chart.

The first task is to try to sort out the reefs I can see guarding the Bight with the constellation of stars which mark them on my chart. The rocks and reefs I can see are not my real concern though. It's the unseen ones, the boomers, the most menacing of hazards in ocean swell, that concern me. A boomer is a rock submerged just below the surface, deep enough that it remains hidden until a particularly large swell passes over it. The danger they pose varies with rising and falling of the tides, and if you happen to be on top of one as the water is sucked out by a large wave, you can be smashed down hard on the rock with enough force to puncture or even snap a loaded kayak in half. I know of experienced guides who have lost boats this way. On my own here in this rising storm alone, swimming would become the best of many bad options.

Not keen to swim, I try to match the breaking waves I can see ahead with the tiny crosses on the chart. The breeze continues to stiffen, darkening the water with cats-paws and pushing up a growing chop making the task more difficult. I plan a dogleg route, aiming first for a rocky bluff on the shore that makes a good landmark, then turning south and running in directly to the beach two miles distant.

I release the kelp anchor and dig my paddle into the black water. It's a hard start into the unexpected current. Fighting my way forward against the stiffening wind, I check my progress against the opposite shore. Within a few minutes it drops to a mere crawl. As I make my turn at the rocky bluff, the beach two miles distant disappears into a blanket of heavy rain. Just before it does, I glance at the compass on the deck of my kayak and take one last bearing. Then my only possible landing site is swallowed up by the rapidly building storm. I grit my teeth, tighten my grip, fix my eyes on the black dome of the compass, and push into the wind. Tricky Raven.

Boas recorded another prayer for such times. Short and easy for stressful situations, it is a prayer to the Sun, one of the many members of the pantheon of Kwakiutl spirits. It also might reflect some early Christian missionary influence:

> *"Press down the sea in your world,*
> *Great Chief Father that it might become good,*
> *that your world be right on the water,*
> *Great Father."*

My own prayers remain of an even simpler sort. Conditions are not bad enough to make much of a believer out of me yet. I grit my teeth and punch into the oncoming gale hoping I am clear of all the boomers. Unable to take bearings off the shoreline, the chart is of little use now. I can only hope that the gusting wind has not blown me sideways off my course. Then one boomer opens its white jaws beside me, sending a surge of adrenaline through my already stressed body. The rest of the paddle is an anxious slog into the wind and the rain.

Finally nearly an hour after I pushed off, the beach appears through the mist in front of me. The last few strokes bring a huge sense of relief as my hull runs up onto the shore. Exhausted from the tension as much as the physical effort, I drag my boat a few yards up the gravelly slope, and pass out on a log, stone cold in the rain.

Some undetermined time later I wake up cramped, wet and cold, thinking about camp and a fire. Instead I decide to stretch my legs. The beach is half-mile long and faces north, sheltering me from the worst of the south-easterly wind that accompanies all the northern Pacific storms. I pull my chart from my boat and start walking to the aptly named Kwakiutl Point, hoping to look out at the sea further on. It's a rocky beach. Along the way small rock crabs scurry beneath my feet, so many of them I have to move up above the tide line to avoid crushing them. In a sandy patch at the end I spot some indistinct footprints the size of my open hand. Must be the kayakers I met a few days ago I tell myself, knowing that it's a lie. I know full well that coastal black bears often feed on the small crabs, but as tired as I am, I'd just rather not think about sharing my beach with one right now. An interested bear could open the hatches on my kayak just as easily as I might open a can of beer.

Scrambling over the rocks I emerge on a small bluff and look out over an ocean that is the nastiest yet of the trip. The heron feather in my cap buzzes in the stiff wind. The storm is obviously setting in.

In nautical terms though, it only a 'moderate gale'. This distinction is drawn from the Beaufort Scale, an archaic but handy method of estimating wind speed for those without an anemometer. It was developed in 1805 by Commander Francis Beaufort of the British Navy to measure the effects of the wind on a fully rigged man-of-war. In its modern form, it is an ascending scale in accordance with the standards agreed upon by the 1939 International Meteorological Committee. They state: when the wind speed is between seven and ten knots, also known as Force Three and a gentle breeze, mariners will see "large wavelets; crests beginning to break; foam of glassy appearance; perhaps scattered white horses". Climbing higher to Force Five, still only seventeen to twenty-one knots and a 'fresh breeze', seamen are told to look for "moderate waves taking a more pronounced long form; many white horses are formed; chance of some spray". That's still reasonable for an experienced kayaker.

Looking out now though, things are a fair bit worse. The Beaufort description "Sea heaps up and white foam from breaking waves begins to be blown in streaks along the direction of the wind; spindrift begins to be seen" seems to fit, putting the conditions firmly at Force Seven, meaning twenty-eight to thirty knots of wind speed. Although I've been out with other guides in Force Eight conditions to practice rescues, these are not the sort of conditions I like to be heading out into on my own. To actually qualify as a *storm* in Beaufort terms, a Force Eleven, the description "small- and medium-sized ships might be for a long time lost to view behind the waves..." is enough to tell me I never want to find myself out there on such a day. Not content, in 1955 the U.S. Weather Bureau added the hurricane category, Force Twelve, with winds over sixty five knots, and the visual clues turned from what was visible to how much could no longer be seen: "the air is filled with foam and spray; sea is completely filled with spray; visibility very seriously affected."

Pushing on into the 'moderate gale' would be fool hardy, so I head back to my kayak to make camp. I pitch my tent during a break in the rain to dry it out and set about making a fire. The wood is so damp that after several failed attempts, for the first time in my memory I have to stoop to using toilet paper to get my fire burning. I'm glad my friends aren't here to laugh at me now, but more than that it's an unsettling feeling, like I don't belong here. I won't be able to shake it off for the rest of the day. After a warm lunch I look up at the waves of rain coming down, and the wind rocking the treetops, and with nothing else to do I nod off into a restless sleep by the fire.

***

Late in the afternoon I awake for the third time today and take a walk to the other end of the beach. In the sand above the high water mark I find wolf tracks, perhaps a day old. They can be distinguished from dogs by the way they tend to put their hind foot closer to the print of the forefoot when running. Further on I find bear tracks down below last night's high tide mark, heading back in the direction of my camp. I follow them back high along the shore, noting their freshness despite the heavy rain. A rocky outcrop blocks my view of my camp, and I half expect to see the bear ripping through my food as I inch around the corner. But just as my camp comes into sight, the tracks stop suddenly and retreat into the woods. I suspect I was watched in my sleep earlier.

Glad to see the wolf tracks, but not so excited about a curious bear, I get a fire going for dinner, resolving to hang the food far from camp tonight, well up a tree with the bowline from my kayak. Still exhausted from the morning's paddle, I feel listless and low, not depressed or discouraged, just deeply tired. The afternoon passes uneventfully as the gale continues to blow, leaving me in a melancholy state. After dinner I measure out my progress. It's a sad tally: just twenty-two miles in five days. Tofino is still one hundred and sixty nautical miles away. At this point, just making it to the Brooks Peninsula would have to count as a success. I slip off early to bed after dinner, happy to desert my own company.

Outer Coast Solo

14. George Hunt

Much like the British East India Company, the Hudson's Bay Company was a virtual empire within an empire, that at one time held title of much of what would later become Canada. In 1849 it added Vancouver Island to its wide holdings. Soon after the London-based company established Fort Rupert near a small coal seam on the northeast coast of Vancouver Island, right in the heart of the Kwakiutl area. Company steamships out of Fort Victoria called regularly and the surrounding Indian villages quickly became the largest and most important on the north end of the island.

George Hunt grew up around the smoky clan houses of the Indian village at Fort Rupert and lived much of his life inside the collision of several cultures. He was the son of an English trader of the Hudson's Bay Company, Robert Hunt, and his wife, Lucy Anain, a noblewoman of the Raven clan of the Alaskan Tlingit people. His parents' mixed marriage, 'in the manner of the country' rather than the manner of the church, was common practice on the coast. For Lucy, whose clan were experienced traders, it was in keeping with the Tlingit tradition of cementing profitable trading relationships with marriage. Likewise, for the Hudson's Bay Company, mixed marriages were the only source of much needed wives for the men and a valuable means of establishing peaceful relations.

From an early age, the young Hunt fell prey to auspicious fainting fits in which he saw visions. At the age of nine, by virtue of his mother's noble Raven Crest, George was called before the fires by the local chiefs to witness and learn the secret dances. While he grew up speaking the Kwakiutl language in the village, at home he spoke the Tlingit language to his mother and English to his father, and Chinook around the trading post. By the age of twenty-one he could read and write -- a remarkable distinction for a native on the coast at that time. Twice he married highborn Kwakiutl women and further advanced his standing in the village. His father, who ran the fort, got him a position with the company. Later he ran his own trading post up in Newetti, competing with Ned Frigon to buy the valuable fur seal pelts. When his sister married the supervisor of the local salmon cannery, Albert Spencer, George got hired as a foreman, an important social position.

It was in the summer of 1886 though, when George met Franz Boas in Victoria, that his major occupation in life was set. The next year they met up again in the nearby Indian village of Alert Bay where Hunt had moved his own family. Boas was finishing his second field expedition to the West Coast and had just a weekend left to collect data and artefacts. He decided to focus on George Hunt. In the short time he "pumped so much out of him that the results of my stay were quite satisfying," wrote Boas in a letter home. Following his visit Boas returned back east to a new teaching position at the university in Worchester. But he was still anxious to further his reputation.

Finally in 1890 the opportunity Boas had been waiting for arrived. He was appointed curator for the Northwest exhibit at the upcoming Chicago exhibition. It was to be the largest exhibition ever held, timed to mark the 400th anniversary of Columbus' arrival in the New World.

Boas immediately wrote to George Hunt, asking him to start collecting Kwakiutl artefacts. He believed they were the 'standard tribe' from which much of the rest of West Coast culture was derived. In order to properly showcase the distinctive cultural group, he instructed Hunt to gather a large troupe of dancers. His plan was that they would actually live in a longhouse on the waterfront of the fairgrounds, right in the heart of one of America's largest and most industrial cities. They should be prepared, he told Hunt, to demonstrate "whatever is asked of them relating to their customs and mode of life, particularly the ceremonies connected with the secret religious societies"[4].

Hunt was eager to cooperate. He would finally have a second chance to travel, after missing his chance to tour Europe with Jacobsen. He soon began combing the inlets and villages of Kwakiutl territory, using money from Boas to buy the elaborate masks, totems, and feast dishes carved in the distinctive Kwakiutl style. Meanwhile Boas engaged a network of collectors in other parts of the coast. The final collection was massive – rare artefacts from the Haida of the Queen Charlotte Islands, including an entire house and 42 foot totem pole, took up three rail cars alone. In addition there was a collection of Bella Coola material, and some Nootka material from Neah Bay. But most impressive of all was Hunt's collection, larger than the others combined.

Three years after he started collecting, Hunt arrived in Chicago with fifteen Kwakiutl adults, male and female (including his brother William's Quatsino wife, the only 'longhead' in the party), two children, totem poles, canoes, three hundred and sixty five material specimens of the winter ceremonials and an entire Kwakiutl longhouse. The collection was judged by one Harvard professor as "the most complete and important ever brought together from this ethnologically most interesting region." For the

---

[4] Cole (1999) p 189

rest of the summer the troupe performed dances and fashioned traditional crafts outside their reassembled house in the middle of Chicago for crowds of curious onlookers.

But within sprawling grounds of the massive World's Fair the exhibit was easily overlooked by the thousands of people passing through each day. Pushed to the remote edge of Jackson Park the ethnological display was a mere sideshow, overwhelmed by the sheer size and diversity of the largest exposition the world had ever seen. They shared the immediate area with an Apache craftsman, a Navaho family in a traditional hogan, four families of Penobscots in their birch bark wigwams, the representatives of the Six Nations in an Iroquois bark house and some British Guanase Arawaks in a thatched hut. Further along on the main stage of the Midway Plaisance there were 280 Egyptians and Sudanese living on a Cairo street, 147 Indonesians in a Javanese village, 58 Eskimos from Labrador, a party of bare-breasted Dahomans camped on a mock west African savannah, plus Malays, Chinese, Japanese, Fijians, Samoans, and an Irish village complete with Donegal and Blarney Castles. Even Jacobsen and Hagenbeck were exhibiting their latest display of wild animals and a few odd leftovers they had yet to flog from their earlier West Coast expeditions.

Hunt quickly realizing that showmanship was the draw card at the World's Fair. One evening he arranged a "sun dance" to draw in a crowd. On a stage in front of the longhouse two dancers had hooks passed through the flesh on their backs. Driven around the stage leaping madly by two others, the pair reached such a frenzy that when Hunt finally walked over and extended his bare arm, one bit a chunk from it the size of a silver dollar. By this time much of the crowd of five thousand had dispersed in horror. The bizarre dance, possibly a mock version of the *Hawi'nalal* dance later described by Boas, did have the desired effect of catching the public's attention though. Shortly afterwards, the Reverend A. J. Hall, the same missionary that had thwarted Jacobsen twice, now on leave in London, learned of the outrageous events via a newspaper report. Incensed by the ridicule of his Kwakiutl flock he telegraphed the federal authorities in Ottawa who had given permission for the show and demanded it be cancelled, but by then it was already to late. Hunt has already cancelled any further performance of the ritual.

Boas for his part was deeply disillusioned by the whole fair. He swore, "never again to play a circus impresario." Despite the scandal raised by the bloody performance, he did manage to spend enough time with the dancers gathering what he felt was an impressive amount of information on the social organization and secret societies. More importantly though, he taught Hunt a phonetic script to record the stories of the Kwakiutl in their own words and language. No longer would he have to be concerned about errors in translation since the stories would now be recorded directly in Kwa'kwala, the language of the Kwakiutl. While the collection of materials stayed in Chicago, at the end of the exposition, the troupe returned by train to the west coast, each man (but not the women) one hundred and fifty dollars richer for their participation.

That autumn, Boas returned to Fort Rupert. On Hunt's advice the day after his arrival he hosted a potlatch of his own. Boas was well aware of the importance of giving generously in Kwakiutl traditions and needed to scotch some rumours circulating about his research in the village. So along with several barrels of molasses and pilot biscuits he presented photographs of the Chicago Exposition. The potlatch was a success. By Hunt's advice, Boas was warmly received and when the normal feasting resumed he was given a prestigious place in the longhouse, seated beside the elders with his notepad on his knee. Up to all hours of the night, sitting with a cedar bark blanket and head ring, and covered in eagle down, he swayed in the smoke and shouted the cries of the dances he now knew well while Hunt provided a running translation.

"You should see me," he wrote home somewhat condescendingly, "using a wooden spoon to eat from a platter with four Indians." Boas was the first of the 'participant observers' in anthropology and one of only a half-dozen Europeans at the time who learnt to speak Kwa'kwala, if only slowly. As recognition of his acceptance he was given a second more playful name. The name was *Me'mlaelatse* – meaning 'where the south wind comes from', reflecting his frequent digestive trouble eating the rich native food such as seal blubber and rancid eulachon oil.

Before Boa departed he hired Hunt as a permanent collector on a salary of seventy five dollars a month. In addition to the masks and feast bowls, Boas instructed Hunt to search for the everyday items of native life, like the particular moss used to wipe a salmon clean, and samples of dried huckleberries preserved for winter food. But more importantly, Boas also paid Hunt fifty cents a page to record any stories, myths, legends and even recipes he could learn.

Traditionally the West Coast people recorded all their history and stories in their memories and passed them on though oral story telling. Despite their intangible nature, the stories were highly valued possessions. Just like the right to fish a certain salmon stream, or the ownership of a large war canoe, they were items of wealth and status closely guarded by the ruling clans. But the Kwakiutl already knew, just as Boas did, their culture was slipping away with disease and dispersion. When Boas wrote them in a letter, "Friends, it would be good if George Hunt would become the storage box of your laws and stories," they responded, helping him fill page after page.

Working in the phonetic script Boas had taught him, Hunt recorded the words of the elders directly in their own language. Over the next five years Hunt sent back two thousand five hundred specimens and Boas returned several more time to the coast, always working closely with Hunt. By 1931, working together Boas and Hunt had collected ten thousand pages of published details of the natives of the north west coast. Together, they assembled one of the most complete collections of any West Coast culture.

In 1900, Boas reached the conclusion that he was getting too old for the rough life of fieldwork. He made what he thought was one last trip to spent two full months amongst the Kwakiutl. By this time his study of the patterns of myths and other aspects of ritual society had lead him toward another revolutionary theory. His limited knowledge of native cultures on the far side of the Pacific, the eastern coast of Siberia, had raised some questions in his mind about the similarities of certain cultural elements. Bows, armour and canoes shared certain unmistakable features. Many oral stories, like the Raven tales shared particular mythological themes. Could it be possible that a link between the two continents once existed and that people had once crossed freely between them?

George Hunt for his part had concerns of his own though that year. One winter's day he was arrested for cannibalism.

15. Hamatsa Society

I wake up early the next morning, and stumble out to check the weather. Climbing up the rocks at Kwakiutl Point, I look out onto dark skies and whitecaps, perhaps worse than yesterday. But the clouds over the mountains are showing patches of blue. There's a raven calling now and until the southeaster lets up I won't be going anywhere. Discouraged, I turn back to light a fire and make some warm tea.

At lunchtime the sky clears some more, and the sun pokes out enough to dry my gear. I start packing up with hopes that the wind will turn too. Above the low clouds, in the breaks I can see higher cirrus clouds blowing in from the southwest – a tentative sign that the weather might be improving.

I finish packing and make a call to push off. Leaving the protection of the south end of the Bight, I cut between a small islet and the shore and emerge at the edge of the open ocean. Here I stop. The whitecaps don't seem to be subsiding. Rather, they seem to be picking up, but it's hard to be sure. Things always look worse from the water than on land. But the swell is over a meter high, well above my head in this kayak, and occasionally up to two meters – more force six or seven conditions making boomers a serious concern. I sit for a few uncomfortably minutes. A few strokes further out and my anxiety level starts peaking irrationally. Instinct takes over. I turn tail and run back toward camp, feeling entirely defeated.

Back home in the shelter of Restless Bight I ask myself how I am ever going to get down this coast? I've got plenty of frustrated adrenaline in my veins. Tucked in behind the high trees, conditions in the shallow bay are far calmer, despite the occasional gust blowing in. A break in the clouds lights up the water, making it seem deceptively inviting. To burn off my pent up adrenaline I decide to practice some 'Eskimo' rolls for the first time on the trip. I'm already wearing my full wetsuit, so I figure, what the hell. I take a deep breath, brace myself for the rush of cold water and tip my kayak over to the right.

Rolling a modern sea kayak has a reputation for being difficult or nearly impossible, but much of the blame for this really rests with older kayak designs. Many of the early fibreglass sea kayaks built on the West Coast had a flat hull shape like a canoe, making them stable, like rafts, on calm seas. But a real seaworthy boat, like a traditional Alaskan design will be rounded in cross section at the middle, allowing you to control it smoothly through your hips in rough seas. Fully loaded and properly balanced, a well-designed touring kayak will sit low in the water, so that much of the weight in the boat is below the waterline, acting like the ballast in the keel of a sailboat, to stabilize against rolling. But once the circular momentum of a roll is started, an experienced paddler can exploit the inertia of his own body weight to follow through. With a flick of a paddle timed with a kick through the hips, theoretically you'll pop to the surface as you follow the natural momentum of the roll through. As a self-rescue technique, a 'bombproof roll' is essential for river kayakers in their much tinier boats. Sea kayakers use them when running in through high surf, where capsizes can be almost unavoidable on rough days. On open water though, rolling back up will just return you to the conditions that capsized you. It is more of a dodging manoeuvre than a rescue technique in rough seas. Underwater, I let the momentum of the roll carry through. I hang upside down for an instant and push my paddle up to the surface on the far side. Then with a twist, I sweep the blade across the surface and flick my hips to carry the motion through. It all takes just seconds. I pop to the surface dripping like a duck in the dazzling sunshine. Encouraged, I throw myself over again, and then again. I keep rolling on both my left and my right sides, until after a dozen, finally I blow a roll and fail to roll up. Hanging upside down in my boat in the frigid water, my arms too cramped to try another and running out of breath, I pull my spray skirt off the cockpit, wiggle out and pop to the surface. In the shallow water I drag my boat to the shore and sit down beside it for a rest.

I feel good, reaffirmed in what I am doing. In physical terms I'm pushing my own limits, exploring the boundaries of my own capabilities. The concept of limits has many more dimensions though.

***

On a cold day in March of 1900, George Hunt was arrested at his home in Alert Bay. The charge was assisting in the mutilation of the body of a dead woman, a violation of Section 14 of the Indian Act.[5] The alleged crime was rumoured to have taken place a few days earlier on the remote village of *Karlakwees*, a Kwakiutl village some distance from Alert Bay.

Allegations of cannibalism and human sacrifice were part and parcel of European colonialization throughout the world. From Columbus onward, Europeans assumed that North Americans were cannibals, and used the excuse of civilizing the savages as part of the rationale for conquest.

---

[5] Cole (1990) p 62

Almost all of the early allegations were based on hearsay, generally the accusations of one village against another. Even when Jacobsen took his Bella Coola troupe of cannibal dancers on tour, he encouraged them to play up the role of wild savage rather than attempt to convey the real meaning of the complex rituals. But the enigma of cannibalism has a long and complex history on the West Coast.

One of the earliest eyewitness accounts by a European appeared in Church Missionary Society letters of a Mr William Duncan, a well-known missionary amongst the Tsimshians on the mainland coast in the late 1850s. As one of the first missionaries to serve when British rule was barely enforceable, Duncan lived and preached almost alone, engulfed by a people and a way of living he could not understand. The manner in which he described the complex rituals in Christian terms reflected his strong moral conviction in the greater purpose of his work amongst the people he saw only as heathen savages. He wrote:

"Sometimes slaves have to be sacrificed to satiate the vanity of their owners, or take away reproach. Only the other day we were called upon to witness a terrible scene of this kind. An old chief, in cold blood, ordered a slave to be dragged to the beach, murdered and thrown into the water. His orders were quickly obeyed. The victim was a poor woman. Two or three reasons are assigned to this foul act: one is, that is to take away the disgrace attached to his daughter, who has been suffering some time from a ball wound in the arm. Another report is, that he does not expect his daughter to recover, so he has killed his slave in order that she may prepare for the coming of his daughter into the unseen world. I think the former reason is the most probable.

"I did not see the murder, but, immediately after, I saw crowds of people running out of those houses near to

where the corpse was thrown, and forming themselves into groups at a good distance away. This I learnt was from fear of what was to follow. Presently two bands of furious wretches appeared, each headed by a man in a state of nudity. They gave vent to the most unearthly sounds, and the two naked men made themselves look as unearthly as possible, proceeding in a creeping kind of stoop, and stepping like two proud horses, at the same time shooting forward each arm alternately, which they held out at full length for a little time in the most defiant manner. Besides this, the continual jerking of their heads back, causing their long black hair to twist about, added much to their savage appearance.

"For some time they appeared to be seeking the body, and the instant they came where it lay they commenced screaming and rushing round it like so many angry wolves. Finally they seized it, dragged it out of the water and laid it on the beach, where I was told the naked men would commence tearing it to pieces with their teeth. The two bands of men immediately surrounded them and so hid their horrid work. In a few minutes the crowd broke again into two, when each of the naked cannibals appeared with half of the body in his hands. Separating a few yards, they commenced amid horrid yell, their still more horrid feast. The sight was too terrible to behold. I left the gallery with a depressed heart.

"I may mention that the two bands of savages just alluded to belong that class which the whites term 'medicine men'. The superstitions connected with this fearful system are deeply rooted here; ... In relating their proceedings I can give but a faint conception of the system as a whole, but still a little will serve to show the dense darkness that rests on this place.... None are allowed to enter that house but those connected with the art: all I

> *know is, that they keep up a furious hammering, singing*
> *and screeching for hours during the day. "*[6]

Fifty years later when George Hunt was arrested, all the Indians of British Columbia were officially wards of the new Dominion of Canada, under the administration of Superintendent Vowell of the Federal Department of Indian Affairs. A liberal-minded man for the times, Vowell and his superiors in the Department of Indian Affairs in Ottawa favoured a tolerant paternalism towards the Indians. Assimilation was an unquestioned policy at the time but Vowell was reluctant to bring down the full force of the law on what he believed to be dying traditions. He openly expressed his view that the best way to assimilate the natives was by education and example, allowing them to see for themselves the superior nature of the white man's ways. It was a view favoured largely by the provincial government, and most whites in the province, who valued peaceful relations with the Indians.

But Vowell's policy of tolerance put him in direct conflict with many missionaries and church groups who were unwilling to tolerate any continuation of the heathen rituals of the savages under white rule. As yet, there had only been one conviction under the entire anti-potlatch section of the Indian Act. Indians were converting to the church in large numbers up and down the coast, and many of the younger generation who lacked wealth supported the potlatch ban themselves. But on one point, both government agents and missionaries did agree. Neither Vowell, nor the department, nor the missionaries were willing to tolerate the infamous "Red Bark" ceremony; the shadowy practice of cannibalism still rumoured to be practiced on the coast. Just five years earlier the Indian Act had been amended specifically to outlaw the cannibalism and animal sacrifice in the rituals. [7]

---

[6] Mayne (1862) p285-287
[7] McDowell p149

Up in Fort Rupert, the local Indian Agent, R.H. Piddock, of the Kwawkewlth agency sided strongly with the desires of the missionaries to shut down the potlatch. But the Kwakiutl refused to heed his attempts at moral persuasion. Already Special Constable Xumtaspi a Kwakiutl, had made a fool of Piddock by dancing at potlatches in his new uniform, wrapped in a cape made from his Union Jack. When word reached Piddock of Hunt's participation in the Hamatsa ceremony he moved quickly to act. Piddock had just recently commissioned Hunt as a special constable, and was incensed by his violation of the law. [8] He sent Agent Woollacott to arrest Hunt, who was soon transported aboard the steamship Coquitlam, along with some native witnesses, to the jail in New Westminster.

In jail Hunt turned to his brother-in-law, S.A. Spencer who ran the cannery in Fort Rupert for help. Spencer drew some money from the cannery accounts and posted bail. The trial date was postponed, allowing Hunt just enough time to return to Alert Bay to recruit his own witnesses.

At the time Fort Rupert and Alert Bay area were strongholds of Kwakiutl resistance to the anti-potlatch law. While many native groups along the coast did convert to Christianity, the Kwakiutl already had a reputation as the most 'incorrigible' tribe on the coast. At least one Catholic mission actually abandoned its efforts to convert them, with one parting priest proclaiming in dismay, "I can do nothing amongst them." Resistance to any suppression of their traditions was fierce. They refused to send their children to missionary schools, or to adopt single family European style housing. As one government agent remarked, "They evince no desire for improvement. They see plainly that innovations will destroy their old, much prized domestic institutions and hence they cling to them more than ever." Despite the ban, the dances continued and potlatching was openly and extravagantly celebrated. Hundreds of sacks of flour, thousands of blankets,

---

[8] McDowell, (1997) p150

sewing machines, outboard engines, engraved coppers, canoes, even motorcars were given away in open defiance of the law.

Finally that spring, in the County Court of Vancouver, before Chief Justice Angus John McColl presiding, George Hunt stood before a jury of 12 white men. The Crown's witnesses painted a damning picture of Hunt's participation in the ritual according to one newspaper account:

> *"The body was placed on a box and two chiefs stood up and spoke calling on prisoner to come and do the carving. Hunt got up and red cedar turban was put on his head, and he went over and went around the house singing in Indian and stopped at the body. The chiefs discussed what he should cut the body with. Saw him take a knife, took the evergreens off and cut the legs off, then the head, and gave the three portions to a chief who handed them to the Hamatsa, named Wys-tla, who handed a piece to another Hamatsa, the trunk was given to a third and the legs to a fourth Hamatsa. They ate all the fleshy parts of the body. A chief gathered up the bones and put them on a buttoned blanket and wrapped them up. When the eating was finished the prisoner stood up and advised the people not to say anything about it, as it was a serious affair."[9]*

By 1900, the use of corpses was widely assumed to have been substituted with dummies and slight of hand. Ironically, many of the most reliable prior accounts of the ritual consumption of human flesh by the Hamatsa had come from Hunt himself. Jacobsen, Boas and the renowned American photographer Edward Curtis all quoted stories related to them by Hunt of various acts of ritual cannibalism that he had witnessed during his life amongst the Kwakiutl. In his journals Jacobsen had speculated that the 1865 gunboat bombardment of the Indian village near Fort Rupert, a

---

[9]Province, March and 18 April 1900, from Cole 1990 p74

mass punishment for the killing of a slave, had already pressured the Hamatsa initiates to substitute old corpses for freshly killed cadavers.

Boas recorded from several Kwakiutl informants that the custom of devouring men first came from the Heiltsuk, a Kwakiutl group from Rivers Inlet on the mainland coast. He found the various oral traditions to be consistent enough to be credible. While recording the marriage history of the noble Gwasilla family of Smith Inlet, which stretched back twenty-three generations, he learned how they claimed to have first received the Hamatsa dances by marriage from Seymour Inlet at a time he estimated to between 1575 and 1600. [10] From there it spread rapidly to other clans and villages. In another account, which he dated 1835, an elite Kwakiutl war party attacked their northern Heiltsuk neighbours, and claimed the Hamatsa dance and the right to perform its rituals, a common right of the victors.

While the specific details of the Hamatsa ceremony varied, most versions shared several common elements. In the Kwakiutl winter ceremonial season those privileged by rank or birth would be initiates of one of four classes. Lowest of all were the sparrows; above them the war spirits, yet higher the seals, and highest of all the Hamatsa or Cannibal class. Each class was further subdivided, into three grades, each of which took four years to pass through. Each secret society held its ceremony once each winter over the course of four days. Thus to become a full fledged Hamatsa, the initiate had to dance a twelve year cycle, four years though each of the three grades, usually after completing several other seasons of dancing in lower ranking societies.

The Hamatsa were the human intermediaries with the chief cannibal spirit known as *Bakbakwalanooksiwae*, which translates as "He who is first to eat men at the mouth of the river" or "man-eater at the north end of the world". As an invisible spirit *Bakbakwalanooksiwae* made his presence known through the

---

[10]McDowell (1997) p132, from Boas (1921) p 836-85

weird whistling sound of the wind blowing through the millions of mouths on his body. During the initiation ceremony when the whistle sounded, the novice would disappear into the woods with his two female companions, *Komunokas*, the rich woman, and *Kinkalatlata*, the slave, each accompanied by their four attendants. After a long period of fasting and seclusion the Hamatsa dancer reappeared. He was in a state of animated ferociousness, his hair, wrists and ankles costumed with hemlock bows, shouting "Hap, hap hap," meaning "Eat, eat, eat" as he tried to break away from his captors and bite people nearby. Eventually the dancer was enticed to enter the house, where over the course of four days he was tamed in the dances, a key aspect of the ritual, overlooked by most early European observers.[11]

While preparing for his trial, Hunt used the money from his brother-in-law to hire W. J. Bowser to defend him. Bowser was already a leading barrister in the growing city, and later went on to become attorney general and finally occupy the office of premier of the province of British Columbia. At the trial Bowser constructed a clever defence. He alleged that another Indian special constable who was a rival of Hunt had set him up and in fact the defendant was only watching the proceedings as part of his ethnographic research. A copy of Professor Boas' recently published book on the Kwakiutl was introduced as evidence, with Hunt's name and role as researcher credited on the inside title page. Thus it was only by chance that Hunt arrived on the island during the middle of the Hamatsa feast. As a prestigious initiate, Hunt was welcomed into the house. In his own testimony, Hunt said, after the body had been brought in and placed in the centre of the room, he was called by name to come and see it. He did so. And when he saw what it was and was turning away the Hamatsa and Bear and Dog dancers snatched the body and ate, or pretended to eat it.[12]

---

[11]Kwakuitl Art, Audrey Hawthorn (1967) p45.

[12] Province, April 19, 1990, from Cole (1990) p75.

At the end of Hunt's trial it took the jury of twelve white men twenty minutes to find him not guilty for lack of convincing evidence. While Hunt was off the hook for dismemberment, he did not escape other consequences. He owed his brother-in-law $400 for legal and other expenses. He returned to Alert Bay, only to take ill with smallpox.

Following Hunt's acquittal, a council of chiefs announced publicly that henceforth, only dummies, not corpses, would be used in the ceremonies, without actually admitting the practice ever existed. Furthermore the practice of biting flesh from the arms of observers would also henceforth be only simulated.[13] Attempts to prosecute the Hamatsa would continue for several years though. In 1904, the new Agent at Fort Rupert, attempted to arrest the ringleaders of a cannibal dance in Quatsino. [14]

By that time Hunt had long given up any public association with the secret society. Instead, he was working with Boas to acquire one of the most sacred spiritual artefacts ever to be removed from the West Coast.

---

[13] MacDowell 1991, p.150 (from Drucker and Heizer 1967, p. 87).
[14] Cole 1990, p 68.

16. Brooks Bay

I wake up at first light, aching with a sore back that has haunted me for years. Thankful to get up and get moving I roll up my bed in the half-light and wander down the beach to shake off my sleep. Not far from my tent I find cougar tracks skirting my camp and heading south. Based on the tide markings they can't be more than a few hours old.

The idea that a cougar, a bear and wolves would all be walking openly along this beach is a good indication of how little this area is visited. Cougars are generally the shyest of the three large carnivores on the coast. Quiet hunters, they spend their days deep in the woods sleeping in the branches of a favourite tree. There are some theories that clear-cuts and other habitat destruction are responsible for driving them down from the mountains to the edge of towns. There they make a menace of themselves snatching cats and small dogs, until finally a conservation officer is dispatched to destroy them. While attacks on humans are uncommon, most summers in British Columbia the newspapers report at least one fatality, usually a child or a lone hiker. Alone on this beach in the daylight I'm not concerned now, but I wonder if I was watched last night at my campfire.

The weather looks like it's breaking so I pack up, eat breakfast and launch quickly. It's not the clear day I had hoped for, but calm enough to try to make a few miles. In the channel heading out once again the swell is less than a meter. The wind, while still from the southeast, is light. I round the point without stopping and start picking my way through the boomers across to some islets directly to the south. It's an invigorating feeling to be paddling once again, after spending yesterday sitting in the rain. My kayak slaps through the small chop, and I hum a little to myself as I push along.

An hour later on the northern side of Lawn Point I pull up for a rest in the shelter of the beach. The first thing I spot is the cougar tracks still heading south along the tide line. I wonder if this is its regular patrol. Grabbing a snack from my food bags I walk to Lawn Point to check the sea further south. It's a flat isthmus of high grass with a rocky promontory sticking out into the open water like a broken finger. I clamber up a knoll and look out for the first time on to Brooks Bay.

It is about ten miles across the open sweep of the large bay to the hulking mountains of the Brooks Peninsula that sits shrouded in a miserable grey mantle of heavy clouds. Thick dark streaks of mist pour down the steep slopes like waterfalls. Beneath the gloomy presence the sea is an intense black like charcoal. It's a cold hostile sight and a stunning splendour all the same.

One legend from this spot, Lawn Point, seems apt for this moment. Recorded in the words of Chief James Wallas, a Quatsino band member, it is the story of a suitable sort of hero for this place. The Man with One Hot Side descended to earth here at Lawn Point. Part sunshine, part human, he was a popular sort of fellow, able to defend his adopted village simply by turning the heat of his body toward his attackers. It would be nice to see him now as I look out across the black water of the bay.

To paddle around the rocky point I'll need to come round the reef that extends a quarter mile out into the rough sea. I can see it is going to be ugly: boomers, chop, and swell are all combining to make a treacherous maze of breaking white waves. But buoyed by my success already this morning I figure I might as well try. It takes me a few minutes to walk back to my kayak and launch. From the shelter of the inner reef, a maze of rocks and channels, I work my way out toward the point. At the edge of the open water I nose my way around the first corner and look out at the open sea. Once again, seemingly inevitably, the wind has picked up. Directly to the south a dark cloud is swallowing the horizon as it rolls my way. Without a moment's reflection, I turn and scamper back into the safety of the beach.

Back on the beach the frustration overwhelms me. I'm sick of waiting in the rain. I'm sick of turning back. I feel like I am on the edge of defeat, but I'm not ready to accept it just yet. Unable to consider another day trapped on a beach, I decide that if I can't paddle around then I'll carry my boat across the grassy point and launch from the far side when the gale dies down. It seems like a rational decision at the time.

I unpack a load of gear from my kayak, hook it onto the two ends of my paddle and hoist it across my shoulders like a Chinese peasant. Then I set off to cross the grassy isthmus of land that connects the mainland with the rocky tip of Lawn Point.

From the shore it looked like it would be easy to break a trail across, but as I push my way in to the shoulder high grass, I soon realize that I have just found myself another tough challenge. Under foot are slippery logs that I have to negotiate with my awkward load across. I stumble alone for a quarter hour breaking a trail, stumbling on the wet logs till I reach the far side.

The far beach is completely unsheltered and thoroughly miserable, with just a sad little campsite cut out in a thicket of stunted trees. With the waves pounding on the gravel shore, just the thought of camping here in the teeth of the storm is completely depressing. But I'm so keyed up about making some miles today that retreat, even in the face of this storm, is not an option. Staying here is only a last resort I tell myself. I'll just hope for a break in the wind.

But before I turn back for my second load, I pause long enough to look out at the mountains of the Brooks. Then it starts to sink in. The sight of the dark mountain range is so daunting I finally start to realize the foolishness of my grand plans. If I can barely get around these short rocky points, then how can I expect to get around the worst obstacle to navigation on the entire west coast of the island? I feel like a fool for even pretending to try. Seven days of paddling and now it comes to this. I had no idea what I'd undertaken. The damn impossibility of this whole misguided undertaking is clear to me now.

Despite my disillusionment, stopping never really comes up as an option. Thoroughly exhausted by the rain and wind and the sheer exertion of the trip, I pick up my second load and begin hauling it across. As the rain starts to pour down, I return for a third load of gear, and then one last time for the final trip with my boat. Although it's only a few hundred meters in the long wet grass, the whole Sisyphean task takes well over an hour, leaving me completely drained. With the moving done I sit down on a log on the beach, completely ambivalent to the storm now raging past me. My mind is almost blank of thought. I sit staring at the impassable Brooks Range.

***

While Boas and Hunt were largely responsible for the best records of the complex Hamatsa ritual, it was one of Boas' students, Ruth Benedict, who finally took up the task of properly explaining ito significance to white audiences. In her seminal book, *Patterns of Culture*, published in 1934, Benedict strove to show how human 'cultures' each spring uniquely from the diversity of human adaptations. She developed Boas' ideas that parts of a culture could only be understood when taken in the context of the whole. In her eyes, whites baffled by the 'savage' behaviour of the Hamatsa or the extravagant giving of the potlatches, could not understand it because they were looking at the behaviour within the context of European morality.

To Benedict, the insider-outsider separation was a fundamental trait of humanity. All humans naturally saw the rest of the world, the 'outsiders', through the lenses of the culture they were raised in. The challenge for Western social scientists was to step away from prejudices of their own worldviews when looking at other cultures. In the 1930s her ideas were a radical challenge to the dominant notions of race-lines, birthrights and genetic superiority currently sweeping Europe.

"Culture is not a biologically transmitted complex," Benedict wrote, "There is no basis for the argument that we can trust our spiritual and cultural achievement to any selected hereditary 'germplasms'. What really binds men is their culture – the ideas and standards they have in common."[15] It was an important revolution in human thought – as important as the ideas of Copernicus that had reduced the earth to a mere satellite of the sun, and of Darwin that had shown man to be little different from monkeys and apes.

Benedict's interpretation of the Hamatsa or 'Cannibal' ceremony was based on the notes of Boas and Hunt. In it she attempted to restore the nobility to the ceremony that the years of persecutions and misinterpretation had attempted to destroy. She

---

[15]Benedict p12 -16

recognized that a central belief of the Kwakiutl culture was that ritual allowed men to cross boundaries into the supernatural realm. Dancing was the central means of reaching the spirit world. In her interpretation of the ceremonies, the significance of the rituals was revealed as one part of the larger worldview. She used the familiar example of the Greek cult of excess to help Europeans understand. She wrote:

> *"The initiation of the Cannibal Dancer was peculiarly calculated to express the Dionysian purport of Northwest Coast Culture. Among the Kwakiutl the Cannibal Society outranked all others. Its members were given the seats of highest honour at the winter dances, and all others must hold back from the feast till the Cannibals had begun to eat.... In their religious ceremonies the final thing they strove for was ecstasy. The chief dancer, at least at the high point of his performance, would lose normal control of himself and be rapt into another state of existence. He should froth at the mouth, tremble violently and abnormally, do deeds which would be terrible in a normal state. Some dancers were tethered by four ropes held by attendants, so that they might not do irreparable damage in their frenzy. Their dance songs celebrated this madness as a supernatural portent:*
>
> > *'The gift of the spirit that destroys man's reason,*
> > *O real supernatural friend,*
> > *is making people afraid.*
> >
> > *'The gift of the spirit that destroys man's reason,*
> > *O real supernatural friend,*
> > *scatters the people who are in the house.'*

"The dancer meanwhile danced with glowing coals held in his hands. He played with them recklessly. Some he put in his mouth, others he threw among the assembled people, burning them, and setting fire to their cedar-bark garments.... This cannibalism of the Kwakiutl was at the furthest remove from the epicurean cannibalism of many tribes of Oceania or the customary reliance upon human flesh in the diet of many tribes of Africa. The Kwakiutl felt an unmitigated repugnance to the eating of human flesh. As the Cannibal danced trembling before the flesh he was to eat, the chorus sang his song:

" 'Now I am about to eat,
My face is ghastly pale.
I am about to eat what was given me by Cannibal at the north end of the world.'

"Count was kept of the mouthfuls of skin the Cannibal had taken from the arms of the onlookers, and [he later] took emetics until he had voided them. He often did not swallow them at all. Much greater than the contamination of flesh bitten from living arms was reckoned that of the flesh of the prepared corpses and of the slaves killed for the cannibal ceremonies.

"For four months after this defilement the Cannibal was tabu (sic). He remained alone in his inner sleeping-room, a Bear dancer keeping watch at the door. He used special utensils for eating and they were destroyed at the end of the period. He drank always ceremonially, never taking but four mouthfuls at a time, and never touching his lips to the cup. He had to use a drinking tube and head-scratcher. For a shorter period he was forbidden all warm food. When the period of his seclusion was over, and he emerged again among men, he feigned to have forgotten

139

all the ordinary ways of life. He had to be taught to walk, to speak, to eat. He was supposed to have departed so far from this life that it was unfamiliar to him. Even after his four months seclusion was ended, he was sacrosanct. He might not approach his wife for a year, nor gamble, nor do any work. Traditionally he remained aloof for four years. The very repugnance which the Kwakiutl felt towards the act of eating human flesh made it for them a fitting expression of the Dionysian virtue that lies in the terrible and the forbidden." [16]

While the Kwakiutl, along with the Nootka and Giksan, continued to defy the ban, the gradual process of assimilation and acculturation finally achieved what the law could not. By the 1940s organizations such as the Native Brotherhood were more concerned with modern issues of social justice such as gaining the vote, better education and medical care. The last of the Hamatsa who could remember the old traditions passed away. The repeal of the anti-potlatch law was no longer a chief concern amongst the new generation of native rights activists.

At the same time a movement was underway in anthropological circles to wipe away whatever traces of the ancient practice remained. For many, the most convenient solution to bridging the cultural divide was to deny that it ever existed. In 1955, a leading scholar on the northwest, Phillip Drucker was ready to erase the stain of cannibalism altogether, claiming, "It is highly improbable that corpses were actually used." Drucker believed that the ceremony was just an elaborate sham. "The Kwakiutl were past masters at producing realistic tricks for stage effects. The smoked carcass of a small black bear, for example, fitted with a carved head, would look convincingly like a well-dried human body at a distance by firelight." [17]

---

[16] Benedict 1934, p177-179.
[17] Drucker 1955, p151 (in McDowell p151).

By the 1970s a movement to absolve all the indigenous cultures of the world of the great Christian sin reached its zenith. It was lead by the cooptional professor, William Arens. Identifying what he called the Cannibal Complex in white society, Arens suggested that cannibalism was actually a universal myth, invented and perpetuated by one group, in this case the white conquerors, to justify their subjugation of the 'others'. To Arens, the significant question was not whether cannibalism had ever taken place, but why one group invariably assumes that the other eats flesh. His published work stirred up fierce debate in the anthropological world, and forced a needed re-evaluation of old assumptions.

But while there was some truth in Arens' argument, he had to ignore a significant amount of evidence to prove his point. And what he could not ignore, he dismissed with a questionable position: despite countless native accounts of cannibalism around the world, since no anthropologist had ever actually witnessed an act of cannibalism, it was unacceptable to conclude it had ever taken place. Arens argued that the second-hand accounts of native informants such as George Hunt, an 'unreliable half-breed', were merely rumours, suspicions or simple accusations. Nothing, but that empirical evidence witnessed by trained (white) anthropologists could be taken as proof. In his paternalism, Arens nearly completed the task the missionary William Duncan set to achieve nearly a hundred and twenty years before, destroying by denial the very essence of a ritual he could not understand.

Finally after years of patient petitions by native rights groups, the potlatch law was quietly repealed in 1951, and in the same year, the first legal Hamatsa dance in 70 years was performed. These days the Kwakiutl still perform the Hamatsa ritual in the village longhouse at Alert Bay. The public version performed for tourists has continued its process of transformation. Copper plates, once valuable trade items are now substituted for corpses and slaves. But this time the change is voluntary, made by those who still own the dance.

***

Lunch is stale pita bread that turns to mush in my hands in the rain. By the time I finish eating, the squall has blown itself out. As I load the boat I realize that if I'd only stopped to rest on the other side of the point to wait out the squall, I could have easily paddled round now. But I'm here now and I no longer feel anything inside me that is either happy or sad. I'm just determined to go forward, as far as I can.

The skies are brightening as I head southeast from Lawn Point. With a ten-mile view across Brooks Bay I can see the weather coming from miles out to sea and for now it looks clear. After a short while I leave the shelter of the shoreline and cross to some islets out in the open water of the wide bay. At the islets I set a course directly across three miles of open water to the entrance of Klaskino Inlet at Heater Point. Just to be safe I take an accurate bearing off my deck-mounted compass as I push off, just in case the storm once again sets in.

Under the grey sky and the distant shadow of the range the normal rattle of my own voice is now absent from my head. In the silence it is easy to notice what else I usually filled it up with, including the imaginary conversations with old friends and companions who I've spent time on the water with, discussing the conditions and evaluating together my decisions along the way. On some occasions when anxiety was overwhelming me I'd turn to them and almost start to speak. Then I'd realize that they were not there at all, and I'd feel lonelier than before. But now all this is gone, an illusion I can no longer sustain. Now I'm alone on possibly the most isolated spot on this stormbound coast and everything - all the decisions, all the motivation, all the bailouts and failures and breakthroughs – every judgement will be entirely my own. I feel a great sense of relief with this hard-won realization. I realize that I am now looking straight at what I have come here to face.

An hour later, still a mile offshore, I pass Heater Point. Buoyed by the surprise break in the weather I make a decision to push on, reckoning I should make as many miles as I can while the weather allows. While the Brooks Range looks just as foreboding and dark, in the strange absence of wind on this leeside of the mountains I feel I am safe. A porpoise and a sea otter glide by curiously one by one, and I spot an eagle on the shore. Their peaceful company in the calm is ironic, considering the one sign of man is the massive clear-cuts from logging at Side Bay and the Klashino. The water here is a thick syrupy brown from the erosion on the denatured slopes. Once again, the white man's work has let the blood of the land bleed into the sea.

Along the shore beaches and possible landing sites are nonexistent. I am committed to my boat for at least the next four miles. It's an almost unbroken line of rocky cliffs. But my confidence grows with every stroke in the glassy swells. From my charts I easily pick out the boomers and avoid them by paddling a full mile offshore. Even that far-off, the sheer slopes of the mountains hang over me, dropping a thousand metres straight into the sea. Surprised by the energy I find in reserve, an hour later I finally turn into the mouth of the Klaskish Inlet. At some small beaches I pull ashore to make camp.

Once on land though, camp seems to give me no rest. I shuffle around cooking and checking my gear, but I can't feel at ease. After nearly a week up in Quatsino, I've come thirteen miles today, and suddenly find myself alone on an empty coast. Across the whole stretch of the bay, there is no sign of any human presence. Looking southwest, the Brooks Peninsula juts out ten miles into the open sea. In my exhaustion I realize I inadvertently picked a site facing south, with little shelter in the likely event of a storm.

That evening in camp, I take stock of my own food supplies. Because of the cold, I'm eating rapidly through my provisions. I have about five days left and I need at least three of those to safely get back to Winter Harbour if I fail to get around. Although the Klashish Islet looks delightful to explore, if I'm going round the Brooks it's got to be soon. I make a decision to head straight out toward Cape Cook, and hope for a chance to get round. I know from Tim in Quatsino that the tiny cove marked on my chart just a mile short of the Cape should be a safe refuge where I can wait out a storm. The prospect of running into some kind of trouble is daunting, but I tell myself if I pay it much heed I'd have no chance at all.

Sitting warm by the campfire looking out at the secluded majesty of the Brooks, it's strange here in this dark bay, like heaven and hell combined. This is the challenge I wanted, but far more severe than I expected. It has made me dig to the bottom of my soul to maintain the motivation to go on. I know if there had been the slightest wavering of intention, I would have turned back. It's like I'm at the end of a long thread that I've been unravelling ever so slowly since leaving Coal Harbour. Now that thread is being stretched to its limit. It's just a tenuous line of retreat that connects me back to that safety.

I know that to make it around the Brooks, at some point I'm going to have let that thread snap, and move beyond the possibility of retreat.

17. Klashish Inlet

The next morning when I wake it's pissing rain. From my damp sleeping bag I can tell by the way the tent is shaking the wind is howling at twenty to thirty knots straight through my unprotected camp. A peek out the door at first light tells me what I already know – more perfect storm conditions, although in the shadow of these mountains it's hard to judge the wind's real direction. I crawl back into bed, shamefully thankful for the chance to rest, but increasingly pessimistic about my plans to round the Brooks.

I feel empty, at the bottom of my soul again. I can now feel my motivation slipping. Happiness and sadness have been replaced with an overwhelming tiredness. There is too much rain, too much anxiety. I realize how much I deluded myself about my ability. Looking back, I realize that despite years of guiding, I've only been on the outer coast in mild weather, and only solo in conditions like this once for a few hours. I've never seen or even expected conditions as continuously challenging as these. I realize that I'm in way over my head.

During my late breakfast the wind continues to blow straight through my camp, threatening to rip my tarp or snap my paddle supporting it. I look around, and wander over to an adjacent beach looking for a better campsite. I stop to rest under a big Sitka and lie down to stretch out my cramped back on a driftwood log.

***

I'm far from the first person to arrive here feeling a bit lonely and dislocated. Some of the oldest recorded accounts of the area come from shipwrecked sailors. Two days past New Years of 1867 two sailors staggered into Fort Rupert with word of a shipwreck in Brooks Bay. Within days a rumour ran round Victoria that the wild tribe of Klashino Inlet was holding five hostages from the wreck of the *Mauna Kea*.

Reaction in the colony was swift; the HMS *Sparrowhawk*, the pride of the Royal Nayy's Pacific fleet, was quickly dispatched to the little-known coast on a rescue mission. Steaming up the protected east coast of the island, the gunship soon reached Fort Rupert and put in for news. The next day she rounded Cape Scott in a snowstorm and pulled into Quatsino to consult with the natives. There they learned that the sailors had already been moved south to Kyuquot Sound. For days the warship tried to round the Brooks Peninsula, but gale after gale kept forcing them back into Brooks Bay. On the fifth day steaming under full power and shipping heavy seas, they made it round only to be turned back at the entrance of Kyuquot Sound by the reefs in the darkening night. Finally, after holding position offshore through the night, at first light the next morning the anxious captain slipped the *Sparrowhawk* between the reefs into the bay and 'rescued' the sailors from Charlie's trading post. One was paralysed from exposure and another was frost bitten, but the rumours of their being held hostage were quickly scotched. Reporting on their treatment at the hands of the Indians, Captain Robertson testified the Indians shared all their food with them until they had no more to spare. With food low, the day after the first two sailors had taken a canoe on their own to Fort Rupert, the Klashino had taken the rest of the crew south to the traders.

A Nuu-chah-nulth tribe called the Classet also once inhabited Brooks Bay, but sometime lost from memory they were pushed out by the Klashino, a Kwakiutl name that means 'people of the ocean'. In the local language, the area was called 'Awlis eik' meaning especially favourable. Divided into four clans, the villages Te't'anetlenoq, Omanitsenoq, Pe!pawi Lenox, and Wis Ents!a were once spread around the shores and up the two sheltered inlets of the bay. The deep waters provided some of the best inshore halibut fishing on the west coast of the island, and when the traders arrived, the Klashino earned a rich bounty in valuable sea otter furs. The people traced their ancestry back to the sea otter woman, the source of their rituals that assured a good hunt. But by the late 1800s the extinction of the Klashino was well under way.

Kwatlimtish, just across the narrow entrance of Klashish Inlet where I am camped, was the first village to be abandoned. In his accounts of the rescue of the *Mauna Kea* Capitan Richardson provided a rare glimpse of the already much reduced tribe. He wrote they were "a very small tribe and rapidly dying off, numbering about 40 of which not more than 12 are adult males." [18]

---

[18]Wreck of the Mauna Kea, Victoria Daily Colonist, 1867, Jan 26, p2

In 1889, when the Indian Agent O'Rielly visited for a few hours to establish the boundaries of the Indian reserves only two houses and a handful of people remained in the entire bay. Most Klashino were already wintering at the amalgamated village of Quatsino. In 1914 a second commissioner met Jim Cultectsum, the only remaining Klashino, in Quatsino. Although Cultectsum still used the reserves for hunting and gardening in the summers and even made a claim for some further lands to be added to the reserves, the commissioner cut off two of the five existing reserves. When Cultectsum died in 1940, the direct line of the Klashino people finally disappeared from the earth, and the reserves passed on to the Quatsino.

Apart from the natives the only other people to inhabit the shores of Brooks Bay have been the occasional trappers, miners, prospectors and a long manifest of shipwrecked sailors. Whites had little use for the rough bay and generally steered clear of its treacherous entrance. One veteran of the coast called the area "the most God-forgotten piece of real-estate in British Columbia." After the *Mauna Kea*, numerous other ships were wrecked in the bay. When the barque *Thos. R Foster* sprang a leak off Cape Flattery, in the winter of 1890, the captain set a course under sail for Vancouver Island, only to beach on the remote tip of the Brooks at Cape Cook. The crew survived for 21 days on mussels, crows, mice, and seaweed before being rescued by the Chicklisaht tribe that inhabited the south coast of the range.[19]

Less fortunate still was the crew of the four-master *Glenorchy*, a formidable 2229-ton ship, sailing for Australia from Puget Sound in February of 1897. Six months later, some wreckage and a ship's lifebuoy washed ashore on the cape but no survivors were ever found. In May of 1893, thirty-six lives were lost and only twenty-five saved as the whaling schooner *Jane Gray* out of Seattle floundered off the cape. In October of 1899 one schooner captain reported a wreck, never identified, lying derelict off the cape. A

---

[19]Brooks Peninsula, p 14

month later the Peruvian barque *Libertad*, had her cargo of nitrates ignite and was abandoned off Solander Island. And in 1901 the barque *William Foster* and in 1903 the sealing schooner *Triumph* were both lost with all lives, along with fishing boats by the score through the years.

Even as late as 1939 rescues in the area were a dangerous proposition. When the fishpacker *Great Northern V* lost her rudder in a December storm that year, the crew cut the scow they had in tow and drifted up the coast for two days in the storm. Without a radio, they finally hit a reef ten miles to the west of Cape Cook, where a crewman, Ted Bernard, lost his life. The two surviving crewmembers, Captain George Skinner and his son Hugh, clung to the remains of the pilothouse as it was blown into Brooks Bay. Unable to walk and without food, fire or shelter in the cold winter storms, Skinner pleaded with his son for two days to leave him and seek help. Hugh finally relented and set out north along the shore toward Quatsino to find help. Able to make only four or five miles a day along the rugged coast, his rubber boots were torn to shreds by the time he was spotted by a search plane. Unable to land, the pilot returned to nearby Winter Harbour and a boat was dispatched to pick up the younger Skinner.

While Hugh was flown to Vancouver to have two gangrenous toes chopped off, a second rescue effort was launched for his father. But the rough winter seas made searching by boat impossible so a party of three prospectors set off by foot down the coast. It took them three days to reach the site of the first rescue and from there they picked up Skinner's trail, finally reaching his father twenty-one days after he first washed ashore. Nearly starved and half-dead from three weeks in the rain, it was still another three days before a boat would arrive to get him out. Within six months, both father and son were back at work on the sea, a testament to the hardiness of the seamen of those days.

***

When I awake from the unplanned nap the sun is breaking through. Encouraged, I eat a quick lunch and watch the sky slowly clear. When the wind dies I pack up camp, optimistic about making some progress, even if it's just a mile or two across the inlet to a more protected site. By the time I launch I've upgraded my plans and set my sights on Orchard Point about two miles distant. From there I'll make a call to keep on going or dig in for yet another night.

It's clear and calm as I start paddling. As I round an islet in the channel I surprise a sea otter fishing during the break in the storm. When he catches my scent in the breeze he startles and then swims away, powerful and calm, rolling on his back and pausing occasionally to scratch his belly with his hind legs.

Orchard Point is calm, so I keep going. I swing out wide from the reef, surprised by my own confidence in the glassy rolls of the swell. I'm learning new limits. I feel like a beginner in a new and unfamiliar environment. Towering above me the mountains of the Brooks Peninsula look majestic with the clouds lifting off the lower slopes just enough that I can see the waterfalls on the mountainsides. Along the shore a broad beach comes into view split by a creek running straight out its middle. It was once called *Le'dzadex* meaning 'having finding of whales'.

Dead drifting whales were an important food, particularly in the springtime amongst the native people of the coast. Chief Nimokwi'malis, a powerful shaman once lived in this area. The chief was a whale ritualist, a specialist who was capable of drawing the mammoth creatures into the bay. To prepare he would sleep in a burial cave surrounded by skulls. Then he would walk down to the water, lay down on a cedar plank flat looking up at the sky and drift out to sea on the falling tide. When the rising tide pulled him in, he would pull in the bodies of dead or dying drift whales. The tribe would then tow the carcasses to the beach to butcher them, then feast on their rich blubber and meat.[20]

---

[20] Brooks Peninsula – An Ice Age refugium

Intrigued by the large lagoon marked behind the beach on my chart, I can't resist a quick exploration. Nervously I paddle in toward the breaking surf at the creek mouth, time the sets and then slip across the sandbar and up the creek, my bottom just dragging on the shallow sandbank. I round a sweeping corner in the sandy channel and come out into a giant saltwater lagoon. The change is profound, like I've entered a land forgotten in time. The water is black and stagnant, only a few feet deep. Dead and stunted trees line the boggy edges of the lagoon, evidence of fluctuating water levels and harsh growing conditions. Further up I see a large flock of ducks and seabirds by the entrance of a freshwater creek. I paddle up and step out of my boat into the shallows of the flowing stream to fill my water bags. Looking up the valley I can't help but wonder what lies beyond. As a result of this discovery, two decades ago the entire mountain range was declared a UN Ecological Reserve.

The first scientific expedition to the Brooks Range was in 1981. A group of researchers spent the short summer of exploring the craggy mountain peaks. On that first trip they discovered thirteen plants unknown anywhere else on the island. They were botanical relics of an earlier age still clinging to life. Nine were previously thought to live only in the more remote Queen Charlotte Islands. Just as intriguing was the discovery that just a few kilometres away, on the main body of Vancouver Island were sixteen common plants unknown anywhere on the Brooks. These plant suggested that somehow, in small pockets on the Brook Range tiny ecosystems clung to life and survived the last ice age 10,000 years ago, and continued on in their isolation to this day. Eventually the scientist deduced that during the Fraser Glaciation, these mountains were covered in ice, but some of the higher peaks became nunataks, an Inuit word for a mountain peak that becomes an island in a river of glacial ice. With only a few square kilometres of land remaining open, the nearby sea tempered the climate just enough to provide an ice age refugium for the relict plants to survive.

I'd like nothing more right now than the time to explore the range, but also I'm anxious to press on, so I squeeze myself back into my cockpit and head back out to the open water. A few miles along the shore at a set of two beaches I jump out and scout about for a campsite. Finding nothing sheltered, I decide to paddle on.

As I push my way out the open coast the pangs of apprehension return, but this time I recognize them a different way. They are not from loneliness as I once thought, but from unfamiliarity with this landscape and all the dangers it holds. I feel like I am cradled in the hand of giant that could close on me at anytime. I have no one to turn to out here if things should go wrong, no radio to call on, no emergency locator beacon on which rescuers might hone, not even someone whose advice I can heed.

Out here today, at this moment, I know any successes or failures will be entirely my own. This is why I have pushed myself here. Rather than feeling apprehension now though, I feel a sense of calmness paddling on this water. I now know what's right for me and how to carry on.

The next beach is the last before Cape Cook, the exposed tip of the peninsula five miles away, so I decide to pull in and make camp. I'm exhausted from yesterday and it is catching up with me. While the wind is calm, a large swell has been rolling in all day and the surf is up on the steep beach, smashing on half-submerged rocks along its foreshore. It's a dangerous combination with a loaded boat and I take a while to scout it out. Finally during a break in the waves, I slip in quickly at the quieter end.

On the beach I find the tracks of black bears, one set big, the other small -- a mother and cub. Judging by their freshness in the light rain I figure they are from today. There is nothing I can do so I keep myself busy in camp, cooking and caching food. Knowing how heavily it could rain here, I pitch my tent between two massive logs, about a meter in diameter each and then string my tarp across it. I've finished all my bread, so I spend the evening baking up a batch of soda bread in the embers of my fire. I don't expect the bears to return, but just to be safe, I drink heaps of tea and urinate everywhere around my camp to warn them of my presence. In truth, it's entirely unnecessary, since a bear can smell almost as well as I can see, but I know I'll sleep more soundly. Then just before dark, the sky lights up with a glowing West Coast sunset, the first of the trip. It is hard to believe this is summer. I slip into my tent soon after dark.

18. Brooks Peninsula

I wake before sunrise and crawl out in the half-light of twilight. Already a blanket of low grey clouds presses a calmness over the water. Looking to the southwest down the peninsula, towards Cape Cook the sky is darker, but visibility is good for ten miles offshore I estimate. I push off an hour later, a little frustrated by the slowness of my departure but patient enough to make sure that today, of all days, everything is just right. I ride my boat out through the surf like a horse with my feet slung over the sides. Once outside the small breakers I tuck my feet in and settle into my seat for what I expect will be a long day of paddling.

My plan for the day is to paddle as far out toward the end of the peninsula as I dare. It's only about four miles to Cape Cook, the westernmost tip of the Brooks where the most severe weather on the entire west coast of the island usually is recorded. The details on the map of the little cove called Kayakers Haven, just before the cape, don't tell me if I'll be able to land there in the breaking swell or a storm. After that there are just two other landing sites for the next thrirteen miles on the far outside -- rocky and exposed creek mouths that would be treacherous in a storm.

I work my way along the coast keeping one eye on the sky to the west, another on the water for wind speed and direction, and a third on the clouds above for signs of high wind aloft. Seeing nothing of concern, I feel confident that I have at least a few good hours. I suspect the light winds I've experienced since I reached the Klashish are a leeward wind effect of the Brooks Range and that things to be worse once I round Cape Cook.

The paddle out to the cape turns out to be easy. I stay a quarter mile offshore, between some islands and the cliffs of the shoreline, and have just a couple boomers to avoid. As a precaution I make mental notes of possible emergency bailout beaches as I pass them and note the various mountains above them to make it easier to find them on the chart later if I have to retreat. But none looks like a nice prospect even in the calm conditions. Out here on the outer edge of the coast the rocky cliffs rise bare of vegetation high above the water, evidence of the battering the storms give the coast.

Just before the cape I pass a massive sea cave and then turn the corner into the small cove called Kayakers Haven. In the small surf the landing is fairly easy, but it's a boulder-strewn beach and in breaking waves it would be treacherous. The tiny cove, ringed by cliffs, is surprisingly tranquil, with a sheltered campsite up the back in the woods and a waterfall providing fresh drinking water. It looks sheltered but the stunted trees revealed that even here the worst of storms have no trouble battering anyone camped out.

After filling a water bag, I launch and head back out toward the cape. Nothing grows for several meters above sea level on the barren cliffs that line the shore. A jagged reef stretches along the front of everything. Beyond this point I'll be committed for at least another hour until I reach my next possible bailout beach. Captain Cook was the first European to spot the point that would later bear his name. Beating up the coast in the *Resolution* in 1778, he called it Woody Point, an unoriginal name that would later be changed on Admiralty Charts to honour his sighting. Ninety years later, the 1864 Pilots Guide to Vancouver Island had the following warnings for captains rounding the Brooks Peninsula:

> *"The cape rises abruptly from the sea to a summit 1,200 feet high; nearly one mile west off it lies Solander Island, which is bare, 580 feet high, and has two sharp summits, between it and the cape the passage is chocked up with rocks and no vessel or even boat should go inside the island. At a distance of 2 miles off the cape and the south side of the Peninsula, the soundings are 20 to 90 fathoms, and as a rule no vessel should approach nearer."[21]*

As I round Cape Cook, Solander Island comes into view on my opposite side. About a mile offshore the island is a smooth green mound, well fertilized from the seabirds' droppings. For thousands of years the island has been home to various species of ground-nesting seabirds like puffins, and rhinoceros auklets, and a large colony of sea lions round the backside. Some of its resident puffins and auklets are fishing in the nearby water. An entire ecosystem has grown up on the rock island in the wet conditions. In other places it might be a guano mine, but here it's protected as part of the Brooks Ecological Reserve.

According to local stories, Solander Island was once a giant blue whale called K'ulis, hunted by two tribes that lived on either

---

[21]The Vancouver Island Pilot, Compiled from the Surveys of Captain George Henry Richards, RN in HM Ships Plumper and Hecate between 1858 and 1864, Published 1864.

side of the peninsula. Each day one of the tribes would paddle out in a great canoe and try to tow the giant whale back to their village to butcher it. But the whale was too large and the next day the other tribe would paddle out to tow it back in the other direction. Eventually, one day K'ulis just sank to the bottom and created Solander Island.

I stop for a minute in the heavy kelp and contemplate my options. My own kayaking guidebooks have little to say about rounding the cape, only to mention that it should be attempted only by the extremely experienced and to keep a sharp knife handy in case breaking waves throw some of the thick kelp across the deck. The advice seems well placed. The woven mats are so thick I could almost get out and lie across them, a sign of the strong currents that constantly wash up and down this coast.

The swell continues to build as I paddle further out, rolling beneath me like the ocean's heartbeat. Light winds blowing from the southeast ripple its surface. I look southwest at a line of cumulous clouds that seem to be moving past. Beyond them, on the horizon, the clouds are darker but not threatening.

I make a quick decision to push on and take advantage of the unusually favourable conditions. If the wind blows up I can turn back and run downwind to the shelter of the haven, or further ahead I could bailout at either of the two creeks. I don't know what sort of beaches they are, but the stars speckling the chart indicate boomers menacingly protect both.

When I reach the second corner of Cape Cook, I finally look around the reef onto the true southwest side of the Brooks, the most exposed section. The swell is predictably larger and the wind slightly faster, blowing just enough to push white ripples off the tops of the waves. I figure it's not a sign of worsening weather, but just the increased exposure, so I make a hasty call to push on.

Strangely confident but not feeling reckless, I punch into the paddle ahead, plotting a course about a half-mile offshore outside the massive reefs of kelp and boomers. A few of the outermost reefs I pass on the inside. Far off in the misty rain to my left, the shoreline is a steep wall of toothy rock, ugly enough that I feel safer the further I am from it. Getting ashore anywhere besides the two creek mouths, still several miles ahead, either by boat or just swimming, is just not an option.

The wind though, continues to pick up, so I start plotting a more different route. To gain some shelter I decide to weave my way inside through the kelp beds and outer reefs, hoping to make quicker time out of the worst of the wind. After a couple miles I can see the point that marks the first bailout beach. I figure this means no turning back now. With the wind slowly picking up, I work forward and within a half hour the beach is directly on my left. From a half-mile offshore it looks like an easy landing. I figure I can run back into it if things get worse further ahead.

The next beach at Amos Creek is two more miles on. I start pushing my pace into the growing wind to stop myself losing speed. Occasionally I have to cross an outlying kelp bed or paddle wide around it. Eventually, by picking out various landforms along the distant shore I think I can make out Amos Creek. This helps predict the boomers. With more reefs and rocks than any other section of coastline I've paddled so far, sometimes I find them and sometime they find me, opening up right beside with a surging roar. A couple of careless readings soon smarten me up.

Out on the open ocean there is a more serious concern though; a darkening cloud low on the water is heading my way. I'm losing visibility quickly, and the distant mountains of Kyuquot I spotted when I rounded the last corner have disappeared from view along with the rest of the horizon, swallowed by the rapidly approaching squall. It's obviously building as I watch it hit the coast a few miles south and head straight toward me.

Amos Creek is still a mile away, making it at least fifteen, maybe twenty minutes away in these conditions. The squall looks five or ten minutes off. According to the bearing I've worked out, to avoid all the boomers and reach the safety of the creek, I need to turn exactly 210 degrees when I'm directly perpendicular to the creek, and run right up it into the shelter of the forest behind. Hopefully the tide will be high enough to let me up it without bottoming out, or I'll have to surf through the rocky entrance. Either way I can't really count on any sort of easy landing.

As I push on toward the creek mouth, the water is now whipped solidly with whitecaps, breaking the tops off the waves. The only part of the entire coast that I can now see in the driving rain are the cliffs directly a half-mile on my left. The creek mouth up ahead and everything else has disappeared into the grey that threatens to envelop me completely.

I'm tired, paddling less than half my normal speed. As I watch my progress past the cliffs beside me I can see I'm making little headway. I can't help but suspect even the tide has turned against me. A few minutes later, knowing I must be near the creek entrance, I start cutting in towards it, sooner than planned, gambling that I'm outside the last of the boomers, and hoping I'll make better time on a diagonal course than continuing straight into the wind and the current. Surprisingly, perhaps foolishly, I don't feel worried. Instead I feel a strange sort of confidence that I am going to make it.

Finally the creek comes into view and soon I'm looking right down it. I look at my compass to confirm my course bearing and notice my course is 40 degrees – a far cry from the 210 degrees I had marked on my chart. Instantly I recognize the carelessness of my mistake. I read the bearing backwards last night when I calculated it. I do a quick calculation to reverse it and get a corrected bearing of 30 degrees. I'm only off by 10 degrees. I correct my course, pull my rudder up and run in for the landing with a small swell breaking behind me.

My boat runs up over the rocks at the creek mouth, just scraping the bottom as I slip up the entrance into the calmness of the forest. Exhausted I pull my boat up on the stony banks.

Figuring that the squall will pass soon, I pull out my lunch and make some tea to warm up.

In the cold rain, lunch is a short affair under the dripping branches of a cedar by the creek. I take a walk on the beach in my wetsuit, oblivious to the rain, eating cookies as I go. Some fresh bear scat is full of tiny crab shells and berries. The whole place has a stunted otherworldliness. The foreshore of the forest is all snags and low scrubby bushes. Thick moss and lichen hang from the branches. The only tall trees are along the sheltered length of the creek.

After about half an hour the wind dies down. I pack quickly and drag my boat across the shallow creek mouth to the sea. As soon as I get underway the rain sets in again, but the worst of the wind appears to have blown itself out. With visibility remaining good, although the southern horizon is far from clear, I can see no reason not to press on. Miles out to sea another small squall is passing by. By chance I see a small sailboat bobbing through the worst. Someone is standing on the foredeck looking out at the sea. I realize that that's the first person I've seen in five days.

***

The southernmost corner of the peninsula, Clerke Point is a long shallow bank of boulders that forces me out almost a mile offshore. Fearful of another whiteout so far away from land, I keep a close eye on my compass as I round the final point. Once clear of the shallow breakers it's four miles down the exposed coast to the first beach. I estimate maybe two hours in these conditions, as tired as I am. I tick off the reefs one by one as I pass them outside. I'm so drained mentally and physically that it is taking all of my concentration just to keep paddling.

When I finally reach the first beach I'm totally exhausted but it offers no shelter for camping. Not caring, I run in through the surf, fearful of capsizing in my exhausted state. Ashore, I string my tarp between some spruce boughs leaning over the beach, strip off my wetsuit and cook a quick dinner on my stove, which ends up full of sand. Too wet and tired to care, my wrists and shoulders cold and aching, I pitch my tent beneath the tarp and climb inside well before sunset.

Outside the rain pours down on the surf and the sand and the tent, like the white noise of a radio blaring with no signal. Inside it's warm, with just a small leak in the floor. I should feel miserable in my damp sleeping bag but I'm exhilarated, even in my exhaustion, to have just soloed the Brooks. The anxiety attacks are gone. I know what my new limits are because I faced them today. Two days ago, no even yesterday morning, I didn't believe I could. Now it seems strange how confident I feel. I should feel scared and alone but I feel safe and at home.

The coast will always be here, and will always be this way. I didn't beat it or conquer it today. It let me round as an act of generosity on its part. In truth with patience and timing born of understanding, I've adapted to its ways, its needs and demands. This is my coast. That's how I've made it through. I feel doubly committed to making it to Tofino to enjoy my bragging rights. But right now it's taking three layers of nylon to keep off the rain.

19. Acous Peninsula

I wake up to clear skies the next morning and shuffle around camp impatient to see the sun rise over the mountains to the east. When it finally spreads its rays across the beach I spread out all of my gear to dry on the sand. A few fluffy clouds decorate the sky. It's the first day of nice weather thus far on the trip. I peel off my shirt and stretch on my sleeping pad in the sun while my gear dries. The naked skin on my back prickles in the heat. It's been almost nine days of rain and clouds since I left Coal Harbour and I've managed to travel only forty nautical miles. Pathetic really. Worse yet, that leaves me with only another nine days to travel another one hundred and sixty nautical miles to Tofino.

My gear dries quickly in the sun and shortly after I launch through the surf and turn my kayak east towards the mountains and Jacobsen Point. Despite the ideal conditions I'm still cautiously wearing my wetsuit, although the gloves and the hood are stored below. A couple miles along the shore I cross the mouth of the Nasparti Inlet. At a small group of islets on the far side I search for a falsely marked passage, before giving up and rounding them on the outside. It take me little over an hour and a half to cover the first 5 miles to Acous Peninsula. I feel confident that at this pace I'll make up the lost miles.

On my chart Acous Peninsula is marked as an Indian reserve, little more than the size of a postage stamp on my chart. Five smaller reserves are scattered on the islands and up the inlets nearby. This is the traditional territory of the Checleset, the northern-most band of the people once known as the Nootka. This language group occupied all the inlets from here to the southern tip of the island, and then across the Strait of Juan de Fuca to a few villages on the Washington State's Olympic Peninsula. In both language and culture they appear linked to the Kwakiutl, yet distinct in their rituals, mythologies and history. Estimates based on glottochronology (tracing the divergence of languages through time) have suggested that sometime 2,400 to 5,500 years ago the two 'Wakashan' languages separated. This seems to suggest (but not prove) a southward migration around the Brooks.

The archaeological evidence of human habitation is equally old, with several digs dating samples of human occupation back four thousand years. While trade routes across the mountain passes could have been another migration route, the larger distinctions between the Nootka and the Salish culture on the far side of the mountains argues against this possibility.

In the cosmology of the Nootka they have been here since transformers brought the land into being. Today the Nootka of Vancouver Island are known as the Nuu-chah-nulth, a name they gave themselves when the thirteen remaining bands formed a political alliance in 1958. The name means 'along the mountains' – a description of their traditional territory. Altogether they have one hundred and sixty reserves, totalling twelve thousand acres. Although it seems like a lot of land, the tiny smallholdings are all scattered piecemeal along the coast, with little potential for economic development. All the geographical qualities that made places ideal choices for a village two thousand or even just two hundred years ago – proximity to the open ocean, defensive position, protected access to land a shallow canoe – are now almost irrelevant, except to kayakers and people in small boats. Access to the highway and a good harbour for fishing boats have drawn most of the Nuu-chah-nulth bands away from the outer coast.

Here at Acous Point the waters are shallow and protected by a maze of islets and reefs that extend out for a mile into the sea. It's a natural harbour perfect for landing a small boat. Through the clear water a white sandy bottom reflects back the vigour of the sun. Cutting across a sheltered channel I run into a couple of kayakers. Fluorescent green paddling gloves leap up and beckon me over. Behind two broad sunhats and matching polarized glasses I find a middle-aged American couple. They look at me expectantly. Not having spoken to anyone in almost a week, I'm not sure what to say.

"Wow, nice boat. Where you coming from?" says the woman. Quatsino, I tell them, instantly feeling like a braggart. For a while I answer their questions about my trip, then I ask them about theirs. They are up from Seattle for a couple weeks and just arrived at Acous Peninsula this morning. They have more gear than experience, but enough trepidation toward the sea to keep themselves safe.

"Do you know anything about an old totem pole here?" asks the woman.

I don't, so she tells me she thinks one remains somewhere on the reserve.

"There was a native guy here in a boat a few minute ago. When we asked him, he just pointed at that beach there and then just sort of took off."

The beach she points to is another obvious village site, now overgrown with a mature forest.

"We had a look, but couldn't find it."

Even from the water I can see a trail disappearing up between the berry bushes that line the shore. So we land. In the forest the short trail turns right along the shore. Nearby I spot the painted ridgeline of a roof that long ago fell to the forest floor. The midden underneath must be at least six feet deep at a bank by the beach. Further along is a thick cedar log covered in moss and punky with age. Along its length I can see the stylized profile of a bear that has fallen face down on the earth. A veil of moss nearly blots out its ovoid eyes. By its short length I guess the pole may have actually been a mortuary pole, a stouter version where the bodies of nobility were set in cedar burial boxes after their death. Like many villages along the coast, this one may have served as a memorial to the people who once thrived here. These days though, the Checleset live in Kyuquot on a larger amalgamated reserve, although I suspect they still use this site for its rich berry picking and for stripping cedar bark for traditional basketry.

Before contact, conservative estimates are that up to twelve thousand Nuu-chah-nulth lived on the coast. Estimates by some native activists are several times higher, up to a hundred thousand. What is documented clearly though is that in just over two hundred years, that population was cut to a mere three thousand, at least a seventy five percent obliteration. Several killers have been fingered in this massive depopulation, but one in particular has to be given the largest share of the blame. The single most lethal killer was the *variola* virus, AKA smallpox, brought by the white man on his ships.

Louis Clamhouse, an Ohiaht from Barkley Sound, south of Tofino, gave this version of the arrival of smallpox in his ancestral village:

> *"There came a ship which entered harbour at N'aqowis. The people went to the ship to see it, and went aboard.... They looked down the hatch, the Ohiahts, and they saw that there was something wrong with many of the white men, the sailors, for they were all groaning... Said the Captain, 'For seven days you will be well. Then you will get that sickness' The Indians did not know what that sickness was. There was none like it in this country."*

Smallpox is spread by droplet inflection, by a sneeze or touching a person or a corpse up to three-weeks old. After infection, a week or two later comes a fever, headaches, aches in the body and a rash. The rash worsens into red spots on the hands, feet and face, eventually spreading to the rest of the body, rising up into lesions that become weeping pustules. In severe cases the lesions become so thick on the body that they flow together into one, bleeding and sloughing off sheets of putrid skin. Smallpox was lethal in thirty percent of cases amongst Europeans. Amongst the natives of North America, it is thought to have been several times worse.

The reasons for its virulence are two-fold. Smallpox is what is known as a disease of civilization; like measles, influenza, cholera, whooping cough and scarlet fever; it spreads quickly and lethally in crowded cities. And like others, it was thought to have first crossed over to humans from domesticated animals, in this case from cattle in Egypt around 1200 BC and had survived in the cities of Europe and Africa until the World Health Organization eradicated it in the early 1970s. In dense populations, over 300,000, it could remain endemic, permanently circulating slowly through the population, striking young and the strong equally, whoever had no immunity. Prior to the development of a vaccine in 1798, the only immunity came from surviving an outbreak. The vaccine was not widely used in North America until 1836.

When a disease of such virulence strikes a population with no immunity, it quickly becomes an epidemic, a wave of unstoppable death. Epidemiologists, those who study the spread of the disease, call the human devastation followed the arrival of Europeans in 1492 in North America the Columbian Exchange. In all seventeen diseases were exchanged. While the native Americans managed to send syphilis and rheumatoid arthritis back to Europe, the worst of the diseases came this way, paving the way for what some have called, without any exaggeration, the worst human disaster in the history of the world.

When Cortez first introduced smallpox to the Americas in 1519, it spread like wild fire through the densely populated agricultural regions of Middle America, levelling the field for an easy Spanish conquest. But there is no evidence that at that time it reached the Northwest Coast. Once it hit the more widely scattered populations of the North America it appears to have died out, a victim of its lethal success. After this first wave of death, the disease retreated, but as inflected carriers continued to penetrate deeper and deeper into the less populated parts of North America smallpox reached farther and farther across the continent. It would continue to breakout sporadically to inflect the following generations.

On the West Coast smallpox did not arrive overland. The mountains proved to be a near impenetrable barrier. Instead it arrived on the Spanish ships sailing up from their base at San Blas, on the Pacific coast of New Spain, now known as Mexico. Conditions onboard Spanish ships were so habitually filthy and notoriously disease ridden that sailors were rarely allowed ashore during the voyages, even at the most remote Indian villages, for fear that they might desert. Malnutrition and chronic illness made the ships' holds floating viral incubators. Because of the poor quality of their rations, the Spanish ships were plagued by scurvy, even on the short summer voyages of only a few months. The cramped living spaces with poor ventilation effectively transported the various old world plagues up the isolated coast. When the Spanish expedition of Quadra came up in 1775, the ships logs recorded scurvy and other unnamed diseases struck down fifty of the crew at one time.

The Nuu-chah-nulth have always blamed the first cases of the disease on the Spanish. It is unlikely the Spanish witnessed its effects, although they must of known that they were spreading the disease. By the time it broke out, they would have sailed on. They would have been well acquainted with its deadly rate of infection after their experiences in Mexico and Central America. But the crewmen of the *Columbia,* a merchant trader out of Boston, recorded the first written account on the West Coast of smallpox in 1791 in the southern Vancouver Island village of Nitinat.

With the English it was a different story. Before the British had a Pacific port, they had to make a sea voyage of almost two years to reach the Northwest Coast. Cook's third voyage was one of the longest journeys in the history of human exploration. The shear time involved prevented them from transporting smallpox and other old world diseases. But when Captain Cook finally did arrive on the Northwest Coast he and his crew off-loaded tuberculosis, syphilis and gonorrhoea. Although the Indians were frequent travellers, if they were ill, they were not likely to set off in open canoes on a long voyage. So for the first hundred years, the diseases were primarily spread by the explorers and then the traders that followed. Later, Hudson's Bay Company ships trading along the coast were a constant source of re-inflections to the native villages. Meanwhile in the north, Russian fur traders introduced smallpox even earlier from the Asian Pacific coast of their empire, but there is no evidence that it spread south at that time.

Once one of these killers was released into a village it was ruthless. With no experience of plague diseases, the native people were virtually defenceless. In the crowded clan houses diseases like smallpox spread rapidly. Traditional treatments such as cold bathing and gathering closely around the sick for shamanic healings actually increased the mortality rate. Eventually, when the natives learned the mysterious spirit was spread by contact, they often pulled their houses down and deserted the sick to die in the ruined villages. But eventually a new strategy of fleeing to neighbouring villages allowed the diseases to spread. Boas recounts a Kwakiutl description of the arrival in one village of the "man with mouths on his body":

> *"A man [came] who now rolled around on the ground, now jumped in the water and went back ashore again. His body was all covered in mouths which all laughed and shouted at the same time."*[22]

The first infections on the northwest coast in the 1770s, were followed by successive plagues in the 1800s, 1820s, and so on, striking each new generation with regularity. By 1835 all the northwest coast villages had experienced major epidemics of meningitis, dysentery, and smallpox. The Hudson's Bay Company began offering vaccines around the trading forts but met a great deal of suspicion from the native people who had no real reason to trust them. Many suspected that the whites were just trying to sterilize them. Then a new disease, measles swept through Europe like a scythe in 1847. By the next year it arrived on the coast. Infected passengers on the *Beaver,* the Hudson's Bay Company steamship carried it up the coast, decimating the locals, both Indians and whites. But it was the smallpox plague of the 1860s that had the most critical effect.

In 1862, along with the gold diggers, the *variola virus* came north on the steamer *Brother Jonathan*, docking on the 13th of March in Victoria. Within two weeks it had spread thought the

---

[22]Spirit of Pestilence, p 28, (Boas 1957/331)

white population of the town. Shortly after, it appeared in the native camps. The press lost no time blaming the most helpless and innocent, the Indians, for the spread of the disease. Plague became a convenient excuse to expel the Indians that occupied the rough shanty towns on the outskirts of the small colonial town. The newspaper, *The Daily British Colonist* condemned "the moral ulcer that has festered at our doors throughout the last four years...[Indians] who have free access to our town day and night." They suggested the townsfolk should remove the entire Indian population to a place remote from communication, "and burn the infected houses with all their trumpery." [23] Not surprisingly nobody suggested burning the houses of whites suffering from the disease.

Some missionaries, along with the Hudson's Bay Company, did attempt to vaccinate the Indians, although the vaccine was in short supply. On some parts of the coast up to fifteen hundred villagers were vaccinated in a single day, possibly saving some entire bands from extinction. But most natives feared the vaccine was a trick to make the women infertile, and many continued to refuse. In Victoria two Anglican missionaries were despondent:

> *"Who should care for these poor savages amongst whom the plague spreads like wildfire? They refused to be vaccinated, nor was there vaccine enough for several hundred miles to go around.... Neither doctors nor nurses were willing to take the risk involved in caring for Indians with smallpox.... The missionary and his helper were little else than grave diggers, placing beneath the sod an average of 4 a day."*

The colonial police chief moved quickly in line with hysterical public opinion, declaring, "The Tsimpsean tribe have one day then to leave this portion of the island, and one of the gunboats will take up position opposite the camp to expedite their departure."[24] Within

---

[23] Spirit of Pestilence, p 176 (DBC 28/April/1862)

a few weeks most of the northern tribes who had come to Victoria to trade had decamped to nearby islands. Colonial authorities decided to push them one step further. The gunships HMS *Grappler* and HMS *Forward* were deployed to force the tribes north, escorting them back to their homes.

At that time smallpox had been on the wane in recent decades. Almost two generations had grown up without any exposure and thus also no immunity. The colonial authorities were well aware that such a move would ensure the plague would spread rapidly to every village on the coast. Rather than take responsibility for the plague and quarantine the camps, they choose the single most harmful possible course of action. The rapid spread of the disease was entirely the fault of white hysteria.

As the people paddled home that summer, chased by the gunships, they succumbed to the disease in a wave of death. On one stretch of beach near Victoria over a thousand bodies were observed lying wasting and bloated in the sun. As the plague spread up the coast, captains reported seeing bodies abandoned on the shoreline of virtually the entire Inside Passage. At Fort Rupert and Fort Simpson, one passing captain wrote, "the Indians where "dying from the smallpox like rotten sheep. Hundreds are swept away within a few days."[25]

A few months later the master on the HMAS *Plumper* passed Fort Rupert and observed, "The once imposing looking village in all its rude uncivilized state is now nowhere to be seen. Of the fine muscular fellows that four years ago numbered 400 men, now not fifty can be mustered and they are mostly of the middle age or older men. The disease appears to have principally attacked the young and strong."[26]

---

[24] Spirit of Pestilence, p 176 (Daily Press 28/ April/1862)

[25] Spirit of Pestilence, p 189 (DBC June 21/1862)

[26] Spirit of Pestilence, p 190 (Gowland, 1862)

The Nuu-chah-nulth were probably amongst the hardest hit by the smallpox in the years immediately following contact, but they escaped the worst of the later plagues of 1800, 1035 and the 1862. That was because from 1800 onward, trade and contact had actually been declining on the West Coast, and only a few ships ever came to call. Across the Americas, major religious and social upheavals often followed in the footsteps of the plagues. In Europe, cults and even the Protestant Reformation had often emerged from the cultural wreckage of plagues.

In 1875 smallpox finally did again reach the isolated West Coast villages, along with the arrival of the men in black cassocks, missionaries who had come to the coast. For the natives, a cultural upheaval was about to sweep over their land and wash much of their culture away.

20. Bunsby Islands

B
ack on the beach I sit down on the bow of my boat to snack on a granola bar. The woman with the big hat emerges from the bush with her camera. She wants to take my photo.

"I may not have done the Brooks but I met someone who has," she says. I grin a bit and say nothing. I'm already feeling a bit guilty about stopping here without proper permission. Despite the fact that the Checlselet no longer live here, it is still their land, what little they have, and none of us have any right to be here.

After the photo, the Americans paddle off and I make the short crossing to the Bunsby Islands, a maze of narrow channels and protected beaches. Inside the shelter of the islands herons are fishing along the quiet shores. I lunch by a tidal pool surrounded by slender trees. There are massive nests high in their branches. To protect their chicks from marauding ravens and crows, herons nest together in large rookeries. For the first time on the trip I feel relaxed, without any apprehension of the paddle ahead.

On the way out after lunch I make a detour toward the outer reefs of the small island group. I spot several sea otters floating on their backs in the kelp. They are the size of a large dog, with long tails, webbed paws and characteristic white whiskers that make them look either comical or wise. From a distance I can see them rolling playfully in the protection of the kelp, but as I near them, they catch my scent, spin over and disappear beneath the kelp. They have a good reason to be shy.

Sea otters were once common on rocky sections of the entire coast of the northern Pacific Ocean. They ranged from Japan, across the Aleutian Islands chain to Alaska and down the West Coast as far south as Baja California. But from the 1700s until 1900, they were hunted almost to extinction for their pelts, the first victim species of the West Coast cultural exchange.

The trade in sea otter pelts began with the arrival of Captain Juan Perez, a senior naval officer from the Spanish base in San Blas, Mexico. In the summer of 1774 he and his crew became the first Europeans to sail up the Northwest Coast of North America. Almost two hundred years earlier, Sir Francis Drake sailed at least as far north as San Francisco, but Perez on the *Santiago* first approached land at the Queen Charlotte Islands. Three Haida canoes paddled out to welcome them and one of his officers threw some crackers wrapped in a kerchief into a canoe.

The next day, twenty-one canoes overflowing with ornamental blankets, cedar bark mats, basketry, hats, carved dishes, boxes and spoons, sea otters pelts and two hundred Haida men surrounded the ship to begin trading. The crew of the *Santiago* offered various items they had brought themselves, including spare clothing, beads, abalone shells, and iron tools. It was immediately apparent that the Haida were experienced traders, who knew specifically what they wanted. One of the two Catholic priests aboard noted their particular desire for iron: "They wanted large pieces with a cutting edge, such as swords, wood-knifes and the like – for on being showing ribands they intimated that these were of trifling value, and when offered barrel hoops they signified that these had no edge."[27] The fur trade on the West Coast had begun.

The Northwest coast Indians were familiar with iron because it was traded down from Alaska by the Tlingit who already had contact with Russians for fifty years. But the Spanish were not traders and they failed to realize the commercial potential of the ad hoc exchange. They returned home, and details of the voyage, like most Spanish exploration, remained unpublished state secrets. It was not until Cook landed at Nootka Sound four years later the seeds of trade began to grow.

From the moment of contact, the 'Nootka' (as Cook named them based on a miscommunication) wanted to trade. In a short month his crew and officers managed to exchange every spare scrap of metal on the two ships for fifteen hundred sea otter pelts, fresh salmon and game, and sexual access to a couple of unfortunate female slaves. (The slaves themselves received little but the first West Coast cases of syphilis and gonorrhoea.)

A year later when Cook's two ships reached Canton, the crew discovered the furs could fetch up to one hundred and twenty pounds each. But they had already sold most of them for much less to a Russian trader who had convinced them they were nearly worthless shortly before they reached the Portuguese port. The crew nearly mutinied and forced the expedition back to the West Coast for another year, but in the end cooler heads and the threat of

---

[27]First Approaches to the Northwest Coast, p 41, (Donald D Cutter, The California Coast, 1969 pp 159)

execution prevailed. By this time the famous navigator, Captain Cook was already dead. Several weeks earlier he had lost his life to a Hawaiian spear.

Six years later, when Cook's official journals of the trip were posthumously published in London, the details of commercial potential of northern Pacific fur trade became public. Amongst the rising class of merchant traders in London the prospect of spectacular profits attracted considerable attention. By all accounts is was a risky venture, requiring wealthy financiers, long risky voyages to uncharted shores, reputably peopled by friendly but dangerous savages, and mountains of profit for the successful.

The next year a merchant trader named Captain Hanna set sail from Macao in a mere sixty-ton vessel named Sea Otter, and dropped anchor at Nootka Sound after a voyage of three and half months. According to one account published in a London newspaper of the time, things did not go so smoothly initially:

> *"Soon after her arrival, the natives, whom Captain Cook had left unacquainted with the effects of fire-arms [not actually true], tempted probably by the diminutive size of the vessel (scarce longer than some of their own canoes) and the small number of her people, attempted to board her in open day; but were repulsed with considerable slaughter. This was the introduction to a firm and lasting friendship. Capt. Hanna cured such of the Indians as were wounded; and unreserved confidence took place – they traded fairly and peaceably - a valuable cargo of furs was procured, and the bad weather setting in, he left the coast in the end of September, touched at the Sandwich Islands, and arrived at Macao the end of December the same year."* [28]

---

[28] First approaches to the Northwest Coast, p 79, (From London *World*, Oct 6 and 13, 1788, unsigned)

Hanna sold his five hundred and sixty sea otter pelts for 20,400 Spanish dollars, a considerably attractive profit at the time. Once news hit London financiers were lining up boats and crews to cash in on the trade. Over the next forty years, three hundred and thirty vessels, flying flags from Britain, America, Portugal and Spain traded on the coast. While initially their muskets and cannons gave them an upper hand against the natives, their hegemony was always far from secure. From the outset of trade, three Nootka chiefs dominated. Maquinna at Nootka Sound, Wickanninish in Clayoquot, and Tatoosh at Cape Flattery. The powerful chiefs quickly monopolized the west coast of the island. Like the salmon in the streams, and the drift whales that washed up on the beach, they claimed the right to trade with the "men in the floating houses" as their property. To strengthen their position they allied themselves through intermarriage establishing a firm control of most of the native population of the coast.

Once the chiefs had adjusted to the novelty of the white visitors, trade was conducted largely on their terms. The traders were often frustrated by the their insistence on conducting long oratory speeches and ceremonies before trading, but had little choice but to submit to the imposed terms of trade. After the initial demand for iron was soon satiated, American traders soon introduced muskets, while others brought clothing, blankets and copper sheets. These items would then be traded or potlatched to other tribes in exchange for sea otter pelts. Once the monopoly was established, the Europeans soon noticed a rapid rise in the price of furs, up to six hundred percent in some places, long before the sea otters themselves began to disappear. By 1791 Wickaninnish had two hundred muskets and Maquinna was trading them across the mountains to the Salish on the east coast of the island. By 1804 Maquinna's wealth included nine wives.

Trade rapidly changed the Indian culture. Prior to the arrival of the Europeans, sea otter pelts were the reserved privilege of the chiefly families. Traditionally sea otters were hunted from a single canoe manned by a single hunter and his steersman. But the lucrative trade with the Europeans meant it was more profitable for the chief to organize large-scale hunts, which soon became the primary occupation of the men.

Typically on a clear calm morning up to twenty canoes would gather in a line a mile wide stretching from the edge of the beach out to sea. As they swept down the coast, when a sea otter was spotted, the hunter would raise his paddle to signal the others, who would bring their canoes around to encircle the creature. The first to put an arrow into it would own the pelt, and those who helped finish it off would be paid off in blankets. Once home, the animal was skinned and the pelt hung with heavy rocks to stretch it, since the traders priced them by length. The trade goods they acquired were status items that soon replaced traditional resources, upsetting the traditional economic structure of the villages.

Relations between the traders and natives soon began to deteriorate, usually due to the savageness of the traders. For the theft of a chisel captain Hanna shot twenty natives in a canoe. The American trader Captain Grey destroyed the entire village of Opisaht, on the suspicion that they were planning an attack. There is still much speculation about the changes brought by the introduction of firearms amongst the natives. Some scholars have speculated that it led to an increase in deadly intertribal warfare. Others claimed this was not the case, saying the native warriors continued to prefer hand weapons in close combat.

As for the poor sea otters, by the early 1800s they were already a rare sight. By 1900 they were completely wiped out except for a tiny remote population in Alaska. Their demise had severe ecological effects. One of their primary foods is sea urchins, spiky round creatures that live in the reefs of the rocky coastline. The sea urchins feed on the bull kelp, a type of seaweed that grows up to forty yards long in large beds. Thick and lush, the kelp forests are an ecological cornerstone of the outer coast marine ecology – an underwater equivalent of the rainforest on the mountain slopes.

After the sea otters disappeared, the sea urchin population blossomed, destroying kelp beds along the coast. For about a hundred and fifty years it remained that way. Then in 1969 the federal government began transplanting a colony of eight-five Alaskan sea otters to the Bunsby Islands. By the early 1990s the population had rebuilt to eight hundred and the kelp beds were reappearing in greater size along the coast.

***

From the end of the reef my plan is to cross directly to Spring Island, about six miles across the open water, but protected by a large number of reefs further out to sea. I figure even at an easy pace, it should take no more than two hours. Before I leave the shelter of the islands I take a long look at the sky for signs of the weather ahead. The morning's sun is losing ground to thin cloud high overhead, but lower to the water the sky remains clear. It is nothing to be concerned about so I head out at a good speed.

On my chart I can see that a series of reefs stretches far out to sea. On the open water the sea is glassy calm. A low swell, less than a foot high, rolls through. My course is nearly arrow straight, marked by only one islet and rocks. About two miles to the northeast the coastal mountains drop down suddenly to a rocky shoreline. Although it seems strange to stay so far offshore, according to my guidebook it is actually safer than dealing with rebounding waves along the cliffs.

With the tide against me the crossing seems to take forever. While the surface of the water seems empty at first, the protection of the outer reefs has created a sanctuary for the creatures of the sea. Halfway across I spot another sea otter sleeping in a raft of kelp, with paws and wheezing snout showing above the tangle. Suddenly it catches my scent in the wind and startles awake before slipping under the surface.

Further along I intersect a pod of harbour porpoises, their round slick backs arching through the water. By the time I start closing in on my destination the bright light of the day is fading toward dark and the sound of engines soon fills the air. Ahead by the islands the channel is filled with sports and commercial fishing boats heading back to Kyuquot for the night, their engines rumbling and whining into the orange sky. I begin to wonder if for the first time on this trip, I'll have to share my campsite. Already I'm missing the quiet of the north.

My destination for the night is the Spring Island, one of the Mission Group of islands, a bucolic mini-archipelago like the Bunsbys, but populated by people, not sea otters. Five of the largest of the islands, McLean, Aktis, Kamilis, Sobrey and Ahmacinnit are Indian Reserves. At one time this was the largest village of natives on the West Coast.

***

Gilbert Malcom Sproat, the first white settler on the entire west coast of Vancouver Island, recounted in his book, published in London in 1868 and marketable entitled *The Nootka – Scenes and Studies of Savage Life*, a detailed account of the last Indian war fought here. Trained as a colonial administration cleric and as a businessman, Sproat had an eye for detail and planning. He was better read than most settlers, and saw the 'noble savages' of the West Coast in a romantic light. Like many educated and cosmopolitan Europeans, Sproat lamented the passing of the 'Indian race', but felt nothing could be done to spot the inevitable forward march of the superior white race. Although it had been over a hundred years since the French revolutionaries cried 'Fraternity, liberty, equality,' few whites considered that none but the noblest savage could be considered their equal.

Sproat interpreted and recorded what he saw and believed in familiar European terms. His writing is in the tradition of explorers who recorded what they observed of newfound cultures without any training and before the development of academic anthropology. In many ways he was the precursor to the much more methodological accounts of Franz Boas on the West Coast. Lacking any formal methodology, Sproat did not record any direct sources for this story, and it is often hard to distinguish between what he actually witnessed and what is speculation and hearsay in his accounts. But in his introduction he does say:

> *"I did not merely pass through this country. I lived among the people and had a long acquaintance with them. The information which I give concerning their language, manners, customs, and ways of life, is not from memory, but from memoranda, written with a pencil on the spot – in the hut, in the canoe, or in the deep forest."*

His account of the Great War of 1855 is a classic war story. It contains all the familiar elements of diplomacy, spying, preparation for war, the drawing of the battle plan, inside details of tactical decisions, the retreat and the consequences suffered. Ten years later Jacobsen republished it in his own book and likewise I could not resist including it in my own. It's also worth noting, that another version, recorded by Nicholson at least fifty years later and based on Kyuquot native accounts, not Clayoquot accounts, is considerably different. The Kyuquot who used to live on these islands referred to this conflict as 'the last war'. Sproat writes:

> *"I shall probably best convey an idea of the native mode of warfare to the reader, by describing an expedition of the Clayoquot against the Kyuquot, a large tribe living on the coast, about eighty miles north from Clayoquot Sound. A bad feeling had existed for some time past between the two tribes, which had been fostered by the chief warrior of the Clayoquot – a restless ambitious man,*

who was always on the lookout for a cause of quarrel. The tribe debated the question of peace or war for several months, and at last agreed to attack the Kyuquot, provided that Shewish, the Chief of the Mowachaht, a tribe living between the expected belligerents, would join the expedition, with his warriors. An envoy was sent to Shewish, in a light canoe, to invite his co-operation, and, before leaving on his mission, the diplomat was instructed to use various arguments that were likely to be effective. After five days passed, the messenger returned with the intelligence that the Mowachaht would join the Clayoquot in exterminating the Kyuquot; or, at least, in reducing them to the position of a tributary tribe.

"There was immediately great excitement in the Clayoquot village. Not an hour was lost in commencing preparations: the war canoes were launched and cleaned, and their bottoms scorched with blazing faggots of cedar to smooth them; knives were sharpened; long-pointed paddles, pikes, and muskets were collected; fighting men and captains of canoes chosen, who, during the night, washed themselves, rubbed their bodies, and went through ceremonies, which, they supposed, would shield them from fatigue and wounds. In the forenoon of the next day, twenty-two large canoes took their departure from Clayoquot, with from ten to fifteen men in each, under the command of Seta-kanim, the great advocate for the war.... After proceeding for twenty miles... [they] reached the village of the Hesquiaht – a tributary tribe of the Clayoquot – who had to furnish six canoes, manned. The fatigued warriors slept in their canoes that night, and Seta-kanim ordered the Hesquiaht to be ready in the morning with their contingent."

The next morning the canoes proceeded north to Friendly Cove, in Nootka Sound, the village of the Mowachaht. Sproat spares no colour developing his characters;

> *"The savage blood in them was up. Their fingers worked convulsively on the paddles, and their eyes glared ferociously from blackened faces besmeared with perspiration. Altogether they were two hundred murderous-looking villains.... At last Seta-kanim rose in his canoe to address the people on shore. He was a tall muscular savage, with a broad face blackened with charred wood, and his hair was tied in a knot on the top of his head so that the ends stood straight up [like the Samurai of Japan – all the rage in Europe at the time]; a scarlet blanket was his only dress, belted lightly round his loins, and so thrown over one shoulder as to leave uncovered his right arm, with which he flourished an old dirk [musket]. Such a voice as he had! One could almost hear what he said at the distance of a mile. The speech or harangue lasted forty minutes, and seemed rather a violent address.*
>
> *"Shewish, chief of the Mowachaht, seemed to lack Seta-kanim's enthusiasm for the attack, and made only a short reply. After a feasting on dried herring roe on seaweed with the Mowachaht, a house-by-house plan of attack was drawn in the sand in front of the village. The detailed intelligence from Quart-soppy, a Clayoquot warrior whose wife was a Kyuquot from the island of Ocktees [Aktis] was used to determine which houses would be the focus of the attack. The next morning the war party, now four hundred strong set off. They paddled till dark to reach a beach just before Kyuquot that day. After a short rest in their canes, at midnight the attack was launched.*

Some Kyuquot fishermen arriving home late caught sight of the approaching attackers and raised the alarm."

Sproat's colourful transcription continues:

"'Weena! Weena! Strangers! Danger! Danger!' resounded through the air before the canoes touched the beach, and the cry was answered instinctively by a hundred half-waked sleepers, 'Weena! Weena! Clayoquot! Mowachaht! Weena!" and already the crack of muskets and the noise of running and shuffling with the houses that had been set on fire now lighted up the front. The Kyuquot retreated into the house of their chief, which they barricaded with boxes and loose planks, and they kept up a quick but not destructive fire on the assailants. Seta-kanim, with the two bearers of his muskets and the party under his immediate command, was well forward in the centre. The canoemen on the left side were inside the Kyuquot houses, and were killing the inmates, and set several houses on fire."

At this point the attackers, discouraged by the unfortunate advanced warning, begin to loose heart:

"Stragglers, shouting and gesticulating, but evidently not relishing the fight, were between the advanced parties and the shore and a large body of the Mowachaht collected near their canoes on the beach..... The attack was a failure: that could be seen at a glance.... Finally Seta-kanim, who had fought in the front, out of cover the whole time, finding himself left with about a dozen men, retired sullenly to the shore. The enemy did not follow and the discomfited assailants paddled away in confusion."

In the end the routed Clayoquot brought home only thirty-five heads [although many more lay unclaimed back in Kyuquot according to Nicholson's version], and thirteen women as slaves. But they lost eleven men, and seventeen were wounded, some of whom died later at home. Back at home Seta-kanim tried to put the best spin on things. He put the heads up on poles out front of the village, and promoted a few courageous warriors with new names at a feast. But eventually the fear of retaliation from a combined force of Kyuquot and Mowachahts got the better of the villagers. Provisions for winter were low and all trade from the north had ended. Few fishermen in canoes dared venture farther than half a mile from shore. A large stockade to protect the village against a counterattack was built from logs and the tribe passed a miserable winter huddled in its confines. Seta-kanim fell from grace and didn't leave his house for three months for fear of being shot by his own tribe.

Thirty year later, Jacobsen, caught up with Seta-kanim's son at a trading post in Clayoquot Sound. It appeared that time had restored his fierce reputation, even given him some celebrity amongst the isolated whites of the coast. Jacobsen's host, a Danish trader named Fredrik Thorenberg now lived on the former stockade site on Stubbs Island. Jacobson wrote of the meeting:

> "I had to find some canoes and Indians to continue my journey. Because of fog we could not go ashore but had a visit from a number of Indians, among whom was the son of Setta Canim [sic], the most powerful chief and most renown warrior of the west coast of Vancouver Island. I was told that Setta Canim, had killed a number of people, including a white trader [a trader named Barney, just prior to the attack on the Kyuquot, according to Nicholson]. He was the greatest gallows bait on the island. This of course raised his status and his reputation so that everyone who came to Clayoquot was anxious to establish

contact with him. I fell for this also, so I engaged young Setta Canim [his son] and three other Indians to take me to kayokaht [Kyuquot].

The next morning the young chief, so boastful on the deck of the schooner, changed his mind. After a night at home talking to his father, Seta Canim, the younger, refused to make the trip to his father's archenemies' village. Jacobsen had a difficult time understanding why since he had already been paid, but Thorenberg diplomatically persuaded him not to bother trying to recover the cash. As for the Kyuquot heads, Nicholson later recorded they too became a bit of an attraction in Clayoquot Sound:

> *"The Scalps [actually the entire skulls] of the victims which the Clayoquots placed on poles and planted along the sand-spit on Stubbs Island, also remained as evidence for many years afterwards. They were seen by sealing schooner crews, who, it is alleged, took some for souvenirs and few were still there when Fred Thorenberg ran the trading post at Clayoquot (on Stubbs Island). Reverend Brabant saw that the last ones were done away with, but even today, when heavy seas change the shape of the spit, the odd one makes its appearance. I remember in 1926, when a group of Japanese school children playing in the sand, found three and brought them to the Clayoquot school teacher."*

***

When I finally reach my beach it's almost dark. I pull into a quiet beach on Spring Island and carry my gear up the shore. As I set up camp the lights of the Indian Reserve on the mainland come on across the water. People, houses, generators and boat engines humming - it all seems so intrusive. Across the water I can see the houses, and hear the buzzing of a chainsaw. All my solitude is gone. There is industry here, fishing boats and clear-cuts with massive road scars and landslides, logged right up to the ridgeline. At least my beach is all my own for tonight. While I boil up some pasta for dinner I check my charts and realize I've done 16 miles today, the longest of the trip. The sky has cleared and the first stars of the trip come out.

Feeling optimistic, I don't bother setting up my tent. Instead I bed down in the pebbles beside some driftwood logs.

21. Father Seghers

In the morning I wake with a sore back from yesterday's paddle. But the skies are clear and that's enough to keep me happy. I'm camped out on a calm beach between two islands and only the occasional cooling breeze disturbs the morning air. Crows are calling. The water is sparkling with ripples and sunlight; the mountains are all blue and hazy in the distance to the south. A tiny curl of six-inch surf is breaking across the reef near the channel entrance.

The sun is a pleasure I can't get enough of and the strain of the trip is obviously catching up with me. I haven't had a proper rest day in nearly a week. The plan for the morning is to take it easy.

Once again I spread the rest of my gear out in the sun to finish drying the remaining dampness and then lie down on my camp mattress to rest my back in the hot sun. Again the skin prickles as it dries. I suspect it's been impregnated with salt. Thankful I'm not under a tarp huddled by a fire. I welcome in the sun.

It was near this spot that two Belgium priests came to erect their first cross. One was driven from Europe by a plague; the other would nearly loose his life when smallpox reached the coast.

***

A flood of tears greeted Father Charles Seghers when he knocked on the rough-hewn door of the Catholic bishopric in Victoria. The slender young priest stood before Bishop Modeste Demers on the wide porch. Eagerly the elderly Bishop welcomed in him. For months he had been eagerly expecting the arrival of Seghers. Almost alone amongst the British Protestants that made up the bulk of the colonial outpost, the lonely Roman Catholic mission was poverty struck, barely able to cover it's own costs, let alone propagate the faith.

By his birth Seghers seemed destined to enjoy the privileged life of the European bourgeoisie. He was born Charles John, the day after Christmas of 1839 in the Flemish city of Ghent. His father was an affluent merchant and they lived well, but even wealth could not save anyone from disease. By the age of eighteen, when Seghers entered seminary school, he had already lost his father and all four siblings to the plague of consumption (as tuberculosis was known in those days), leaving only he and his mother alive. After two years of tonsures and tutoring at the Jesuit school he received his minor orders in the Bishops Chapel of St Baaf's Cathedral of Ghent. Shortly after his graduation, his mother followed the rest of the family to the grave.

At twenty Seghers was pale, skinny and coughing up blood. But what consumed him was a passion to do missionary work in

America. Charles feverously believed that forsaking the comforts of European parishes that attracted most of his classmates for the harder and dangerous missionary in America was an act of courage for which God might restore his health. The Paris Central Committee of the Society for the Propagation of the Faith desperately needed young priests to spread the word of God amongst the pagans of the new world. And so, despite concerns for his health, the pale orphan with a reputation for devotion was admitted to the American College for training. Three years later he was ordained. He closed all his affairs, said his farewell to his family at the mausoleum and boarded a steamship for the New World, expecting never to return.

From his first trip at sea, and for the rest of his life, Seghers was seasick every time he stepped onto a boat. He took it as God's will, and suffered stoically all the way across the Atlantic on a steamer. At the isthmus at Panama, he crossed the mountains by train over to the Pacific and boarded a second steamship overflowing with 1,200 Americans infected with fever of the Californian Gold Rush. In San Francisco he lodged with two Roman Catholic priests who had already failed in their own efforts on the northern coast. They advised him to stay in their prosperous parish since the Indians to the north were just too savage to save. Undeterred, Seghers prayed to his God to give him just five years of life to do his work on the coast. In his letters to his superiors back home he wrote of his ardent desire to die like his patron, Saint Lieven, a martyr amongst pagans in a far land.

In Victoria, Bishop Demers was eagerly waiting the arrival of his new priest. The bishop was desperately fearful of recently arrived Anglican priests who spoke openly of establishing missions on the coast. But when he opened the door to the enquiring knock, he quickly realized he had a new worry - the young priest the seminary school in Paris had sent him was obviously sickly and weak, clearly unfit for the arduous life of a missionary on the remote coast. To make the best of the situation the bishop assigned the young father to simple parish work in settlement.

Seghers was disappointed not to be given a mission, but took the parish work with as much enthusiasm as he could muster. But he soon discovered that among the tents and shanties of the gold miners, another god was worshipped, and it was not sought in the promises of a priest, but sparkling in the bottom of shallow pans. In his letter home to his bishop in Ghent, Seghers wrote he was frustrated by the difficult parish service. The gold miners, particularly the French Canadians, were "worse than the infidels, angered by the mere presence of a priest. They think of nothing but gold. They speak only of money. These white men are so immoral that one often fears for Victoria, and dreads the chastisement of God."

Seghers' ardent desire to work amongst the Indians, spreading God's word amongst the savages, before the Protestants and Methodists could pervert them, never waned. Yet he was repulsed by the Indians he saw around town, "Truly it seems to me that these Indians have hardly any resemblance to any of the other descendants of Adam. Their language is an atrocious jargon, their persons so offensive, so untidy." Most unchristian of all in his eyes were the "squaws", dressed in crinolines and hats, pimped by their drunken husbands who sat for hours hunched under blankets on the edge of the streets, he wrote.

In Seghers' eyes, it seemed obvious that unless the Indians could be converted to the Roman Catholic faith, they would be completely debased by corrupting influence of the colony, or worse. "These wretches are persecuted by the whites, and whenever they show a wish for revenge they are threatened with the severest penalties. And there is not a single priest to teach them heavenly doctrine and preserve them from the crimes which return upon their own head. The bishop thinks that a war of extermination between the Indians and the whites will be waged, as it was in the eastern states. The death of the last Indian will end this murderous conflict," he wrote.

After four years of the parish work, Seghers fell ill once again with the consumption that had killed his family. For five days he coughed up blood. The doctors came and went from the log house he shared with the bishop. Able to do nothing, they left him for dead. But after even the bishop lost hope, Seghers declared the Blessed Virgin would cure him. Soon after he recovered miraculously and the bishop decided the two should travel to Europe to meet the Pope and raise funds for the mission.

A few years later when Bishop Demers died, the Pope, impressed by the young man's ardent devotion, appointed the young priest bishop of Vancouver Island, the youngest in North America. Seghers must have hidden his sickness from his Holiness. At only thirty-three, he believed he had only a few years left to live. Immediately upon his appointment to bishop he began plans for the first missions on Vancouver Island's west coast. Shortly afterward, on April 12, 1874 he departed north on the schooner *Surprise*. He was accompanied by a new arrival, another young Flemish priest fresh from the missionary college in Paris, Father Brabant.

Brabant was everything Seghers was not. He was tall, muscular, and blessed with boundless stamina and a solid constitution. But he shared Bishop Seghers' feverous desire to spread the doctrine of the faith amongst those they believed to be the savages of the coast.

"Nothing in the world could tempt me to come and spend my life here, were it not that the inhabitants of these shores have a claim on the charity and zeal of a Catholic priest," [29]Brabant once wrote.

Sailing from village to village up the coast on the *Surprise*, by their own accounts, the two priests were surprisingly well received. Brabant wrote in his journal that the Nootka, by now familiar with

---

[29] Mission to Nootka, p10.

the white traders and navy gunships, welcomed the strange visitors in flowing black cassocks, who came not to trade or to settle, but spoke of a God above all other gods. To some degree the villagers might have recognized and accepted them as shaman, special envoys of the white men. Aided by Indian interpreters who excelled in their ability as storytellers, in the doctrine of creation, and the tale of the great flood, the two priests offered a new order that was not altogether unfamiliar. The teaching of the sign of the cross caused great excitement, as did the hymns and catechisms. Hundreds of children were baptized as they sailed from village to village up the coast.

Eventually the schooner finally dropped anchor here amongst the Mission Islands, just close to my camp. Here their warm receptions suddenly ended. So wrote Brabant:

> *"Here not an Indian could be seen on the bay, nor, in fact, outside of the camp. It was pronounced an unusual thing, as the captain stated that these Indians used to meet him out at sea, and literally crowd the deck of his schooner on any other occasion. Nomucos, our Kyuquot cook, was also at a loss to explain, and his shouting and calling for the Indians had no effect. However, at last a small canoe was launched at Aktese [the island across the channel from my camp], two Indians got into her and paddled quickly to the spot where we were at anchor. Every little while they would stop and listen to the shouting of our Indians.*
>
> *"'We are afraid,' was the first sentence we could hear them utter. Our savages reassured them and when at last they got on board they explained the whole mystery. They had heard of our arrival, but the story got mixed up. On board the schooner was a living man who would cut the children on the chest, and another who would rub something over the wound and it would be healed. Then*

the first man would begin killing the Indians and upon the Indians' trying to kill him, he would turn into a stone or become a stone man,"[30]

The two priests were ignorant of the political intrigues amongst the native groups on the coast, and never suspected that rival groups to the south may have tried to keep the priest to themselves by instilling fear in the northern villages. But they would soon learn first hand how important an understanding of local politics could be. The next day, after scotching the rumours of mutilation, the two priests entered the main village and baptized one hundred and seventy-seven children in a single day, their most successful day yet on the coast. Two days latter, with an escort of forty-three 'savages', they headed up to the Checkleset camp at Acous, where I stopped the day before. They were flattered to be accompanied by such a large party of strong young men.

Upon their arrival the Kyuquot men began singing the hymns the priests had taught them. Brabant writes:

> *"The Checklesets came rushing out of their houses, and seemed quite stupefied, but did not come to the beach till they were called upon to do so. It took them a long time to assemble in the Chief's houses and when assembled by His Lordship, although seemingly attentive, it was quite evident that everything was not 'all right.' The evening and darkness soon put a stop to our work; then we began to look for room to sleep."*

Unbeknownst to the priests, the two villages had been at war for several years. That night at Acous, the Kyuquots slept in a circle round the priests, with knives tucked in their hands.

The next morning the two Belgians priests taught catechisms and hymns, but even the sign of the cross failed to impress their

---

[30] Mission to Nootka p 18.

nervous hosts. The Checkleset mocked the Kyuquot interpreter and openly taunted the priests. In the crowded longhouse even the ignorant priests soon realized the situation was quickly becoming dangerously tense. Just as they started to make plans for a quick getaway a storm set in, making it impossible to launch the canoes. Trapped in the village, nervously Brabant and Seghers retreated outside to huddle under a large tree in the rain to recite prayers. Shortly a Checkleset summoned them back to the clan house. Brabant wrote in his journal what happened next:

> *"We pretended not to understand, but at last His Lordship concluded to follow the savage and so we re-entered the Chief's lodge. It was quite a sight. To the western side of the camp sat the Chief in a very prominent place, and on each side sat an elderly man holding in his hand a long rod, which seemed to us to be a mark of authority. Everything was still, the men on our side, the women and children on the other. A seat was shown to us on the right side of the Chief, where we were requested to continue our instructions. But none of the young men could interpret and not one of Kyuquots was about, nor, in fact, could be gotten. This seemed very strange."*

What the priest did not know was that the Kyuquot men had been lured into another house with the promise of feast, and then barricaded inside while the Checkleset summoned the priests. When the Kyuquots finally broke out and returned to the main house, "Angry words, speeches and gesticulations were the order of the hour." The next day the storm abated just enough to let the two priests and their now rowdy escort slip away. They had faced the first resistance to their proselytizing on the coast.

The Checleset would remain fiercely resistant to the priest for many years. When Jacobsen, was collecting in the area several years later he met a third priest, Father Nicolai, who was building a mission at Kyuquot. In his usual hyperbolic manner, Jacobsen notes relations between the three parties remained largely unchanged. His account of the situation also offers a peak at the colonial version of justice on the coast:

> *"The next day we had an example of how dangerous this area can be for a white man. The missionary, Father Nicolai, who had been visiting the neighbouring village of Tschuklesaht [Checleset] came back and related that the local Indians, who were regarded as the most aggressive on the west coast, had threatened him with axes and knives. When the howling, enraged mass moved toward him he stepped forward and told them in a quiet voice in their own language that they could kill him, but if they did a gunboat would soon appear whose captain would most certainly hang at least half the population of the Chickliset. This helped; for the Indians knew that whenever such a crime was committed, like this proposed murder of Father Nicolai, the guilty had been punished together with innocent. So they desisted but told him that he must leave at once and not try to convert them, since they were well satisfied with their own religion."*[31]

Shortly after Father Nicolai abandoned the coast missions due to 'illness', but even Brabant believed he was not ill, but 'sick at heart at the discouraging state of affairs here.'

---

[31] *Alaskan Voyage*, p 66.

22. Kyuquot Sound

After few hours snoozing in the sun, I rouse myself and shuffle round camp picking up my gear. Over lunch I empty out my three food bags to see what needs restocking. This afternoon I'll paddle to the village of Kyuquot for lunch and some shopping. It's getting hot now and I suspect a northwesterly might blow up this afternoon. Happily I put away my wetsuit for the day and I pack my boat and set off through the islands toward town.

On the way in I pass the Indian Reserve on Aktis Island. A few houses line the shore but the grounds are overgrown and there is little sign of life. Then a young couple appear on the beach and launch a banged-up aluminum boat. When they pass me on the water they pull alongside and stop for a word. She has straight black hair and he has thick red curls and fair skin. Both speak with the same West Coast accent, one that has nearly died out, that rolls words up in wide vowels.

"Where you coming from?" they ask, and I tell them of my trip down the coast. Even for residents and natives the idea of paddling so far in a kayak seems to make an impression. I ask them about themselves. It turns out they are just heading out fishing for the day, trying to catch the last of the spring before it's done. On the West Coast, 'spring' refers to the late summer salmon, not the time of birds and flowers that follow winter. The Nuu-chah-nulth name for the late summer was actually *sats'amit*, meaning of course "spring Salmon". I ask them about the houses and they say most are abandoned; some families come out for a few weeks in the summer, but only theirs is occupied year round. They seek a simpler life, away from the main village.

I cross Nicolaye Channel and head toward Village Island. Houses, fishing lodges and then a log cabin Red Cross 'hospital' appear on the small islands nearby. Kyuquot is the largest village on the coast without road access. As I paddle into the harbour one half of the village is on one island where a boardwalk connects the houses that hang at the water's edge. There are orchards and picket fences and several wharves. The other half of the village is across the harbour on the mainland. It is treeless and rests on a giant midden – it's the Indian Reserve. The houses are stacked densely and farther back from the shore. A few neglected fishing boats are tied up on both sides. I feel conspicuous as I paddle across the harbour. As I do, some local white kids come wakeboarding through in an old water-ski boat. Kids here would learn to run outboards before they could ride a bike.

On the white side of town is 'Charlie's Restaurant and Bed and Breakfast', a big white building with a new cedar veranda. I pull up on the pebble beach out front and climb up the steps to the deck and step into the dining room. It's a typical small town diner with a burgers and fries menu. I order a burger and fries, and coffee, then sit down inside in front of the big windows. It's delightful.

While I wait for my lunch I strike up a conversation with the young couple at the next table. He's wearing heavy work clothes while she has the look of a hippy. Her long brown hair and piercing green eyes, the curves of her body beneath the soft fabrics of her dress, all those signs of femininity remind me how long it's been since I left Rosie. The man looks at my clothing and quickly deduces I'm a kayaker. That means to him I'm also a radically unreasonable eco-tree-hugger.

"You look at a clear-cut - you see destruction," he informs me almost from the outset of our conversation, "but when I look at it - I see jobs."

"How much have you worked lately?"

"Well, since the new regulations came in, just one month since the fall."

That's almost a year of unemployment. The contradiction seems to escape him, but not his companion. She looks more likely than me to lie down in front of a logging truck.

She says, "My father was a hand logger with his own boat. We used to live on the boat in the summers while he hauled the logs out off the shoreline. Without clear-cutting the hand-loggers would still be working. He did it the right way."

They seem an odd couple. Perhaps they don't usually discuss logging much. Perhaps they are not even a couple, but just friends, but I don't want to pry enough to find out. The cook's wife brings out a plate with my burger and fries and sits down to join us while she has a smoke. She tells me the fishing is slow and most of the kayakers have already left. So today is their last day for the season. It wasn't even the last week of August. Tomorrow they'll shut for a week of cleaning and then the short summer's work will be over. Hopefully they had enough to clear the mortgage for another winter. Maybe next year they wouldn't bother opening at all. Now that the fishing boats didn't come by, they were hardly making enough to make it worth their while. Everyone was moving away to Tahsis or Gold River or Zeballos, anywhere with road access, or further, across the island or to Vancouver where you could get a better job. Not much for the young people here anymore.

After lunch I wander down to the government pier to see if the store has opened, but a sign hanging on the door says it will only be open for two hours in the afternoon. I wander down to the loading area and find some schoolboys from the reserve having a swim while they wait. Immediately they surprise me. The most outspoken one soon introduces himself as Clifford.

"Want to see me jump over that wharf," he immediately offers. I look down. Ten feet below us is the finger wharf. It's eight feet wide.

"No." I say, but I know he is not really concerned with my answer. He steps a few yards back then takes a run for the edge and launches himself out into space. He barely clears the timber rail below with a big splash. When he climbs back up, he shows me some scars on his back from when he broke his shoulder doing the same thing a few years ago. Happy to have an audience, he jumps again, and a few of the other kid join him this time. When they get bored with it, we chat for a while and they tell me about a store on the other side.

As I turn to leave Clifford calls out, "Hey you, what's your name?"

"Mike," I shout back.

"See you later Mike," he shouts. He sounds dead certain that we'll meet again. But I guess if you live out here, you don't expect people to be coming and going as much as I do.

I stretch my legs along the boardwalk and peak in the yards of the lovely old cedar-sided houses that line the shore. Early in the century the so-called Japanese current that circulars around the Pacific Ocean came closer to shore along the West Coast, making the summers warmer and longer. Some of the older houses still have small orchards with stunned fruit and picket fences, remnants from the settler days. It takes only a few minutes to walk out to both ends of the village so I decide to paddle across and see if I can find the stores on the reserve Clifford mentioned.

As I return along the wharf I meet an older Kyuquot native man, also waiting for the store to open. A small gathering seems to be taking place. Nobody seems to have much else to do. When I mention the store on the reserve he tries to dissuade me from visiting. "Its just a juke store, not a real one," he says. I ask him about work and he tells me he was a commercial fisherman but now with the fish gone there is no work for him. Then he just shrugs his shoulders and looks away. Afterwards I feel like an ass for asking him.

23. On the reserve

It's just a short paddle across to the reserve. Down on the beach a few guys are cutting up an alder tree for firewood, smoking as much as the chainsaw. Some of the kids playing around soon spot me in my kayak and immediately scream into the water trying to climb aboard. Before they manage to capsize me, I get my bow to the beach. As soon as I stand up, a girl of about five is already climbing in my seat between my legs. I retreat to the safety of high ground while kids swarm all over my gear. I chat with the guys cutting wood for a couple minutes then one of the older boys, a fellow named Clive wanders over to meet me, obviously looking for something to do. I ask him about the store and it turns out there are actually two, although one is closed, the other is open and just a short walk away. He offers to show me the way. The rest of the kids seem more interested in my kayak than me, so after tying it to the wharf, I follow Clive up the slope of the midden into his village.

There are only a few gravel roads on the reserve. We take a short cut through some vacant land. Bright laundry hangs on lines stretched in every direction. Only a few of the houses have a distinct yard of their own. The rest sit scattered on the commonly shared land. Under one house a big Rottweiler is growling on a bone. Clive makes a wide circle round the perimeter. I make a wider one, not trusting the rusty looking chain.

The store is a no-nonsense plywood affair. A hand-painted sign says Judy's, after the proprietor I presume. Inside behind the small counter are two teenage girls. The two narrow rows of shelves are half-stocked with food. Empty packing boxes are scattered everywhere in disarray. I asked about granola and get a shrug in response.

"I don't know. Have a look around, maybe..." says one with a smile.

I wander round the two aisles and get lost in the boxes and soon forgot what I wanted. In the end I pick up a box of cookies and wander back to the counter and ask about pens. They giggle a bit and rummage around in some draws under the counter until they finally pull one out. They scratch it on a nearby box to make sure that it works.

"How much?" I ask. The older teen looks down at the cookies and pen and shrugs her shoulders.

"Two bucks," she finally says.

"You just made that up, didn't you," I ask with a laugh.

"Yup," she says.

"I'll take two ice cream cones too, a double-scoop for Clive"

Clive orders bubble gum flavour; saying that last time he ordered tiger-strip it gave him hives. I avoid the tiger strip too. (Always trust your guide.) While the girls discuss which of them will make the cones a few people wander in and out, discussing trucks for sale in Winter Harbour and Gold River. We watch each other curiously from the corner of our eyes. Then a big red truck rolls by with two kayaks in the back. Clive says it means the teachers are back in town. Schools starts again in a week.

Clive and I wander back toward the beach, past the Rottweiler now out on patrol. It lunges as we pass, and I thank the chain for holding. Perhaps it likes ice cream? On the beach by the red truck a young Caucasian couple is busy unloading the kayaks. The man is wearing a T-shirt from the guiding outfit I once worked for in Tofino. I introduce myself as a friend of a friend.

It turns out Chris and Sally are school teachers. They tell me that they've just returned for their second year of teaching on the reserve. I ask if they enjoy working at such a remote school.

"We felt so welcome our first year here we decided to stay another. We just arrived and fourteen people just showed up on the beach and carried all our stuff up to the house," says Sally.

Chris is much more plainspoken about life in the last Vancouver Island fishing village without road access.

"In the summer and winter it's two different places, it gets so serious instead of fun. We arrived in February when it had been raining for months, really wet winter weather, and every one was grumpy and wanted it to stop raining. I asked the other teachers what they do and they said nothing, like no outdoor activities, just work and go home. A lot of teachers come here to make a start; many leave after a year, but some like the remoteness. The principal spent twenty years in Cape York, teaching in the remote aboriginal communities of outback Australia."

The population of the school, which is built on the hill above the reserve is ninety percent native with around two hundred students. A few years ago there was ninety percent employment and ninety percent alcoholism as well. It looked like a functional community, says Chris, but in the winters it wasn't. Now with the commercial fishing nearly shut down, it has ninety percent unemployment, but also ninety percent dry. Alcoholics Anonymous is doing well in this town. Still says Chris, he sees the community as struggling with its history and its future. The older generation is amongst the worst hit by the changes.

"There is a void in their lives. One kid just told me that his grandpa tried to kill himself the other day, after he had a fight with his wife," he says.

While many Canadians are aware of the hard lives of people on remote Indian reserves, few really understand the reasons these communities are so plagued with social problems. That's because as a nation we are blind to their history. Conveniently for the rest of us, our academic historians and popular writers wrote the Indians off as irrelevant and nearly dead, back before WWII. The 'Indian Problem' as it was known, when it was known, was believed to be solving itself, via extinction and assimilation. It was wildly believed the Indians who survived would see the wisdom of the white man's superior ways. They would go to schools, become Christians, move off the reserves, trade their official status card for full citizenship and the right to vote and forget about superstitious and backward old ways. Assimilation, a gradual uplifting of the primitive Indian to the white man's level, was their only hope.

But it didn't happen that way. For some reason, the native people who had lived here for so long without the white man's ways did not want to change, at least not in the particular way the white man wanted them to. This surprised the white man. He gave them God, school, and a chance give up the old ways for some thing he believed was better, and the 'ignorant savages' said 'No'.

Rather than ask why the native people rejected the white agenda to destroy thousands of years of culture, the federal Department of Indian Affairs developed a program of forced assimilation for Indians who would not accept it voluntarily.

Nobody called it cultural subjugation or genocide back then. The first step was to put a stop to the native land rights movement that flourished in the 1920s. Many Canadians believe that the native land rights movement is a modern phenomenon but the United Native Brotherhood was actively campaigning soon after the First World War when it began making legal challenges to the land seizures that had taken place in British Columbia. In response the Department of Indian Affairs was outraged that the court system was granting its wards a voice of their own, and in 1927 they made it illegal for natives to put land claims before the courts, and thus shut the land rights movement down for over 50 years.

The result of the legislation was that unless the Indians gave up being Indians they couldn't vote, or own land off reserve, or fish from a motorized boat. In 1927 Canada's 'Indians' now had fewer rights and freedoms in their own land than any immigrant stepping off a ship in Halifax, (such as my own father). The government had made them an underclass of 'aliens' on their own land.

Then a problem developed. Indians were no longer dying off as conveniently as before. In fact, from the 1930s onward, a lack of new diseases saw reserve populations start to increase for the first time since the arrival of the whites. Since the reserve system was assumed to be a temporary measure, put in place by the white governments to ease the process of assimilation, the government had little interest in improving the living conditions. As the population swelled and native people continue to resist the increasing pressure to assimilate, many reserves became overcrowded. Often two or three extended families shared a single three-bedroom house.

Then suddenly in the early 1950s, a growing concern about the living conditions on aboriginal reserves mysteriously developed. Provincial social workers starting removing kids from families where they deemed the children were living in poverty. Nobody considered improving conditions of the overcrowded reserves, or building better houses. That would involve spending money on the worthless Indians, an unpopular cause that no politicians could risk championing. And since Indians could not vote or were even recognized as proper citizens, they were of no concern to the mechanism of Canadian power and democracy. The real reason for the sudden concern with Indian babies was the recent transfer of a particular power from the Federal Department of Indian Affairs to the provincial government welfare agencies. The provinces now had the right to seize Indian children and move them to foster homes or even charge a fee for their adoption to white families. This was a financial bonus for the provinces because for every Indian child the provincial social workers could apprehend, the federal government guaranteed handsome transfer payments to the provinces. Within a few short years native kids rose from one percent of all apprehensions to 40 percent nationally.

By the 1960s the forced adoption program was booming, so successfully that it was later named the 'sixties scoop'. The kids were never placed with other families on their reserves since the houses built by Indian Affairs did not meet the standards set for foster homes by the government. Instead adoption agents took the children to virtual Indian baby clearing houses, shipping thousands south to the U.S. for a lucrative five to ten thousand dollar 'fee' each. Of the thousands scooped in B.C., many went to Chicago, Detroit, and the Midwest. The removal of children was so extensive that native leaders today claim that barely a single native family in Canada avoided loosing a child to the 'welfare'. None of the parents ever saw a cent of the 'fee'.

Worse yet was the fate of those children that were deemed unmarketable and rejected by the agencies. Often too old for adoption, they ended up in government run foster homes. Some estimates are that 85 percent of native foster kids were sexually abused in those institutions. Of course, back on the reserves, the parents were shattered. The families, social structures, culture – the entire emotional fabric that holds a community together - was targeted and destroyed in the final solution to the Indian problem.

It's a national shame that deserves to be more honestly remembered. That was assimilation.

***

Back at the beach the kids have lost interest in my kayak. I say good-bye to the schoolteachers and the guys with the chainsaws, and I push off the beach before the kids have a chance to notice me again, eager to get back to the store and not miss the short opening hours.

Back on the other side the tiny on room store is crowded. Everyone is doing their shopping at once. It is an-everything-in-one general store - post office - government agent - booking office -floatplane terminal, in a space the size of most of families' living rooms. The shelves are cramped with groceries, clothing, fishing gear and engine parts. I pick up some bread mix for baking bannock in my fires, granola, pasta, cauliflower, carrots and few cans of tuna. On these long days of paddling I have neglected to make time for fishing. I pay and I head down to the beach to pack up my boat. Then I remember I need to make a call.

I walk up to the telephone box on the pier and pull out my calling card. My mother is happy to hear I'm alive. I tell her that I'm uncertain but hopeful about making it to Tofino in the remaining time.

"Rose phoned the other day, asking how you were doing," she says. Afterwards I consider calling Rose in Australia, thinking how nice it would be to hear her voice. But in the end for some strange reason I don't understand or choose not to I don't call, telling myself it would be too strangely out of place. Anyway she's most likely left for work I think as I walk back to my boat. It seems I have adjusted to my solitude out here.

***

213

Before Seghers and Brabant left Kyuquot, the bishop decided to erect what they believed incorrectly to be the first Christian cross on the west coast of Vancouver Island. Perhaps it was intended to serve as much as a sign to the Protestants of their claim on the souls of the local savages as much as any other purpose. In any event, the festivities involved a strange synthesis of traditions. Brabant wrote in his journal:

> *"On May 1, we had the happiness of offering up the holy sacrifice of the Mass in honour of the Blessed Virgin Mary, putting our new mission under her special protection. His lordship having noticed the good disposition of the Kyuquots had, before going to Checkleset, asked the Captain of the Surprise to make a large mission cross, which we found ready upon our arrival. The cross was twenty-four feet long, with the cross-piece in proportion. It was the work of not only the Captain, but Peterson, the Mate, a Swedish Lutheran."*

> *"Before proceeding to plant it, we were called to the house of the Chief, where we found all the men of the tribe assembled. After asking our permission, they began to sing some of their savage songs with great solemnity. Then they showed us a mask, the handiwork of northern Indians, most ingeniously made; as well as a number of beads held in great esteem by all the Indians on this coast. Beads are sold by one tribe to another at greatly exorbitant prices. After a speech from his Lordship, condemning all Indian superstitions in general, several important men got up and promised to go by our instructions.*

> *"After this we proceeded to the blessing of the cross. It was placed on three canoes and about fifty young men took charge. An immense number of Indians followed us in canoes to the foot of a small island opposite the shore, then unoccupied and seemingly abandoned. It was*

beautiful to see the Indians struggle to carry the heavy burden, preceded by his Lordship. When it was raised, fifty muskets were fired off as if to announce a great triumph to the savages on the Kyuquot Islands. And there it now stands in sight of the tribe."[32]

***

I have had a productive afternoon in town, but I'm now anxious to get underway. I still have a lot of miles to make. But as I paddle past the last house at the edge of town I get stopped outside a small sawmill. A bearded man in a tool-belt and red suspenders flags me down as I paddle under his pier. I'm no longer surprised by such friendliness, but he seems to have the overly enthused manner of a proselytizing Christian. I listen carefully as he tells me about his sawmill which he set up inside the old school house. Then rather shortly, he runs off to get me something. When he returns from his house, slightly out of breath, he reaches down and hands me a colourful pamphlet. It's a catalogue of nutritional products he sells locally by mail order.

Paddling out of the harbour there's a light wind behind me and the tide is in my favour. Just outside of town I stop on a quiet beach amongst the islands and change into my wetsuit. Then I leave the shelter of the islands behind and run down the open coast in the fading light. I make a quick crossing of the entrance to Kyuquot Sound and put an easy five miles between me and the town before pulling into a small pebble beach just before sunset.

It's another clear evening and I can't be bothered to light a fire or set up my tent. After dinner I just sit quietly in camp watching the stars come out. Close to nightfall I stand up to stretch and startle some creatures that have wandered in close to my camp. I wander over to investigate with my flashlight and find two sets of tracks, one big and one small, bounding away in ten-foot and five-

---

[32] Mission to Nootka, p 20.

foot leaps. What a life to be a deer, always running, never in safe territory. But even the emblematically brave eagle has no rest. Just before sunset I watch some seagulls chase one away from a tree just above my camp. I can't help wondering if possibly this is the small beach that Seta-kanim and his warriors rested at before launching their midnight raid on the Kyuquot. It's not long before I fade off to sleep

24. Nootka Sound

When I wake a heavy dew is covering my sleeping bag. The last of the stars still are pinpoints of light in the western sky but the east is already starting to glow. In the half-light I zip open my sleeping bag and startle a large buck that is feeding down the beach. Bleary-eyed, I turn on my stove and brew up a strong cup of black tea. It is a nice change to be camped on the pebble beach, without sand throughout everything. In the half-light of the breaking dawn I enjoy the luxury of tea in bed before the long day ahead begins.

Even though it looks like another fair day lies ahead, I want an early start this morning to get safely round Tachu Point, the headland that separates Kyuquot Sound from Nootka Sound to the south. I need to make some miles while conditions are calm. Although the high pressure will mean clear skies, once a strong high-pressure system starts to build with this sunny weather, the heat over the land will start to draw the air off the ocean in katabolic winds. They will strengthen in the afternoon as the sun heats the land. In the summertime these northwesterly winds can make paddling a real challenge, kicking up white caps that keep most paddlers ashore. Once I'm safely round the point, I'll be happy to have the northwesterly at my back, but till then I'm happier if conditions stay calm. But I'm also anxious because yesterday in Kyuquot I heard that a low-pressure system might be moving on to the coast. Those are two good reasons to be keen to get around Tachu Point into Nootka Sound, about a day's paddle away, as soon as possible.

I take a walk and stretch my back, and watch the morning arrive. Over breakfast I watch a bright red and white Canadian Coast Guard cutter hum past. For a while the stout boat runs along the inside of the protecting islands, before it turns west, straight out to sea and disappears into a thick wall of sea fog that has drifted in from farther offshore. The fog is another phenomenon of warm summer days. It is much different from the mist that comes with rain. It forms when hot humid air from the south is drawn over colder northern currents. Inside it, visibility is rarely more than half a mile. According to the Nuu-chah-nulth *Annis* the Crane is the guardian of the fog which he keeps in a box. When he is commissioned by the creatures of the world, Crane releases the mists, sometimes a little bit, sometimes a lot, depending on their requests. It's the crane, or more accurately heron, feather in my hat that is my constant reminder that timing and patience are critical for my success on this trip.

The fog is obviously a concern for me, but for now it is hanging back a mile offshore, just a wall of grey cloud floating on the water. I pack up and slather on sunscreen and put an extra water bottle on deck and launch. On the water I turn south after the coast guard cutter and start out down the coast. It's a beautiful calm day and under the blue sky the water reflects like a mirror. For the first hour the fog offshore seems to burn away. In my wetsuit I soon work up a sweat, and the sealed cuffs and collar on my dry-top turn it into a torso sauna. Since conditions are so calm I stop just at the last sheltered spot inside the protecting reef and balance carefully as I pull the jacket off over my head. Once my head is out of the neck seal, then I work my arms out of the tight latex cuffs. Although it seems like a simple procedure to remove a jacket, I am well aware that if I capsized alone here with my head and arms both trapped inside, it could easily be deadly.

From the shelter of the reefs I cut out to the unprotected open ocean, into the glassy rollers just before Tachu. On the beach a small swell is breaking in steep curls - the most surfable waves I've ever seen on the West Coast. I'm tempted to take my kayak in for a run, but the chart shows rocks, not sand, on the bottom and I back off. Surfing a loaded sea kayak is good fun, but I don't want to risk smashing my boat or my head on the rocky bottom while things are going so well. From the water, the view back along the mountains is a marked contrast to the beauty of the shoreline – a disgustingly huge clear-cut runs virtually uninterrupted for miles down the coast, leaving nothing standing its wake. How many salmon streams were destroyed for this? At least the deer, and thus the cougars will be prosperous with the easy foraging, but that hardly justifies such avarice destruction. There seems no limits to man's greed in this land.

Once safely round Tachu Point, I pull into a small bay named Yellow Bluff. I've done eight miles already this morning, and drunk two litres of water in the hot sun. Now I'm desperate to answer nature's call. While in the woods I find an old squat, wrapped in torn tarps and plastic sheeting, falling into the mossy forest floor. Perhaps native fishermen or hunters used to come here to get away, or even surfers drawn to the nearly perfect break back around the point. This bay is an Indian Reserve, so I don't want to linger. Back out in the sun on the pebble beach I down a quick snack and push off. At the next bay I pass an active logging camp, portable trailers on gravel pads and large machinery scattered around the yard.

Along the shoreline I turn south for a quick crossing to Catala Island, a marine park at the entrance to Esperanza Inlet. The wind and the tide and the swell are all behind me but it seems Heron has also opened his box a little more. The foggy fingers scratch at my back as I run across open water to the islands. But as I surf along in the following sea with the wind and current at my back, I feel like I have wings of my own. Warily I keep an eye on my bearing on the deck compass. Just as I arrive at the island, the grey swirls finally envelop me.

Inside the clutch of the fog, I can see the blue patches of the sky above, but the shoreline that is only a hundred yard to my right is just a grey outline of treetops against a luminous white. Instinctively I close the distance between shore and myself until it is just a few paddle lengths off my side. Then I start to skirt the island, looking for a place to land. Shortly, I pull into a pretty little bay. As I paddle in the mouth of the bay I cross a shallow sandbank and just as I do the fog blows away. It's like a curtain has been pulled to reveal a world of brilliant greens. Shaped like a natural amphitheatre, a semi-circle of logs rounds the bay like grandstand seating.

On the beach I take my lunch out of my kayak. I know the tide is dropping and in the shallow bay I don't want my kayak to get grounded while I stop, so I tie a rock to the bowline to use as an anchor, and then toss it out into the middle of the bay and push my kayak out after it. This way the receding tide won't leave it aground, forcing me to drag it over the barnacles when I want to launch again. With the morning's goal of rounding Tachu safely and easily behind me, it is time to relax. I take a refreshing swim in the shallow warm waters and scrub off the grime and sweat of twelve days in polyester and nylon. Afterwards, clean, warm and relaxed, I lie face down naked on a big warm log in the sun and immediately fall asleep in its embrace.

***

Gilbert Sproat was also the first white to record a detailed account of the religion of the Nuu-chah-nulth. To most white observers the unrestricted polytheism of the Nuu-chah-nulth cosmology was evidence not of a deeply connected spiritualism linking the land and sea, but of a childish immaturity. Even Boas was hard-pressed to learn much about their religions. Since rituals were largely done in secret, like most white observers, Sproat tended to underestimate their significance. He wrote:

> *"In speaking of the religion of the Aht [the tribe near whom he evicted to set up his sawmill in Barkley Sound], I use the word simple for want of any other. What I refer to is among them rather a certain form of worship or propitiation of deities according to old usages, and not, of course, a system of religion in our sense of the word, containing a body of morals and spiritual truths. No attempt is made by any class of priest, nor by the older men, to teach religion to the people – there are no doctrines of religion in which they could instruct the people."*

Although Sproat several times mentions a particular habit of ritual bathing that he often observed, he was never able to grasp its intense significance to the Aht. With so much inherent secrecy even Sproat recognized he was having a hard time getting a straight story. He wrote of the difficulty of getting the Aht to speak openly of their religion:

"A traveller must have lived for years among savages, really as one of themselves, before his opinion as to their mental and spiritual condition is of any value at all. The fondness for the Aht for mystification, and the number of 'sells' [hoaxes] which they practice on a painstaking inquirer going about with notebook in hand, are unexpected and extraordinary on the part of savages whom we regard as so mean in intelligence. They will give a wrong meaning intentionally to a word and afterwards, if you use it, will laugh at you, and enjoy the joke greatly among themselves. They generally begin by saying that no white man is able to understand the mysteries of which they speak."

While the Kwakiutl peoples used the winter dance ceremonies as a foundation of their culture, the Nootka cosmology lead them alone to the water's edge to seek spiritual power. At secret washing spots they went alone or with family or apprentices to practice *Uusimch* – a complex process of ritual bathing. A week before I came on this trip I had driven to Victoria to see a new exhibit at the Royal British Colombia Museum. Entitled '*Huupu Kwanaum Tapaat, - Out of the Mist*', it was the first time the Nuu-chah-nulth had participated as equals in the planning and presentation of a museum exhibit of their culture. The opening section spoke of the central place of ritual bathing in their culture. A quote from Tim Paul, a Hesquiaht, described *Uusimch* this way:

"Everything and everyone are connected. All things in the physical world originate in the spiritual world. Success depends upon effective communication between the two realms. When our people sought spiritual power, called Uusimch in our language, they visited a sacred pool knownas uusaqulh where they used special medicines called tich'im. Some of the prayer pools are just about

behind the mountain. Some of them are, well, just above the mountain. And they have no trail; they don't show a trail because they are sacred places. You have to know where you are going."[33]

Louis Roberts, a member of the Ucluelet band, described it this way:

"I was taught how to Uusimch by my grandfather and father. This consisted of bathing in the sea, scrubbing the body afterwards with tree branches and singing songs of prayer in our own native language. Each family had it own Uusimch. Some did it for a few hours each day for a period of time, others continually for as long as eight days. There was so much secrecy about what branches and herbs to use and the contents of prayers, so much secrecy that Uusimch was carried out in a secluded area."

Seeking *Uusimich* was a deeply private affair, a ritual of preparation that purified the body before undertaking any important activities, anything from berry picking to whaling to war. The particulars were passed within families at locations that were closely held secrets. Depending on the activity, it included fasting, sexual abstinence, ceremonial bathing in cold streams or the sea, and scrubbing the skin vigorously with hemlock bows and other plants until the skin bled.

***

After lunch I make the two-mile crossing of Gillam Channel over to Nuchatlitz on Nootka Island, the largest island on the west coast of Vancouver Island. The fog that had worried me in the morning continues to wander in and out. The crossing is a bit rough. The

---

[33] Tim Paul in Out of the Mist, RBCM, 1999, p 25.

outgoing tide and wind clash in near opposite directions pushing up the waves in steep short sets. Two sports fishing boats bang past through the chop, heading in, chased off the fishing by the fog. Then a coast guard inflatable flies past, heading out to sea and straight into the fog under the all-seeing eye of the radar. I wonder what poor souls are lost out there now.

When I reach the protection of Nootka Island, I slip into a shallow harbour between some islands to see what remains of Nuchatlitz, once one of the main villages on this section of the coast. On my chart there are three small reserves, including two smaller islands. The main village was apparently on a small peninsula between them. All that remains of the village are a couple of houses falling into the earth on the barren midden. From the water the village looks like it is literally sinking into the earth that its residents once created. On my chart is a small cross, but I see no steeple on the shore. The lives of the people and the work of the missionaries seem long past here now.

***

From Kyuquot Seghers and Brabant headed north on the *Surprise*, hoping to reach Quatsino, but bad weather at the Brooks drove them back. So instead Captain Frank turned the *Surprise* south and coasted into this bay at Nuchatlitz. Brabant wrote boastfully of the reception they received:

> *"May 3. – Early this morning we were taken in a canoe, by the Chief of the Nuchatlahts and a crew of young men, to the outside camp, where the Indians were at this time living. The reception given to us by the Nuchatlahts was something never to be forgotten. The news of our arrival had preceded us. The Chief had made a new house and a wharf about two hundred feet in length but only about four feet in breadth, had been constructed*

[The villagers themselves had little or no use for a wharf, instead pulling their canoes up on the beach.] Although the Indians deserved credit for making such extraordinary preparations, we had to measure our steps and movements least the whole structure should break down. Inside the Chief's house the ground was covered with white sand, our path and the room which we were to occupy were laid with new mats; the walls were hung with sails of canoes and piece of calico. Twenty-nine sea otter skins, valued by Captain Francis of the Surprise *at close to two thousand dollars, were hanging in a line opposite to where we were sitting, and exciting our admiration."*

However it was soon obvious a great welcome did not mean the priests would be successful in their work. The villagers had their own local affairs that took precedence over the agenda of the travelling priests:

> *"The Ehattesaht Indians had come across and joined the Nuchatlahts. In the afternoon a disturbance between the two tribes took place. Our interpreter was of little account, and our success was not in keeping with the great preparations they had made to receive us. However, before we left, harmony had been restored."* [34]

As in every other village, Father Brabant failed to record any evidence that the natives already had a complex religion of their own.

* * *

According to native oral histories, it was in the villages of the outside of Nootka Island that a man first learned the rituals that

---

[34] Mission To Nootka, p 21.

allowed his clan to become the actual hunters of whales on the coast. While the claiming of dead or dying drift whales was common, here at the mouth of the Esperanza Inlet, and at the entrance to Nootka Sound a lack of salmon streams forced the local people to look to the open ocean for food. Twice a year the big *ma?ak*, longer than all but the greatest of canoes, and the *sixwa?ox*, or 'sore face', along with *?ihtop* and great *kotsqi*, or 'mussels on the head', passed along the coast on their annual migrations.

George Hunt recorded this story from an old man named Moyes, a Mowachat from a village at the south end of Nootka Sound. It tells how the rituals and skill of hunting the humpbacks, greys and killer whales came to the coast, passed from Thunderbird to a great hunter of black bears named Ts!ok'tbeel.

***

"*Once there was a man whose name was Ts!ok'tbeel [whose name meant true hunter of bears]. This man was the chief of the ts!awen of the Mots!adox (Mowachaht) tribe; and this chief, Ts!ok'tbeel used to go up to the great mountain, whose name is Nots!e ts!awen or Seen-All-Round. This great mountain has three long peaks on the top of it; and this man used to go up as high as the foot of the three peaks; he went up there to hunt for black bear, or tsemest; and he used to kill lots of bears up there.*

"*One day, he thought that he had better go up higher than he generally did, and he went on until he came to the snow; then he got up to the top of the great mountain; and as soon as he came to the top of the mountain, there he saw a great house, with four great whales outside of its door. Then he stood up in the place where he first saw the house and he said to himself, "I will go and see whose house this is; for if I don't go, it will bother my mind, so I will go" and he went toward the house; and when he came inside of the house-door he saw a pretty woman sitting near the fire inside of the house. She was treeing, or boiling, whale-blubber to get the oil out; and as soon as she saw him she said pointing to the farther side of the fire, "Come in, stranger, and sit down there". Then Ts!ok'tbeel went and sat down where he was told to take his seat.*

"Then she spoke very kindly to him, and Ts!ok'tbeel looked round and lo! he saw lots of whales hanging up by their tales; and they were all split open from their noses down to their tails; they were hanging over the beams of the great house.

"Then Ts!ok'tbeel began to think that the pretty woman was the only person in the house, and he got up and sat alongside of her, and was going to put his arm around her waist to make love to her, but she said, 'Don't do that; for my husband, although he is a long way from this house, could see everything that's going on inside of it; and even when he's inside of this house he can see what's going on all round the world. Now, he has seen you come into this house;' and while she was speaking to Ts!ok'tbeel, lightning came through the roof of the house; and the woman said, 'My husband, the chief of this house, is coming home now; and I think that you had better go and hide in the corner of this house; and I will cover you with this mat, or lehal.' Then he went and lay down on the floor in the corner, and she covered him with a mat. 'Now,' she said, 'you lay still for some time. He is angry towards strangers that come into the house.'

"Then she went and sat down where she was sitting before. She had not sat there long when her husband came in. He had his Thunder-Bird mask and his skin on; and the man lifted the corner of the mat to see the great bird come

in. Then he saw that the great Thunder-Bird had HaEL!ek all over his breast. The great Thunder-Bird stood up and took his head bird-mask off; and afterwards he took his body-skin off, and then he hung it on the right-hand side of the house from the door. After he hung it up he came and sat down on the opposite side to where Ts!ok'tbeel was lying and he faced the place where he was hiding. Then he said to his wife, 'Ask that man to come out from under the mat; for I saw him when he came into my house first.'

"Then the woman went to the corner of the house and she took the mat covering off Ts!ok'tbeel, and she said, 'You had better come and sit down on this side of the fire where my husband can see you.' Then he came and sat down where he was told. Then the Thunder-Bird man, Dodotsyadogwes said to him, 'What made you come up here where my house is; for I never saw anyone come here before; and don't be afraid to speak to me, for I will not hurt you; I will do good to you.'

"Then Ts!ok'tbeel said, 'I am a black bear hunter on the lower part of this mountain, and I have always been hunting there; but this morning I thought I had better come up to the top of this mountain to see if there were any more black bears here than there are in the lower part of it; so I came up to this place and found your house here. Then I thought I had better come and see whose house it was, and when I came up to it, I came inside of its door, for it was wide open; and I said to myself, 'Now I am this far I will go in and see what is inside of it'; and as I came in I saw your wife sitting alongside of the fire; and when she saw me she told me to come in and sit on the opposite side of the fire to her.'

"Before he said any more Dodotsyadogwes asked Ts!ok'tbeel if he was a strong man; and Ts!ok'tbeel said, 'I am not as strong as you are; yet I am stronger than any

of our people, and that is why I came up to this mountain; for I am said to be the strongest man in our village.'

"Then the great man Dodotsyadogwes asked him, 'Are you strong enough to lift up the largest whale in the sea?'

And Ts!ok'tbeel said, 'No, that I could not do.'

Then Dodotsyadogwes said, 'Now, as you have come into my house I will give you strength to carry two large whales;' and he said to his wife, 'Will you build a fire under my stone kettle and let the water boil in it?'

"Then the pretty woman took some fire from the large fire of the house, and she took it to the left-hand side of the door of the house. Then she put fire under the great stone kettle, and in a short time it began to boil. Then Dodotsyadogwes said to Ts!ok'tbeel, 'Now, we will go to that corner and I will wash your body, so as to get all the skin off, which makes you weak;' and he went to the corner where the great stone kettle was now boiling. Then Ts!ok'tbeel went after him, and when they came alongside of it Dodotsyadogwes told him to take his bear-skin blanket off, and Ts!ok'tbeel took it off, and when he was naked the great man Dodotsyadogwes said, 'I will put you into this boiling water;' and he took hold of Ts!ok'tbeel by the two arms and put him into the boiling water; and he was dipped into it four times until the skin of his body all came off. Then he was taken out.

"Then the great man Dodotsyadogwes took four bunches of hemlock branches, common fern, and flag-grass: these were all tied together, and he took the man Ts!ok'tbeel, saying, 'Now, you come to this corner of my house,' (that is, to the right-hand side of the house from the door) and Ts!ok'tbeel went after him; for there was no pain in his body. There he found cold spring water; and he was told to get into it and to dive and rub the bunch of hemlock, fern, and flag-grass on his right-hand side.

"After he had told him what to do, Ts!ok'tbeel went into the spring water, and he dived. Then he began to rub the bunch of hemlock on his right-hand side. When he had finished he was given another bunch, and again he dived, as before; and when he came up he began to rub on the same side. When he had finished he took the third one of the mixture of hemlock branches, fern leaves, and flaggrass, and dived into the well of spring water; and when he came up again he began to rub his left side.

"When he was finished Dodotsyadogwes said to him, 'Now this is the fourth time you will dive, and you had better stay under the water as long as your breath will let you; and when you come up, keep on rubbing with this bunch until your body gets very warm.' Then he gave the bunch of hemlock branches to Ts!ok'tbeel, and took a long breath and dived. This time he stayed down a long time, and when he came up he began to rub it on his left side until his body was red and very warm. Then he stopped rubbing. Dodotsyadogwes told him to stay in the water; and he went and took from the rear of his house something that looked like three pieces of soap, and he brought it to where Ts!ok'tbeel was still standing in the water. Then he gave him one of the pieces of yew-wood, or wedabet, or body-strength-giver, about three inches long, which looks like soap.

"Then Dodotsyadogwes said to Ts!ok'tbeel, 'Now, take this and dip it into the water and rub it on your body.' Then Ts!ok'tbeel took the wedabet and did as he was told to do; and after he had rubbed it on his body the great man said, 'That is enough with that one. Now take this one also, and rub it as you did with the first one.' Then Ts!ok'tbeel took the second piece of wedabet and dipped it into the water, and he began to rub it on his body until he was told to stop. Then the third one was given to him, and

he was told to rub his body all over with it as long as he did with the other two pieces. Then he took it and dipped into the water and rubbed it on his body for quite a long time, until he had white skin on his body.

"Then the great man Dodotsyadogwes said, "Now, all the skin that you had on your

body has come off, and you have a new skin that has no smell to it, as your other skin had; for I could smell you while I was on the other end of the world; and your body also has strength to carry four large whales,"

"Then Dodotsyadogwes said, 'Will you come and sit down. Then we will eat together, so that when you go home you can tell your people that you have seen people who lived on the top of the great mountain Notg!e ts!awen, or Seen-All-Round; and that you have eaten with their chief Dodotsyadogwes, or, Only-One-Heard-By-All-Round-The-World; and after we have finished eating I will give you some food to take home with you,' and they sat down to eat what the pretty woman cooked for them. It was the back fin of a whale that she cooked; and when it was put into a wooden dish, or mage, and put down in front of the two men, Dodotsyadogwes said, "Now, we will eat this, for it is my chief food, hereafter you will live on the whale's blubber-flesh; for I will give it to you," said he, as he took the first piece, Then he began to eat it; and then Ts!ok'tbeel took one piece, and began to eat also; and he liked it, for it was the first time that he had tasted a piece of whale's blubber.

"After they had finished eating the great man Dodotsyadogwes got up from his seat, and he took down one of the largest whales that was hanging up, and doubled it up into a ball, Then he kept on squeezing it until it was turned into the shape of a salmon about three feet long. Then he took four pieces of cedar withes and made a

sling out of it, and then he put one end of it through the whale's mouth and the other end was tied round to the salmon-shaped whale's tail. Then he took another large whale down from where he took the first on, and that one also he began to fold up into a round ball; and after he had made a round ball of it, he squeezed it until it was the same length as the first one.

"Then he took some more cedar withes, as he had done before, and he put the other of the cedar-with rope round the tail of it, and he tied it in this shape; and after he finished it he said, "Now I have shown you how to wash for good luck, or osemts!a [uusmich]; and how to eat good whale's blubber and flesh. So now get ready and I will take you down to the foot of this mountain peak; and these two whales I have given you to take home with you; and now you can take hold of the slings on each of the whales in each hands and carry them; and I will put my arms round your waist. While I am carrying you and flying downward you will have to shut your eyes. If you attempt to open them, I will get weak, or lose my strength. Then we should both die, but as long as you keep you eyes shut we shall be all right." And he took his Thunder-Bird skin and his Thunder-Bird mask and put them on.

"When he was ready, he said to Ts!ok'tbeel, 'Now you take these two whales out of my house. Then there I will pick you up, although they look as small as two large spring salmon now; but the weight of them is there still.' So he tried to lift them up; but he was now a strong man. And he lifted them up and carried them out of the house. Then he put them down just outside of the house-door, where he was told to put them, and very soon Dodotsyadogwes came out of his house. He was now dressed in his Thunder-Bird dress; and he said to Ts!ok'tbeel, 'Now, take hold of the sling of these whales,

one in each hand, and I will put your two arms round your waist and fly and carry you halfway down from the height of my mountain; and now be sure and keep your eyes shut; or, if you open them, there will be sure death to you and me; for if you attempted to open your eyes while I am carrying you, I should lose my strength and, of course, I would have to let you go. Then you would be killed, for I never carry a whale alive; for, if he was alive, I could not carry him; so you will have to pretend to be a dead man while I am carrying you,' said he, as he put his arms round Ts!ok'tbeel's waist.

"Then he flew downward, and Ts!ok'tbeel had to keep his eyes shut. In a very short time he was brought more than half-way down from the top of the mountain. Then Dodotsyadogwes said, 'Now, my Friend Ts!ok'tbeel, when you get home, you take these two great whales down to the beach in front of your house, just above half-way down from high tide; and when the salt water comes up and touches the whales, or covers them over, they will grow to their full size; and when the tide goes down you can begin to cut the blubber off; but the first thing you do, ask your speaker to go and cut the fins off the backs of the two whales and have them cooked: these must be brought out to you, and you must eat them before any one cuts the whale's blubber off, for, if you don't do this, the whales will not be fat at all; and you will also have to keep away from your house until you have eaten the cooked fin. After you have eaten, you can go into your house, and your people can go and cut the two whales up.' Then he flew away and went out seaward.

"Ts!ok'tbeel took the two whales up as he was told to carry them, and went home; and as he came out of the bushes from behind the houses, he saw all of his people sitting in a summer seat, just outside of his house; for they

were looking for him to come home, as this was his fourth day out. When they saw him going down to the beach with his load, all his people watched him; but they did not say a word to him; because they thought that he had met with some kind of supernatural spirit; for he looked like a young man, and his skin was very white now.

"After he had put down the two whales about half-way down from high-water mark, with their heads up from the salt water, he sat down at high-water mark, and then called one of the old speakers to come down to where he was sitting. When the old man came down to him, he said to him, 'Now I want you to go up to my house, and there you will find my knife and you must sharpen it; then, when the tide comes up to those two fishes, you will have to go and cut their back fins off; and then you must cook them. After they are cooked, you must bring them to me where I am sitting on this beach. Then, when the tide goes down, all our people will have to go and take a piece of the fish in my name.'

"Now the tide was coming up, and the old speaker went up to the house, and it was not long before he came back with the L!OtS!EM, or mussel-shell knife, already sharpened. Then the tide came up, and as soon as the salt water covered the two small whales they grew into two large whales. Then the old speaker said, "Now I see that you have met with some kind of spirit; and that is how you have got these two great whales."

"Then Ts!ok'tbeel said, 'Yes, I have met a man who lives on the top of that great mountain, Notg!e tg!awen; it was he who gave me these two great whales. Now, will you tell my people to get their knives ready to cut the blubber off these two great whales when the tide goes out, and also tell our people who gave them to me; for it was he, the great chief Dodotsyadogwes of the mountain; but before

you tell our people about this, go and cut off both of the fins from the backs of the two whales and cook them. After they are cooked, bring them to me and I will eat them here; for if we don't do this, there will be no fat on the whales."

"Then the old speaker went out in a canoe (tg!abeets), and he cut off the fins, and then cut them into strips. Then he went into the house and there he cooked them. After he had finished cooking them he brought them down to where Ts!ok'tbeel was sitting, and Ts!ok'tbeel ate them.

"By this time the two great whales were left high and dry on the beach. Then the speaker spoke out loud and called all the people to get their knives sharpened and to come and cut the blubber from the two whales, and he also told them how Ts!ok'tbeel got them; and he told them that there were people who lived on the top of the great mountain who ate with Ts!ok'tbeel while he was living four days on the mountain.

"Then after Ts!ok'tbeel had finished eating, all the Tgawenaedox, or brother tribe of the Mots!adox tribe, came down and began to cut out the blubber of the two great whales. After they had finished cutting off the blubber, the chief Ts!ok'tbeel went up into his house; and after four days all of the blubber was taken from the two whales and carried into the house. Then all the people came into Ts!ok'tbeel's house; and they all thanked him for the great feast he had given them.

"Then they asked him if he would try to keep on giving a whale-feast once every year; and Ts!ok'tbeel said, 'Yes, I will go up to the mountain again and find out from my chief Dodotsyadogwes if he will show me how to kill whales.' And all the people were pleased to hear him say that he was willing to try to go after whale hereafter.... Then Ts!ok'tbeel gave another feast of whale to his people,

and that is how all harpooning began, and from that, all the west coast."[35]

***

After Ts!ok'tbeel learned the secrets from Thunderbird, the ritual hunting of whales soon became a central aspect of Nuu-chah-nulth culture. Killing a whale was a glorious undertaking that provided not only food, but also immense prestige for the chiefs. One recorded twenty-three successful kills in his lifetime, but most others, despite the purity of their preparations, managed much less. As the ritual skill of the hunters was passed down from father to son in the chiefly families, it was also passed through the marriage of daughters to clans and other villages, and so it spread amongst the noble families of the coast. The young son wanting to follow in his father's path prepared himself with five years of nightly rituals during the four moons of spring at the family shrine in the woods, before he would be allowed to throw the harpoon for his first kill. But it was such a complex ritual that it never spread beyond the Nuu-chah-nulth. Even the warrior Haida, in their massive open-ocean canoes never learned how to bring in the mammoth beasts. Apart from closely linked Makak and Ditidaht groups to the south, no other culture south of the Eskimo-Aleut groups in Alaska all the way down to Terra Del Fuego at the tip of South America hunted whales despite the migration of the creatures twice a year.

The killing tool itself was a three-metre harpoon crafted by carvers who specialized in the tool. The following description was recorded by the anthropologist Drucker:

> *"The Nootkan whaling harpoon, complete with shaft, fore shaft and head, was nearly twenty feet long. The heavy seasoned yew shaft was three or four inches in*

---

[35] The Yuquot Whalers Shrine, p180-187, from Franz Boas Papers, American Philosophical Society, Philadelphia, Hunt Manuscript 419-38.

diameter, and tapered at its ends. It was made in three sections so skilfully joined that it appeared to be a single flawless piece of wood. Two pieces of elk horn and shell were lashed together, the lashing also forming a lanyard with an eye splice for the main line. When the shell broke on a strike, as often happened, the elk horn pieces remained as barbs. The shell cutting blade was easily replaced with a spare, but Mokina [Maquinna, one of the long lineage of chiefs sharing the same name] treasured the elk horn base, which has belonged to his father and his grandfather. [36]

Even if the entire crew had been meticulously devout in observing the rituals, hunting a forty-five-foot whale from a canoe was still dangerous work. In the village the chief would wait at his shrine for a dream or an actual sighting of a whale offering itself up before launching the hunt. Before sunset, the crew would lift the special canoe, itself thirty-five feet long, and carefully cleansed for the event, up on poles and carry it down to the water's edge.

It was a long paddle through the darkness to where the whale was awaiting them far offshore. With the first light of the morning the gear was carefully checked, the two main lines of strong cedar bark twine were carefully coiled in the canoe, and the skin bladders were inflated and lashed to the line's end. Then the chief would take out one of the harpoon heads, perhaps a favourite one passed to him from his father or grandfather and attach the forward end of the line. At first light the canoes would spread out. When a 'Noble Lady' was sighted, the first to spot it would raise his paddle, a silent signal for the others to approach.

Mentioning the whale by name was strictly taboo during the hunt. It was also particularly critical at this point that the hunter's wife did not stir as she lay back in the quiet of the house under her best cedar bark blanket, lest she upset the canoe. Young noble

---

[36] Drucker, Cultures of the North Pacific Coast, p136

women were raised from birth to be a hunter's wife, carefully trained in the complex restrictions of the privileged position. When the hunt was underway, her actions controlled the whale, which had itself already chosen to receive the hunter's harpoons. If she moved suddenly, tripped or rolled over as she lay, the results could be catastrophic for her husband and his crew out on the open sea. The rituals of preparation for the hunter's wife were closely guarded family secrets.

As the creature rose briefly each time to the surface to breath, the canoes would close in. The chief's steersman would manoeuvre his canoe slowly up the right side, waiting patiently just by the tail flukes where the whale could not see them. The steersman, often a brother or uncle, waited until the flukes were almost touching the canoe, then whispered the signal. Then the chief rose at the gunwales and drove the harpoon down hard just behind the whale's front flipper. A solid jarring on bone told him if he had planted the head deeply enough.

As the whale thrashed spasmodically, the canoe pulled quickly away, the lines running over the gunwale of the canoes, the floats one by one following the giant beast as it dove for the shelter of the deep. The shaft of the harpoon was collected on the surface and sent by a fast canoe immediately back to the village, while the others waited for the whale to resurface. One by one, more harpoons were driven in, adding more floats dragging on the weakening creature. If the rituals had been properly observed, it would head for the village to die by the beach. If someone had erred in their preparation it might head out to sea, meaning a long tow of several days to get it to the village. The manner of harpooning with floats was remarkably similar to the technology used by other whaling nations around the world at that time, yet developed uniquely here on the coast.

Once the creature finally expired, and could no longer be persuaded to swim closer to the village, it was time for the kill. Chisels were used to severe the tendons of the huge back fluke.

Once the floats and lines were arranged to keep it afloat, the chief took a lance and slipped between the two ribs protecting the whale's heart. The noble lady had given herself up

One of the crew would quickly jump in the water and sew the mouth up to stop it from taking on water during the long tow home. As they neared the village other canoes arrived to help them tow. Back in the village, preparations would get underway for dividing and rendering the blubber into oil for winter feasting. Once on the beach speeches were made by the hunters and crew and then the hunter claimed a large piece just behind the head. Then each local chief in order of rank received their pieces. The harpoon maker, the crew, and the other paddlers were all rewarded in turn, until finally the carcass was turned over to the rest of the villagers. By evening only the ravens, eagles, crows, and seagulls, beach crabs and various forest creatures remained to clean off the bones, to which the warriors of the village later returned to collect ribs to make clubs.

***

Today, I can't see any sign of occupation on the reserves of Nuchalitz, but elsewhere amongst the islets, I spot two large groups of kayakers, both camped close together on the same island. Anxious to avoid them, I paddle on, toward a secluded little bay behind the Indian reserve, thinking it might have a more private campsite. Instead I find a small collection of houses perched on the rocky slopes. As I paddle past the wharf of one I spot a young girl of about five years, with a summer hat knotted in a bow under her chin. At the water's edge she dangles a simple fishing line into the water. Precociously, she ignores me as I drift up in my boat. An elderly man appears from the house and makes his way down the steps.

"Hello" I say.

"Frank," he says as he leans over to shake my hand. Frank calls himself an American, but has been living here since retiring ten years ago. While we talk the little girl pulls her fishing line around the dock to stand close enough to listen, still refusing to acknowledge the visitor.

"Granddad, I need a better worm," she announces.

"But you have one,"

"I need a better one"

He leaves me for a moment and runs up to the garden and returns moment later with a fat wriggler.

"Do you want to do it this time?"

She screws up her nose and he picks up the hook as he continues to talk to me. I ask him about the fishing.

"We used too have a thing going here on the rocks, mussels and oysters and clams, but now the sea otters have cleaned them right out. They eat everything, from sea urchins to geoducks. There are only a few killer whales left to take care of their numbers. I'd consider them a pest now."

Frank turns out to be a great source of local knowledge. Like most retired folks he knows plenty about the goings-on in the neighbourhood.

"This used to be one of the biggest fishing stations on the whole West Coast," he says sweeping his arm across the bay. "There are some old ruins of the gas tanks of the filling stations round the corner and there used to be fishermen's squats all in these spots with alders. But then they just packed up and left, sold out when all the herring were gone, must have been in the 70s. That's why this land was put up for sale. Two of my neighbours made a living farming oysters, I reckon they could make more pumping fuel at a gas station in town."

I ask about the church marked on the chart in the Indian reserve and he tells me it's just in ruins these days, The natives had moved out about ten years ago to the mainland village of Zeballos to try to combat problems with alcoholism and drug abuse, but he says a few old fellas still live up in Queen Anne's Cove. There are also still some missionaries living round the back of Nootka Island at the old hospital he says. That sounds intriguing,

An hour has passed and the sky has turned overcast by the time I finish talking to Frank. The predicted low pressure has arrived. That means a storm is likely to blow tonight. I beg off and say goodbye to Frank and paddle around the islands and pick a camp away from the other kayakers for the night. In a small opening under some trees I light a fire to cook my dinner just as a light rain begins to fall.

After dinner the rain gets heavier so I kick the fire out and set my tent up in the same spot under the tree. After carefully pegging it out to prevent leaks, I crawl in, mindful of the increasing number of drips already. This old tent has served me well for many years, but this trip I suspect may be its last. I know I am leaving with one foot in my past on this trip. The strain of the long wet days has become routine. I'm older now and not as eager to endure these cramped quarters. Still there is a romance for me now in revisiting it temporarily, but I would not want to return to guiding as way to make a life. Tomorrow I'm hoping to take an inside route around the back of Nootka Island, but already I'm missing the solitude of the outer coast.

25. Queen Anne's Cove

When I wake it is still dark and I can hear a storm howling outside the tent. I lie in bed to avoid facing it until daylight and restlessness drives me from the damp tent. When I pop out I'm thankful to discover it is not raining, at least not yet, just windy. I put the stove on and make tea, have a walk down out to the point to check out the conditions on the water and begin my morning routine.

I'm moving slowly, and my enthusiasm is limited, but when I finally start packing, I take some pride in being the only kayaker venturing out that morning. The rest seem to be battening down their tents to wait out the storm. I wonder how long they are ready to wait. I am glad to leave them behind. I hate kayakers right now.

They seem like such an invasion of my coast. I feel a smug sense of superiority to them, and strong desire to set myself apart. Such hubris on the water is a dangerous thing I know, but I can't help feeling a growing sense of pride as I push off under the darkening sky.

My plan is to take a break from paddling the rough waters of the outer coast for a while and go round the inside of Nootka Island instead. On the chart the detour adds an extra day to my route, but with bad weather setting in, I would have to wait to head down around the outside anyway. So I kick off toward Queen Anne's Cove, on the north side of the entrance of the Inlet. It's roughly four miles across the mouth of the inlet. The mountains seem to be funnelling the wind and I get a good ride in from the southeaster blowing on my back. At least for once the storm winds are blowing in my direction. With a good flood tide rushing into the channel, I take little notice of the rain that has begun falling on my back. I'm bundled up in neoprene boots and gloves, long synthetic underwear, semi-waterproof kayaking pants, a warm shirt, a fleece jacket and a kayaking anorak. I'm warm and I'm happy to be making miles on such a lousy day. I soon drop into a vigorous paddling rhythm.

The storm limits visibility, but the crossing goes quickly. On the far side I round a small island and the sheltered harbour of Queen Anne's Cove Indian reserve comes into view. Backed by steep hills that disappear quickly into the clouds, and ringed by a rocky shoreline with one small beach in a tiny bay, it's a seven-house village with a single finger wharf floating out front. The houses look in good shape and the beachfront is covered with scraps of ropes and boat parts, crab traps and old nets, and a large tarp covering what appears to be a boat of some sort. It's the typical detritus of a West Coast fishing village. As I paddle in I spot a woman cleaning an open sports fishing boat tied to the wharf. I can't tell if she is deliberately ignoring me or if she hasn't seen me arrive.

"Hi," I say as I drifted up to the wharf, pulling back my rain hood to reveal my face. She smiles a big smile at me but says nothing. "Lousy weather" I try.

"Yeah," she says looking around as if she just noticed the downpour, "It's not so bad." She is standing in rubber boots, shorts and a wet cotton sweatshirt with a wolf on it.

"Is this Rogers' Fish Camp?" I ask, reading the name off the side of the boat.

"No, it's down Port Eliza," she says pointing further down the narrow inlet. Just then a man appears from the wheelhouse of the only commercial fishing boat. He is wearing a T-shirt, shorts, and cropped hair. He introduces himself as Tim, and his quiet companion as Jennifer, his wife. We chat for a while. He's a fishing guide at Roger's camp around the corner.

"How is the fishing this year?" I ask him.

"Pretty good really." He's the first person to say that to me, which surprises me, until I remembered that all guides will tell you that. We chat about guiding for a while, about dealing with clients with more money than brains, and the strange preconceptions people have about life on the coast. I ask him about the sea otters.

"They cleaned out all the urchins," he says, "There used to be enough in this bay to feed five families for the summer. They looked like a kelp bed, a whole herd of them floating along, They must have moved on when they cleaned this area out. Now there are none. You used to see a whole raft of sea otters, 250 at a time, but it's down to about a hundred now."

I know the males often travel far down the coast in search of new territory to colonize. I tell them I've seen them as far south as Clayoquot Sound, outside of Flores Island.

"The chiefs used to hunt them for their regalia. I'd like to do that," says Tim. I ask him about the Makah, the Nootka band just across the Strait of Juan De Fuca that separates Vancouver Island from Washington State. In recent years they have taken up whaling again, claiming a cultural right to practice their traditional hunt as part of their treaty rights. A U.S. court decision recently ruled in their favour. Tim's obviously got mixed feelings on the revival of the hunt.

"If you are going to do it, you need to do it right, with all the ritual and fasting. You can't just harpoon a whale and then shoot it. You got to pick the right one, not just anyone, but look for a weak one, like the wolves do. I don't know how they do it there now, so I can't say if it's right," he says.

Many of the skills the whalers used fell into disuse after the arrival of the whites. Most of the reasons for this were economic. Whaling was a risky activity that brought uncertain returns. Hunting sea otters, and later, fur seals, was an easier source of trade items that replaced traditional resources. At the same time, by the late 1800s American whaling boats operating from Boston had reduced the migratory herds to a fraction of their past population.

After a while I remember why I came and I ask about the church. Tim points to the hill behind us where it sits all grey and weathered, the square steeple tilting and covered with verdant moss, the yard overgrown with blackberries bushes.

"My grandfather and great-grandfather built it," he says, "One summer the whole village fishing fleet saved all its money for the season to buy the supplies to build it. A travelling priest came round every so often, and stayed for three or four days in the area at different churches. They were Catholics. Now it's just used for storage. The kids play in it."

I ask about having a look and he waves toward an overgrown path past the last house on the beach. I land my kayak and scramble up the hill. The path is overgrown with berry bushes so thick I have to get down on my hands and knees to crawl though at some parts. Eventually, scratched and dirty I emerge from the tangle by the white siding of the church's back wall. The front step faces out at the ocean and the worst of any incoming storms. Imposing but totally unsuited for the coast, presumably the missionaries liked the way it once dominated the small cove. Today the front door of the weather-beaten church is off its hinges and the front-steps are a treacherous affair

I step carefully up and look around inside. Little remains to indicate it was ever a sanctified place. The windows are missing and huge puddles of rain cover the linoleum floor. An outline marks the spot where the altar was removed. The kids in the village have been painting graffiti on the walls. I wander past, into the priest's vestry where there's a collapsed pool table in the centre of the small room. Back out front, I snap a fuzzy picture in the rain and then head back down. I wonder what was the fate of those who once came here to preach, and those who came to listen. Those are stories likely lost forever as the forest reclaims the space.

When I emerge from the bushes a big Rottweiler pup is barking at the stranger. I quickly make friends with him, and once his tail is wagging I wander back to my boat. Then I remember my water is running low, so I grab my bags and walk up the steps to Tim's house and knock on the door. His wife Jennifer answers and shows me in.

The house is overflowing with kids and boxes of clothes and belongings piled high on shelves on every wall. A massive rack of elk antlers hangs above a large colour TV which is playing the closing credits of a Pink Floyd concert video. Japanese glass floats hang in bundles all over the walls. Every ten seconds little faces peer round a corner at knee level to see the visitor. Jennifer tells me that the house is Tim's uncle's and that they are just visiting for the summer while Tim fixes up the water damage in one of the other houses for them to live in. They are the only two families out here. They don't want to live in Zeballos where the rest of the band has moved.

"It's technology that made them move," says Tim. "They wanted cable TV. Satellite is good enough for me," he says with a grin.

I thank them for the water, and head back down to my boat. As I'm packing up, Tim's uncle Martin comes by to chat and look at my boat. Martin is dressed up in a red Mackinaw jacket, a hunting cap and dark green work pants. He looks a lot like my father, who is about the same age and has identical taste in clothes. I ask him about the church but he shakes his head dismissively.

"All that was before my time," he says. He seems to care less than Tim. But I suspect he is hiding what he knows. Many say it's his generation that suffered most under the missionaries. Why open old wounds for the casual interest of a passing stranger?

Tim appears from the house to see me off. He takes a look over my kayak and asks me how much it can hold. I offer him a chance to paddle it, but he declines with a laugh, saying it's a lousy day for a swim. We chat about kayaks and canoe carving and he points to the blue tarp high on the shore. He and his uncle are carving a dugout for salmon fishing. We wander over and lift the blue plastic tarp to reveal the rough shape of a hull. It's hewn from a single cedar log about twenty feet long and three feet in diameter. He confesses his uncle only remembers the basics. The finer details of the process are unknown to them.

As a coastal people, canoe building was a central part of the Nuu-chah-nulth culture. From birth, infants were nursed in canoe cradles, ensuring that they would be confident paddlers, and old chiefs were often laid to rest in the branches of a tall tree in their favourite canoes. The anthropologist Eugene Arima recorded eight common types of canoes in his studies of the Nootka people (whom he called 'The West Coast People'). The subtle variations are a testament to the extent of the technical innovation of the people. *Shitl'ats* was a beamy long canoe, used to transport household goods between seasonal village sites. Two could be covered with the planks from the house, creating a large barge for transport up the quiet inlets. *Witaqsats* was a war canoe, the same length but narrower for speed. *Tl'isol* (meaning 'white-face') was a huge war canoe with painted ends and high wide prow to shield against arrows, up to sixty feet long. *O'otaqsats* was a whaling canoe, *Yashmaqsat* was a sealing canoe, built narrow and fast to be paddled by a small crew, while *hw'aka'atlasats* was a sea otter hunting canoe, just a little shorter and more manuverable to chase them inshore, while the more common *hashmahats* was a three-person utility canoe, small and wide. Smallest of all were the *chitssats*, a trolling canoe, and *taka'odiyak*, a one-man 'sit in the middle' canoe for odd chores and just getting around.

Canoe building began at the end of the summer when the trees were soft with sap. After completion of the necessary *ussmich*, the canoe maker would paddle up the back of the inlets with his apprentice, perhaps a son or a nephew, to find a tree that was offering to become a canoe. (Only a fool would paddle out to sea in a cedar that wanted to remain a tree.) There at the foot of the mountains where the rain fell heavy grew the tallest straight-grained cedars. With stone axes, fire and wet clay, and later with steel chisels, they felled the tree, cleaned the branches and there in the woods they shaped the hull. The outside was chipped off and then the inside hollowed out. To maintain an even thickness along the length, small holes were bored with a hand twist-drill, made from the bone of a deer, bear or eagle. Then the carver returned to the village for more men to help roll it to the water's edge and tow it home. In some villages, for good luck at this first launch it was overcrowded till it sank.

Through the winter the carver and apprentice worked on the hull on the beach in front of the village. With the shape carved, they flared the sides by lighting a fire underneath and filling the inside with water and hot stones. As the wood softened and expanded inside and contracted on the outside, they slipped hemlock thwart poles in crossways to hold the flared shape. Next they fitted the high prow and stern pieces, lashing them on with cedar twine, giving the canoe a sea-worthy shape. A characteristic notch in the bow headpiece was the resting place for the hunters harpoon. Next the outside was scorched to remove any slivers, holes were patched with pugs and spruce pitch, and the surface of the hull was sanded to a slippery smooth finish with a natural sandpaper like dogfish skin. A hemlock or alder solution was painted on the inside to protect the wood from burrowing insects. In the case of war canoes, a final touch was to paint the bow with the crests of the clan. Once the floorboards, mats, and tackle and water boxes were fitted, the seaworthy craft was ready to launch.

The Clayoquot, along with the Nitinat were the most famous canoe builders. Jacobson even bought one of their war canoes from a Fort Rupert Chief, long after it had been traded and potlatched amongst several nobles. But during the cultural upheaval of the last century the tradition of carving managed to pass from the last generation to this one in only a few families.

I mention to Tim that I know two Clayoquot brothers named Carl and Joe, mutual friends, who live in Tofino. The two learned to carve in their father's boatshed. Since then they have done much to revive the tradition on the coast, teaching whites and natives on the beaches close to town. Tim says now he wants to learn from them how to finish the canoe. I tell him I hope some day he does.

The storm is still blowing just as hard, but it feels like time to go. I pull on my spray-skirt and pick up the bow of my boat with the plastic toggle. It slips backwards into the shallow water, rocking steady like it belongs in the sea. I step across it and settle into the familiar seat. Just as I push off, Tim asks me when I'll be back. I say 'Not soon', and instantly regret it. But what else can I do? Since I began, this trip has been about completing something left undone, rather than beginning something anew. I've got a plane ticket, a ring and Rosie pulling me back to a beachside flat in Sydney. I wave back to the house as I paddle off, gritting my teeth against the incoming storm.

26. Ehatisaht

The storm doesn't let up and I paddle for several miles alone in the mist. When I reach the main channel I turn east, away from the ocean and the storm I can see building out there, and toward the shelter. Inside the inlet the steep slopes of the mountains hem me in, protecting me from the worst of the storm, which I can see rocking the trees higher up the forested slopes. Several sports fishing boats buzz past, heading in ahead of the building tempest outside. Then a floatplane buzzes low overhead just beneath the clouds, heading out. Ten minutes later, still with a full load of passengers, it drones past again returning back up the channel. I suspect it is full of loggers trying to make an unsuccessful landing at the camp I passed a few days ago.

Ahead is an old native village site of Ehatisaht. One of my older guidebooks says there is a totem pole, one of the last of the old ones on the coast, still standing there. What is interesting about totem poles is that Captain Cook spent a month in this area and neither he nor his officers ever recorded seeing a single one. Inside the houses they did find elaborately carved corner posts, which they speculated had mythic but not religious significance. In fact the tradition of carving crests into tall poles and erecting them in front of the clan houses actually came from far north up the coast from the Haida, either by trade or by marriage during the cultural renaissance stimulated by the wealth brought by the fur trade to these villages. Trading furs gave the people access to sharp iron and steel carving tools, which allowed the clan chiefs to hire specialized carvers. Poles began appearing in front of the villages and soon had a prominent role in the culture. By the time the collectors arrived, the poles were considered so spiritually important that few owners would willingly part with them for any cash offers.

Today as I approach Ehatisaht I see just a pebble beach backed by a tall forest. Behind that is a short steep gully that disappears quickly into the shear wall of mist. There are no houses, or poles. The forest has grown mature enough to hide almost all trace that humans once inhabited this place. But floating on the water out front of the former village site is an elegant wooden sailboat. The boat is a hand built masterpiece, every inch obviously painstakingly crafted, bedecked with intricately carved woodwork. Across the transom is 'Mystic' and Oregon. Walking on the deck I see a dread-locked fellow in s tie-dyed shirt, so I paddle over to say hello.

The conversation begins in the usual way.

"Where you coming from?" asks the man through his thick beard. Prompted by the sound of a stranger's voice a woman emerges from below. She says hello with a European accent, and is dressed plainly. They both appear to be roughly my age. We converse for a while as they look down at me pitifully in my tiny boat in the rain until they finally invite me aboard for coffee to warm up. After a morning of battling the storm, I'm a happy to climb aboard.

Down below two large dogs are kicked off the dinette seats to let me sit down. The woman stands while she makes coffee, while the man tells me about their summer of sailing. He spent nine years building the boat by hand in his backyard, and she just met him a few months before they departed. They came up a couple months ago from Eugene, Oregon and have spent the summer sailing up the inside coast of Vancouver Island. Now on the return leg down the outer coast, with luck they would be home in a week or two. The distances seemed incredible to me. Although the man keeps talking of their big plans, I can already see the woman is less certain of the relationship after a summer in the boat together.

We get talking about the missing totem pole and he shows me a picture of it in his cruising books for the area. After locating its most likely position from the deck of the boat they pile into their rowboat and I into my kayak and we paddle over to shore to look for it along the shore. It quickly becomes obvious it is nowhere to be found, but as we walk the beach we stumble into an old graveyard, overgrown with blackberries. Some of the gravestones though are as recent as 1995. I realize it is time we should be going.

Jacobsen once landed here, in search of whale bone war clubs that he particularly coveted. Including the three clubs Jacobsen sent to Berlin, only a handful of the intricately carved chiefly possessions still exist. Like many early collectors, he mistakenly believed that bone carvings and stone tools were more ancient, than the commonplace woodcarvings. When he arrived in the middle of winter, before he could trade, he had to wait for several days while a ceremonial dance was underway. Just by chance he recorded a rough account of the most important winter dances of the Nuu-chah-nulth, the Wolf Ceremony. He wrote:

> *"The next morning I left Muchalat after this weirdest New Year's Eve of my life and spent the first day of 1882 getting back to the* Favourite *with my friend Captain Frank. The first days of the new year were spent organizing the new trading post, while I listed and packed my collection. By 6 January we were ready to leave Nootka Sound and continue northward to our next port of call, Esperanza Inlet, where I had been a month before. We landed at the firm's post at Nuchatlitz, and I rented a canoe and two Indians, who happened to be the same who went with me in December from here to Hesquiat, and we went deep into Esperanza Inlet to Ehatisaht. "*
>
> *"When we arrived, in darkness, we found the people from Mowachaht [from Yuquot] visiting to take part in a big feast and dancing, which I had the privilege of attending.... As the invited guests enter the house their names are loudly announced, and each is assigned a seat. When he enters each guest is given a bundle of shredded cedar bark with which to clean his feet. The chiefs and the most distinguished guests arrive last. After the guests have been placed all around the fire, the meal is cooked in large wooden boxes filled with water that has been heated with hot stones. When the water boils, the food, principally meat is put into the boxes and cooks very quickly... Before the meal begins a small cedar-bark mat is laid before every guest. The host walks around during the meal to see that every guest is well served, while the hostess and her helpers pass the food around. During eating there is little conversation, for that is not considered in good taste. Each guest receives his portion on the mat. The meal usually consists of dried fish and is served in finely carved bowls.*

Freshly cooked fish is eaten with a wooden spoon, and the other food is held with the fingers. The teeth of these Indians are worn down almost to the gums because of the large amount of sand in the dried fish that is their principal food. A favourite food for feasts is whale blubber. The portion of food for each guest is so large that only half can be eaten, so they take the remainder home. After the meal every guest is given a strand of shredded cedar bark to wipe his mouth and hands. The meal is foiled by speeches and conferences. Women are seldom invited to these gatherings, but they have their own feasts, to which friendly neighbours are invited. There are also feasts for those not so highly placed."

"The west coast Indians are supposed to have a greater variety of dances than the north coast people – it is said they have fifty-three different dances. In Ehatisaht there was a dance leader who arranged the performances. There were round dances as well as set spectacles.... For an individual dance he would give the performer his beat with his rattles. All the dancers were in full regalia, with the men's faces painted black and red, the women's in red alone.... Three naked Indians represented wolves, and for this the first held a well-carved wolf's head in his hand while the other two covered themselves with a canoe sail and stood bent over. This represented the body of the wolf. The third man, half-naked, was at the end of the sail and held in his hand a so-called foxtail, which he held behind him and moved like a tail. This three-part figure moved in unison, looking like a six-legged being. This giant would open and shut his mouth and ran toward the audience, which fled from him in terror all through the house."

"After this scene another dance began which reminded me of the terror of the cannibal Hamatsa on the north coast of Vancouver Island. A naked Indian representing a

slave or a prisoner of war was led around the fire, his captor carrying a large dagger with which he made motions as though he wanted to cut open his victim's abdomen. The slave was very frightened and tried to escape, but he was caught, and in pantomime his captor carried out his threat and supposedly slit him open and then caught his blood and then drank it. During this pantomime all present screamed and danced. After the dances I bought some of the masks and accessories, unfortunately at considerable expense, since these pieces were considered very valuable. To my great sorrow I could not acquire the costume of the firebird [Hotloxom, Thunder-Bird, the great eagle]."[37]

***

There is obviously no totem pole here now. I'm cold and wet and now feel guilty about trapping around without permission in a graveyard, so I head back to my boat. Alone, I grab a quick snack standing in the rain, shout good-bye to the sailors and push off. When I look back I can see they have wandered to opposite ends of the beach, and neither looks interested in returning to the confines of their boat. The open cockpit of my kayak now feels much larger than it previously did.

Past Ehastisaht, the storm seems to mellow out in the deep shelter of the inlet. A few more hours pass under my paddle stokes. Sports fishing boats cruise past on the far side of the mile-wide channel. By the time their wakes reach me they are already long out of sight. The landscape is a dull mix of brown and greens and half hidden shapes. I'm cold wet and hungry. In the rain I soon find myself singing a little rhyme to keep myself going. It goes:

Grim, ... grim,

---

[37] Jacobsen, p 63-65.

Grim, ... grim,
Grim determination,
Will get me through!

Repeating it endlessly, somehow in the silly rhyme I find a reason to keep going. Still, I have no choice. The slopes of the mountains drop straight into the water along the sides of the inlet and there are precious few spots to land a kayak, let alone set up a camp. According to my chart, the next possible campsite is an hour away and I am beginning to wonder what sort of place I'm going to find for the night. As I round another point I find myself turning almost straight into the storm again. I pass a salmon farm, identical in every aspect to the one in Quatsino Sound, but not a soul stirs on its rain-lashed decks.

Further on at Haven Cove, I turn in, hopeful to find a campsite. It turns out to be pretty, but the shoreline is flooded by the high tide and there are no dry spots large enough to stick a tent. So I push on. When I come back out into Hecate Channel, the storm seems to have passed, but the rain continues. The *Mystic* motors past far out in the middle. On the back deck under a tarpaulin, the dreadlocked captain waves and toots a blast on the air horn that echoes off the steep mountain slopes. I'm soaked through now and I can feel a deep chill is setting in. Even the bones in my legs are starting to feel cold. I should have worn my wetsuit today. I put my paddle down and pull my chart back in front of me and begin searching for another possible camp.

27. Esperanza Mission

cross the channel is the Esperanza Mission. Curious, and
looking for a diversion from the endless paddling and the
rain, I cross toward the collection of white houses and
buildings. A massive boat shed dominates the water's edge. Smoke
is rising from the chimney and an old sport boat is halfway up the
slips. I can hear an engine running and see figures moving inside.
As I coast past rubbernecking, a figure appears beside the boat on
the slips dressed in a black overcoat and cap. He waves and shouts,
"Come inside and get out of the rain."

It doesn't take long for me to get ashore. After tying my boat up
under a long pier, I walk up the grassy slope to the side entrance of
the shed. The smell of burning cedar hangs in the air. Inside the

shed I find a group of several men and one woman huddled round a wood stove. A few more are winching the boat up the slips. After a minute, the figure in the black wool cap turns from his position at the winch and says, "Oh there you are. Dinner's at six. Grab a bunk across the yard."

A bit surprised but grateful, I step back out into the rain and walk back down to the shore to unpack my kayak. Across the yard I open up the door to one of six small cabins on the edge of the clearing. Inside is a simple and purposeful six-bunk arrangement, with a table and chairs under the one window at the front. The price stickers from the lumberyard are still stapled to the plywood walls and back of the front door. On some shelves at the back I find two versions of the Bible, and under a vase of fake flowers on the table a laminated sheet of memory verses.

Built like a hermitage, the cabin is a palace to me. I can stand up while getting dressed and sit in a chair at the table. I soon have my wet clothes hanging all over the beds and chair. There is no heat but it hardly matters. Thin calico curtains decorate the only window. As I skim the memory verses, a bell starts to clang. I check my watch. It is nearly six o'clock. I put on my least fetid shirt and pants, then my raincoat and rubber boots and step back out into the rain.

It's a short walk from the cabins to the main hall, and along the way I pass a couple of old houses. As soon as I enter the big double doors, the man in the hat spots me in the doorway and welcomes me to his table, introducing me to the people he is sitting with. Dinner is being served in the gymnasium tonight because the dining room was getting a new floor. Dean it turns out is the resident missionary, one of the Shantymen that has run the mission for about sixty years. He says most of the others are volunteers who have come up for a week from Seattle to put in the new floor. Once the introductions with the rest of the table are complete, Dean sends me up to the buffet table to fill up a plate with roast chicken, potatoes, soggy three-veg and gravy. I have all sorts of questions for him, but by the time I return to sit down he is just slipping away,

"Enjoy your dinner, I'm heading back to my house where my dinner and family are waiting," he says.

Once I sit down, I realize everyone is waiting for me. A redheaded fellow beside me, Paul, rattles off a quick grace and then for a couple minutes we all are hungrily attentive to our plates of food. But soon Paul wants to know about my trip. So I talk while we eat. He's impressed to learn I am some sort of local, and he tells me he's lives in nearby Tahsis, and has worked in forestry most of his life.

"Now life there is going down hill. It's just single guys who can afford to work only five months or less a year. They don't care about advancing their careers. It is just becoming more redneck - too many men without women. The social life is just Hockey Night in Canada and a case of beer," he says.

Now out of work due to shutdowns at the mill, he lives in a trailer without electricity.

"When I became a Christian I lost a lot of friends," he admits with some scorn.

The other couple at the table along with their two kids are residents of the mission for six years, but not actually missionaries. To join, they had to fill out an application to see if they had the values and beliefs of the Shantymen. Then they had to find some sponsors back in Seattle to pay their living expenses while they were here. It just took a summer for them because they came from strongly religious families. What their sponsors gave them was essentially their wage, from which they paid rent for a house on the mission.

The mission itself was only 62 years old. It was originally owned by the Nootka Mission Society, since it was part of the vows of the Shantymen not to own property, but ten years ago it was reorganized into one legal body. Originally the mission ran a hospital that relied on government funding, but the funding ran out in 1975 and the hospital became a dental clinic for ten years, before that shut too. These days the mission tries to generate its own funding by running a gas bar for boats. At certain times of year they run drug and alcohol rehab programs for local families, youth camps in the summer, which are very popular with local kids, community outreach programs, a bible group in Tahsis, and a youth group in Kyuquot and Zeballos.

After diner I pitch in gratefully with the dishes. A good stiff drink would make it a perfect evening, but I don't think I'm going to get one around here. So instead, already a bit overwhelmed by all the conversation I head back to my cabin after the dishes are done and retire exhausted. Within minutes of climbing into bed I'm sound asleep, oblivious to the drumming of the rain on the roof.

***

I sleep in the next morning until the ringing of the bell summons me to breakfast back in the gym. After a double-serving of French toast and 'lumberjack' syrup, I pack up, say my thanks and press a donation into the wet hands of one of the kitchen volunteers. As I walk down to water's edge, Dean approaches.

"You should get better weather shortly."

He's checked the weather forecast for me. I never even asked him too. I thank him for his hospitality and he waves it off.

"Enjoy the rest of your trip. Now I've got work to do," he says, pointing at the boat shed with his chin. By the time I launch, I can already hear the winch lowering yesterday's work back into the water.

The rain is holding off and the sunshine Dean promised seems to be arriving early. Across Hecate Channel I can see the remnant pilings of two ruined piers, salmon canneries and pilchard reduction plants that once flourished back in the inlets. A short paddle around the corner is the tiny settlement of Ceepeecee, now just a collection of old buildings and a modern floating fishing lodge.

Once, about 400 people, natives, immigrants, mostly women, lived and worked here, employees of the Canadian Packing Corporation (thus the name), a subsidiary of the California Packing Corporation. In 1925 the waters off the West Coast suddenly became alive with schools of overgrown type of sardine called pilchards. George Nicholson, a local historian, postmaster, justice of the peace and coroner, Department of Mining recorder, registrar or births, deaths and marriages, marriage commissioner, Department of Transport air harbour licensee, and commercial agent for the Standard Oil Company of B.C. and the Zeballos Trading Company and the representative of the Department of Veterans Affairs, at Zeballos, at the time, recorded the following account of the industrial explosion:

"Boiling schools acres wide suddenly appeared only in the inlets of Barkley, Clayoquot, Nootka, and Kyuquot Sounds. The sardine industry in California was in full swing at the time, and within a couple years 26 reduction plants opened all through the inlets. Built at a cost of quarter million dollars a piece, sites were at a premium, requiring good penetration for pile driving, shelter for boats and docks, and above all, a plentiful water supply. Construction crews would ask any price for their hire. Victoria and Vancouver shipyards worked night and day building seine boats and scows, while fishing companies vied with one another in a mad scramble to cash in on the bonanza. Meanwhile the pilchards continued to show up in greater bulk."

The huge reduction vats were shortly cooking down hundreds of tonnes of the oily little fish a year. It was said of the pilchard that if you left them in the sun in a bowl, within twenty-four hours, only the skin and backbone would remain in a bowl of oil. Sales in the fish oil quickly reached $2 million annually, used for fertilizers, cattle and poultry feed, margarine, 'milady's cosmetic preparations' and high-grade paints.

Then as suddenly as they arrived, after just a few years schooling every summer in the sounds, the pilchards mysteriously moved offshore where only the larger boats could reach them. In 1944 the numbers suddenly dropped. In 1946 not a single one was seen. Just as quickly as it had boomed, what remained of the industry was shut down, or switched to fishing lower grade herring. Nevertheless, in the age before conservation strategies and ecological theories, the disappearance puzzled many, including Nicholson:

> *"The fishermen point out that during the years they fished them, the sea would frequently be alive with pilchards and, overnight, they would disappear for weeks at a time, only to return in greater quantities than ever. They just seemed to have a habit of disappearing when they felt so inclined and reappear if and when they saw fit.... They only appeared off the Island's west coast when the temperature registered a degree or two higher than the normal summer average and when a certain form of microscopic feed made its appearance.*
>
> *"These two points, however appear to have little or no bearing in the subsequent disappearance, for many summers have since come and gone with both water temperature favourable and this feed showing up, but still no pilchards. Our fishermen blamed the California sardine industry for catching every pilchard (sardine) that came their way. From San Francisco to the Gulf of California the coastline was dotted with sardine canneries with a fleet of boats numbering in the thousands, fishing anywhere from the beaches to one hundred miles out to sea. However, one satisfaction Canadian pilchard fishermen*

derived out of the existing state of affairs, was that the sardine fishermen of California found themselves in the same boat. Like the pilchards, the sardines have gone and that industry too.

"Another theory is that they fled the shore of the North American continent altogether. They have since been reported showing up in waters adjacent to New Zealand and Australia and in the Indian Ocean."

The pilchard plants once shared these back inlets with numerous salmon canneries as well, but by the 1970s almost all of those had also closed. These days most salmon caught on the west coast of the island is processed at fish plants in Tofino, and then transported frozen to distributors across the island.

***

It seems odd to me, floating past in my kayak, to imagine the industry that once hummed at the bottom of this shadowed valley surrounded by these steep mountain walls. From the water I can see the yard of the remaining houses is crowded with the rusting memorabilia of the bygone age, remnant equipment from canning and forestry. I pull up at the dock in front of the floating sports fishing lodge tied up to the wharf. Someone spots me from inside and soon a middle age woman appears at the door to great me. She seems happy to talk and I am soon deep in conversation with Laura, the chambermaid from Tahsis, the small logging town up the back of the Tahsis Inlet. Years ago, Tahsis was only accessible by boat and plane, but like many communities on the inner reaches of the coast, the coming of the roads changed everything.

"Father always said that when the road went through it ruined that place," says Laura, "Before the roads you could only bring in an Austin Mini because the streets were so narrow. They had these crazy narrow little streets that no other car could fit down. Since they were private roads they issued special licences and licence plates. Since everyone relied on subsidized flights to Vancouver to get in and out, there was a feeling of community. Then after the road went in it was every man for himself."

I ask here what it was like to grow up in an isolated West Coast town and she thinks for a while before responding.

"There was just one type of job then – forestry," she says, "The two mills ran three shifts a day – they never shut down. The town was essentially socially segregated according to job status - management, tradesman or mill worker. As a woman you had no career options though, only office work, cleaning or waiting tables, so most of them got bored and moved on."

She tells me things were toughest of all for the natives who lived in the community of whites, many of whom felt it necessary to put down the natives to prove their own superior worth.

"At school if you were an Indian you got strapped ten times worse for the smallest infraction. They did everything they could to stop my brother from being friends with one of our Indian neighbours. Even today the natives know which schools are bad and they won't send their kids there."

We chat for a while longer about the sport fishing industry until the sun start to come out. Under the parting clouds my mind shifts to paddling and so I take my leave. Within a few miles I pass through a narrow tidal channel and come out in the long straight stretch of Tahsis Inlet. For the rest of the day I paddle into a light wind between the heavily clear-cut steep slopes on both sides.

For many families, including my own, logging and fishing were the means to establishing a life on this coast. So it was for my father. Work in the logging camps was what drew him to Vancouver Island a half a century ago.

***

In 1948, my father Hugo was just 21 years old, and living in a Displaced Persons camp in Germany. The Soviet occupation of his country, Estonia, made it too dangerous to return home. His family had fled to Sweden in a small open boat across the Baltic, but my father, like many young demobilized soldiers was stuck in the refugee camp under the protection of the newly formed United Nations Refugee Commission. Just as he finally made contact with his family through the Red Cross by mail, news spread through the camp of an offer to immigrate to Canada. For one year he would be required to work as a lumberjack. Then he would be granted landed immigrant status and be set free in the new country. With twenty-one other Estonians he enlisted for a new life in a new land. Together they boarded a United States Navy liberty ship that once transported American troops to the war. For a week they swung in the hammocks as it lumbered across the Atlantic. Ashore at Halifax, they boarded a train for a lumber camp in north Ontario.

My father still recalls how they all mistook their first regular meal in the camp as a welcoming feast, tables of meat, soups and pies – more food than they had seen since weddings before the war. They ate triple-helpings and stuffed extra pork chops down their shirts to eat later that night in the bunkhouse. But when the feasting continued right through the next day and into the one after, they knew they had come to a good life. All through that first long northern winter they worked in the woods and shared a twenty-man bunkhouse, making plans by the massive woodstove. With their contract fulfilled a year later, they were free to go, residents, but not yet citizens of their new home.

With five others, my father took the wages they had saved and put their limited possessions, mostly Swede-saws, axes and other lumberjack gear, on a freight train heading west. Then they piled into a Chevrolet one managed to buy and followed some friends who had already found better work on the British Columbia coast. At Vancouver they kept going, and boarded a ferry to Vancouver Island. From Nanaimo they drove west to the mill town of Port

Alberni. There they caught the *Uchuck*, a small passenger boat that took them out to the isolated Sarita River logging camp, on the edge of the island's west coast.

The camp boss must have taken one look at my father's big frame and immediately known what to do with him. He started work the next day as a 'powder monkey' on the road-building crew. Every morning a man would push a 70 pound box of dynamite off the back of a truck at the end of the road. My father would strap it onto his back with a 'Trapper Nelson' pack frame and set off into the woods, teetering along the fallen tree trunks.

His boss, the 'powder-man', showed him how to set a trail of charges under each massive stump. At the end of the day, they would stop and light the last charge. The time-delay fuse would give them just enough time to run back and light the next. And the next 30 or 40 down the line. As the charges started to blow, he had to keep well ahead of the chain or risk having the exploded stumps rain down on him. More dangerous yet was working with dynamite without gloves. Handling the sticks all day allowed the skin to absorb the nitroglycerin. The effects made the old-timers a little crazy. They all kept smelling salts handy in their lunch boxes for when they passed out.

The camp at Sarita River in Barkley Sound was like many coastal camps of the time. It had a bunkhouse for the single men, and a small village for the families. For socializing there was the community hall where movies where shown. Passenger steamships from Victoria like the *Princess Maquinna* would stop in regularly. On the rare occasions it tied up overnight a dance might be held. At Christmas, Woolworth's leased the entire *Princess Maquinna*, and turned it into a floating department store. With his saved wages my father bought his first transistor radio. He could get two stations from Victoria on a good night.

Six months as a powder monkey was enough to get him a promotion and a long-term din in his hearing. So he started working on a road crew as a grader's assistant. After a year his friends wanted to move on. Once again they pulled up stakes. This time they headed to Vancouver for better jobs. Eventually most attended university at the growing UBC campus that I would also attend. But for the rest of his life, and the first sixteen years of mine (until he took us back), he would talk of the island as 'God's country' and speak of it as his home.

At nearly every creek mouth along the shore there is the remains of an old wharf or pilings, remnants of cannery or logging operations. Two of the camps are still active, and the peaks to the west towering above me still have snow on the summits. All day long boats pass me in the channel and the rocks have sharp barnacles that scrape the bottom of my boat when I land for a break. The *Uchuk III*, one of the last of the old freighter passenger ships servicing the coast passes me here, the tourists all pointing from the deck. Late in the day, I pull into a beach on Strange Island, just short of my intended destination.

28. Refugees and invaders

IN 1999, another boat, or rather a ship, arrived in this same spot, also just short of its final destination. Many of the passengers had paid $38,000 dollars for the trip, which worked out to about a thousand a day over the course of the thirty-eight day trip from Fu Jain, China. But conditions were far from luxurious. The ship itself was a rusting offshore fishing boat, about a hundred feet long, painted blue all over, without any markings or identification. Of the 123 people aboard, not a single one carried any form of identification. By the time the unnamed ship reached

Nootka Island, human feces covered most of the deck and was driving people from the hold below.

The ship was first spotted by some U.S. police officers up on vacation to do some salmon fishing. They notified the Royal Canadian Mounted Police who sped to the scene in their Suburban trucks, rubber zodiacs, and the pride of the force, the *Higgit*, the fastest offshore boat on the coast. The RCMP soon had the smugglers' ship surrounded. When rumours reached Vancouver and Victoria of the ships arrival a circus of photographers, reporters and cameramen soon began chartering floatplanes out to the remote sound. Soon the flotilla of police was also surrounded. Back in Victoria, the newspaper headline the next day ran "Immigrant smuggling ship snared – largest refugee scam on the West Coast broken up." [38]

The jagged coastline of British Columbia has long been a smuggler's paradise. In the early days of the fur trade rival traders played cat and mouse amongst the inlets. Later during Prohibition Canadian bootleggers operated out of West Coast fishing villages, running illegal spirits down to the Washington coast. More recently the coast has been a popular entry point for drugs, particularly heroin arriving from Asia. The common technique is for a nondescript mothership to sit just outside the legal 200-mile zone offshore and offload shipments to smaller boats during the night, which then run into remote drop-off points along the coast. But this ship was different. This ship was intended to be abandoned once it reached the coast.

Once the boat was finally boarded, and a doctor had a chance to give the bewildered passengers a clean bill of health, the illegal immigrants, as they were officially called, since they had yet to file any official refugee claims, were quickly bussed down to Victoria to be held at the old naval barracks in Esquimalt. Initially the detainees had little to say about the mysterious circumstances of their arrival, but after the RCMP removed the suspected

---

[38] Times Colonist, Wed., July 21, 1999. p A1

ringleaders of the smuggling operation to Vancouver to be processed separately, more details began to emerge.

It turned out none of the women had paid for the trip, but were promised jobs as soon as they arrived. It was not known how many of them were aware these jobs would likely be at the less glamorous bottom pit of the sex trade. Many were expecting to claim refugee status and then to be released into the community, to await hearings. Statistically only 50 per cent could be expected to actually show up at the refugee hearings. Most would leave Canada and head to larger cities in the US where jobs and contacts were already awaiting them. With an average US$28,000 debt hanging over their heads to a Chinese triad that made regular house calls on their family back home, Canadian dollars were not worth the effort. It was not unusual for people in their situation to take three generations to fully pay off the loan by sending money back home.

In the media frenzy that followed, the dangers of illegal immigrants ran front-page on the newspapers. Pundits and politicians warned of connections to Asian organized crime triads, enslavement of the women in prostitution via drug addiction, Canada's role as an illegal entry point in to the USA, the cost to the public of legal fees, private security, policing, and processing the detainees. Rising to the top of the media scrum, the federal immigration minister vowed a crackdown on people smuggling and talked of establishing integrity in the immigration system. "Now is the time to draw a line in the sand and let the world know Canada will not be an easy target." In a July 30th Editorial, the Times Colonist newspaper, the bastion of conservative Victorian sentiment, picked up the popular position:

> *"It is absurd but it's the law that though the people may come here illegally, once they are ashore and claim to be refugees, they are here legally. We can and should find ways to hold those who arrive unbidden on our shores*

until they are determined to be refugees, to fast track those
who come by the boat load and block avenues of appeal
that allow bogus ones to remain so long that we can't get
rid of them. "[39]

Voices speaking out in favour of welcoming the refuges were few and far between. Francisco Rico Martinez, President of the Council of Canadians, an umbrella organization of left-wing activists, countered that Canada had a proud heritage of welcoming refugees in massive resettlement programs. Martinez pointed to the 60,000 Vietnamese boat people who were welcomed in a massive resettlement program in the 1970s, and the 5,000 Kosovar refugees welcomed in the 1990s. The 123 Chinese would only be a tiny fraction of the 25,000 refugee claimants that arrived in Canada in a typical year. The irony of the situation, that a city of immigrants only a hundred and fifty years old was so xenophobic seemed lost on the public at large.

When people ask me where I am from I am stumped by the question. I was born in a distant corner of Australia, a place I have only returned to once, for a brief month. But we left when I was two, and we moved to Canada, by way of Scotland, eventually ending up in the suburbs of Ottawa. Later when my father retired we moved out to Nanaimo on Vancouver Island's east coast. Now just months past thirty, I am building a life back in Australia. In truth I most often feel from nowhere in particular. What would it take for me to be able to call this place mine, to be able to say that I am from here, I often wonder.

***

The distinctions between immigrant, refugee and invader strike me as exceptionally arbitrary now. But if anybody would have appreciated a 'fast track' process to return unwanted immigrants, it

---

[39] Times Colonist, July 30, A15.

would have been the residents of this coast, the First Nations people about 200 years ago. Gilbert Sproat recorded this frank account of his reception as the first white settler on the coast when he sailed up the Alberni Inlet at the back of Barkley Sound:

"In August of 1860, I entered Barkley Sound, on the outside or western, coast of Vancouver Island, with two armed vessels, Woodpecker *and* Meg Merrilies, *manned by about fifty men, who accompanied me for the purpose of taking possession of the district now called Alberni."*

"Reaching the entrance of this inlet, we sailed for twenty miles up to the end of it – as up a natural canal – three-quarters of a mile wide and very deep, bordered by rocky mountains, which rose high on both sides almost perpendicularly from the water.... Near a pretty point at one side of the bay, where there was a beach shaded by some young trees, the summer encampment of a tribe of natives was to be seen. Our arrival caused a stir, and we saw their flambeaux of gumsticks flickering among the trees during the night.

"In the morning I sent a boat for the chief and explained to him that his tribe must move their encampment, as we had bought all the surrounding land from the Queen of England, and wished to occupy the site of the village for a particular purpose. He replied that the land belonged to themselves, but that they were willing to sell it. The price not being excessive, I paid him what was asked – about twenty pounds' worth of goods – for the sake of peace, on condition that the whole people and the buildings should be removed the next day.

"[The next day] no movement was then made, and as an excuse it was stated that the children were sick. On the day following the encampment was in commotion; speeches were made, faces blackened, guns and pikes got

out, and barricades formed. Outnumbered as we were, ten to one, by men armed with muskets, and our communications with the sea cut off by the impossibility of sailing steadily down Alberni Inlet (the prevailing breeze blowing up), there was some cause for alarm had the natives been resolute. But being provided, fortunately, in both vessels with cannon – of which the natives at that time were much afraid – they, after a little show of force on our side, saw that resistance would be inexpedient, and began to move from the spot."

Here Sproat does not record the number of natives killed or injured to drive them off their land.

"Two or three days afterwards, when the village had been moved farther on to another place [Somass], not far distant, I visited the principle house at the new encampment, with a native interpreter."

'Chiefs of the Sheshahts," I said on entering, "are you well; are your women in health; are your children hearty; do your people get plenty of fish and fruits?'

'Yes,' answered an old man, 'our families are well, our people have plenty of food; but how long this will last we know not. We see your ships, and hear things that make our hearts grow faint. They say that more King George men will soon be here, and will take our land, our firewood, our fishing grounds; that we shall be placed on little spot, and shall have to do everything according to the fancies of the King George men.'

'Do you believe all this?' I asked.

'We want your information,' said the speaker.

'Then,' answered I, 'it is true that more King George men (as they call the English) are coming: they will soon be here; but your land will be bought at a fair price.'

'We do not wish to sell our land nor our water; Let your friends stay in their own country.'

"To which I rejoined: 'My great chief the high chief of the King George men, seeing that you do not work your land, orders that you shall sell it. It is of no use to you. The trees you do not need; you will fish and hunt as you do now, and collect firewood, planks for your houses, and cedar for your canoes. The white man will give you work and buy your fish and oil. [Dogfish oil was a popular Indian industry at the time]'

'Ah, but we don't care to do as the white men wish.'

'Whether or not,' said I, 'the white men will come. All your people know that they are your superiors; they make the things which you value. You cannot make muskets, blankets, or bread. The white men will teach your children to read printing, and to be like themselves.'

'We do not want the white man. He steals what we have. We wish to live as we are.'

"I spent some months very pleasingly directing the first work of the settlement. The vessels discharged their cargos and the carpenters worked on shore preparing timber for the houses and buildings.... The place the Indians had moved to was about a mile distant, and our conversation naturally was very much about them. In the evenings we sat round the fire discussing their dispositions and probable intentions, and the Indians did the same about us in their new encampment."

"We often talked about our right as strangers to take possession of the district. The right of bona fide purchase we had, for I had bought the land from the government and had purchased it a second time from the natives. Nevertheless, as the Indians disclaimed all knowledge of the colonial authorities in Victoria, and had sold the country to us, perhaps, under the fear of a loaded cannon *pointed towards the village, it was evident that we had taken forcible possession of the district. The American woodsmen, who chiefly formed my party, discussed that whole question with great clearness. Their opinion generally was that our occupation was justifiable, and could not be sternly disputed even by the most scrupulous moralist. They considered that any right in the soil which these natives had as occupiers was partial and imperfect as, with the exception of hunting animals in the forests, plucking wild fruits, and cutting a few trees to make canoes and houses, the native did not, in any civilized sense, occupy the land.*

"It would be unreasonable to suppose, the Americans said, that a body of civilized men, under the sanction of their government, could not rightfully settle in a country needing their labours, and peopled only by a fringe of savages on the coast. Unless such a right were presumed to exist, there would be little progress in the world by means of colonization – that wonderful agent, which, directed by laws of its own, had changed and is changing the whole surface of the earth.

"I could not, however, see how this last-named fact strictly could form the groundwork of a right. My own notion is that the particular circumstances which make the deliberate intrusion of a superior people into another country lawful or expedient are connected to some extent with the use of the soil, and with their general behaviour as a nation. For instance, we might justify our occupation of Vancouver Island by the fact of all the land lying waste without prospect of improvement.... The whole question of the right of any people to intrude upon another, and to dispossess them of their country, is one of those questions to which the answer practically is always the same.... The practical answer is given by the determination of intruders

*under any circumstances to keep what has been obtained;
and this, without discussion, we, on the west coast of
Vancouver Island, were all prepared to do. It can easily be
supposed we spent many anxious nights in our remote,
isolated position at Alberni.*[40]

What Sproat was clearly claiming was the right of conquest.
Despite his claims of moral right, his forcible eviction of the
Sheshahts was clearly illegal even under British law. The Royal
Proclamation of 1763, asserted the Crown's unilateral sovereignty
and protection over all the Indians to the west of the existing
American colonies. At the same time, in the spirit of the
Renaissance, it also acknowledged the Indians continued to own
the lands that they used and occupied. It began:

*"It is just and reasonable, and essential to our Interest,
and the Security of our colonies, that the several Nations
or Tribes of Indians with whom We are connected, and
who live under our Protection, should not be molested or
disturbed in the Possession of such Parts of Our Dominion
and Territories as, not having been ceded to or purchased
by Us, are reserved to them, or any of them, as their
Hunting Grounds ... If at any Time any of the Said Indians
should be inclined to dispose of the said Lands, the same
shall be Purchased only for Us, in our Name, at some
public Meeting or Assembly of the said Indians."*

About ten years after he evicted the Sheshahts from their land
in the Alberni Inlet, Sproat was actually appointed Indian Agent
for the entire province of B.C., and made responsible for laying out
reserves across the province. In his new position he was somewhat
sympathetic to the natives, and actually enlarged some of those
laid out by his predecessors. But shamefully for the next hundred

---

[40] Sproat p 3-9.

years later, the provincial government of B.C. used the argument laid out by Sproat to deny First Nations' claims to the land.

***

A look at my tide charts tells me to expect a very high tide overnight. I pitch my tent high on the beach on a platform made from pebbles. In big red letters on my chart, right across this beach I had previous written 'BEARS' – advice I gleaned from a guidebook before I left. As night falls, I slip into my tent and strip off my clothes. As I do I catch a fetid smell I can't recognize. I remember hearing how much the thick fur of a bear stinks, so much so that even humans can often smell them as they approach. I lie dead still and listen. Outside I hear some rustling not far away like stones being turned over. I suspect it is a bear following the scent of my meal into camp. I make a quick decision to burst from my tent and head straight for my pots and pans, which I can bang to make noise to drive it off. Just like in ice hockey, with black bears, a good offence can be the best defence. In the half-light I spring out of my tent stark naked and streak across the beach in the starlight toward my kitchen, expecting to be facing down the bear. But there is nothing about. And there is no smell.

Curious I stop and listen. Down along the shore small waves are lapping through some pebbles. I chuckle to myself and crawl back into my tent, embarrassed by my own 'bearanoia' once again. In the corner along with the rest of my clothes lies my favourite blue polypropylene paddling-shirt, reeking like an old dog. Obviously it's time for my first laundry day tomorrow.

29. Friendly Cove

In the morning over breakfast, I flip through my journal and make sure I've kept accurate count of the days. I still have about 60 miles to go, and about four days to make it to Tofino. Fortunately the weather is clear with just a light south-easterly making small chop on the open stretches of water. I'm looking out at clear blue skies to the south and a band of cloud to the west. Against the light wind and tide I push off for the Indian Reserve of Yuquot at Friendly Cove. The Mowachaht people operate a simple campsite on the reserve for the summer, which is popular with sports fishermen. My body is still tired from the past three hard days. It feels like I'm paddling through molasses and I'm not enthused. As I pull my paddle through the dark water I daydream about sitting down for a meal in a restaurant in Tofino. I realize that I have not had a day off paddling since the north side of the Brooks, so I resolve that a rest day is in order for tomorrow.

Along the shoreline I soon pass the old Nootka Cannery, now a small sports fishing resort with nice new cabins, a gas bar for boats, and a lodge. Nearby is Boca Del Inferno, a small tidal rapid leading into a hidden lagoon, so named by some Spaniards. It is tempting to try and run the rapids into the lagoon just for fun but today the tide is running in so fast that I know that I'll be trapped inside until it turns, so I paddle on without entering. High above, a pair of eagles calls a fledgling from a treetop. A few more fishing camps appear at Jewett's Point and one more in Mackay Passage.

When I finally reach Yuquot the prow of my kayak gouges a shallow wedge into the beach as I run up on the pebbles. In the cockpit I lay my paddle across my neoprene spray skirt. The effort of lifting myself from the seat is enough to put me off standing for the moment, so I sit for a while to look around and flex my cramped hands in relief. I am only just becoming aware of how deeply exhausted the last few days of paddling has left me. Beside me at the water's edge I can see a light rain has begun falling, leaving perfect rings on the still water and chiaroscuro dots on the pebbles of the beach.

Looking up from my reverie I can see the small cove is several hundred yards across. The beach itself is all pebbles and some sand faced roughly east. Atop a rocky headland that protects the cove to the south, a lighthouse is perched with its outbuildings. Closer to me sit two weathered old houses just a few steps above the beach. Beyond the north end is the thick tangle of the West Coast rainforest.

Seeing no one around, I lift myself from my kayak seat and step out into the shallow water on the edge of the beach. I step to the front of my boat and haul the heavy craft a few meters up onto the beach and secure it with the bowline against the rising tide.

I had expected Friendly Cove to be busier. A feeling of abandonment about the place is only enhanced by the same chilly grey sky. Behind me I hear the putt-putt of a one-cylinder diesel marine engine. A tubby white sailboat that had been shadowing me for the past three days down the passage behind Nootka Island is just motoring in. A moment later a smoky little sports fishing boat appears round the point and slows into a graceful arc as it enters the small cove.

As the sailboat weighs anchor, the runabout pulls up alongside the second wharf in the cove. The wharf itself is little more than a mottled collection of rough logs, planked just above the waterline with rough-cut timber. It stretches out into the cove like a tangle of gossamer on the dark water.

This must be someone from the Indian band, I think, since there are no other boats on the wharf. I turn and wait for the occupants to get out. As the engine cuts out I hear a few voices and then a giant blue cooler is hefted out onto the wharf. A young white girl appears with a rope in her hand and begins tying off the boat. Fishing gear follows in the grip of a teenage boy. Surmising it is other than whom I had hoped for, I walk out to greet them.

By the time I reach the small fishing party the boy has already hacked off the head off the massive spring salmon he has pulled from the cooler. Seconds later the belly is slit and pink and grey guts spill onto the silver surface of the cedar planks. By the look of his clothing it isn't the first fish he's cleaned in recent days.

"Pretty good fishing," I say to no one of in particular. From inside the boat comes the reply.

"Ah yeah, been all right today. Got more than we need really, but once they start biting who can stop eh?"

It is an older man, presumably the father of the two teenagers. Like the others he is dressed in a fishy mismatch of tracksuits.

"You kayaking, eh? Where'd you come from?" he asks as he steps up onto the crowded planks.

"North, Quatsino Sound," I reply.

"Long way to come in a kayak"

"Yeah, I could sure use a couple days rest."

"Bet you could – its pretty good camping here – just go up and see Ray in the house. He'll set you up. There is no one else here right now. Just us three fishing like mad. You should of seen it last week though – the place was packed out."

"I didn't think anyone was home. No boat on the wharf."

"No Ray's boat is broken. It's over in Gold River getting fixed, so we're taking him in tomorrow to pick it up, do some shopping. Do you need anything from town by the way?"

I decline the friendly offer, and take my leave from the three and the mess of guts and pink meat and severed heads and walk up towards the house. As it leaves the beach the ramshackle wharf turns to a rough staircase covered with asphalt shingles heading up toward a high barricade of berry bushes. Above on the plateau of the massive midden, two houses sit in a clearing. Scattered all around is a universal sort of human detritus. Old fridges stand alongside a small collection of derelict outboard engines. Long forgotten bicycles and children's toys lie scattered in the weeds.

One house, a once vivid greenish blue now sits peeling and obviously abandoned. The other, a larger two-storey house is obviously inhabited. I step up onto the porch and knock on the weather-beaten door, unsure of what or who to expect. Some rustling inside precedes the encounter. An older native man opens the door. He is dressed in a red Mackinaw jacket, dark green pants, wool socks and worn leather boots. In his hand he is holding a hunting cap, like he is just on his way out.

"Hi ya," he says

"Yes, hi. I was wondering about camping," I begin

"Oh yeah?"

"Yes, I just arrived in my kayak and the fellow down on the wharf said to talk to you about campsites."

"Yeah."

"So is there a spot here I can pitch my tent?"

"Yeah."

"Um, great, - how much is it for a night?"

He names a price and I mutter something about coming back with my wallet.

"So just up on the hill I guess?"

"That's right"

"Ok, thanks."

"Yeah"

I head up to the campsite to check it out. The clearing at the top of the hill is dominated by two features. The first is the concrete foundations of a large building long since destroyed. The second is an incongruous white church, sitting proudly on the highest point at the south end. Just behind the clearing the land drops away quickly to a second beach, this one steeper and open to the Pacific Ocean to the west. The entire village site is on a narrow isthmus, which connects with a rocky outcrop to the south topped by a lighthouse and several buildings. Such a position with a snug harbour on one side and the open ocean on the other would have been an excellent village site. Looking over I can see the vast grey emptiness of the sea stretching to the edge of the earth.

I spend an hour hauling my bags of gear up from my kayak and setting up my camp by a picnic shelter in the clearing. Nearby a big dome tent and a plastic blue tarp serve as kitchen and home for the fishing family. It's warm and windy on the hill at Friendly Cove. The earth is all black. The entire isthmus is a midden it seems, piled perhaps twenty or forty feet deep. My eyes scan the ground for trade beads, but I wouldn't be the first to search for them here.

***

Captain Cook, the great explorer of the Pacific Ocean was just a month out of Hawaii when crewman in the rigging sighted land. Now on his third and final fatal voyage of exploration in the Pacific, this time to the uncharted Northwest Coast of New Albion [North America] in search of the fabled Northwest Passage, he was almost as far from England as it was possible to go, without leaving the surface of the earth. Well provisioned after a long stay on the recently 'discovered' Sandwich Islands, he was held offshore for another twenty-two days by storms before he was able to approach land. In the rough weather he missed the wide entrance of the "pretended Strait of Juan De Fuca" that separates Vancouver Island from the mainland of North America. Thus when he finally drew close to land just north of here, he was unaware he was approaching an island, not the mainland of North America. In his log he wrote:

> *"Sunday, 29th March - At length, at nine o'clock in the morning of the 29th, as we were standing to the North East, we again saw the land, which, at noon, extended from North West by West, to East South East, the nearest part about six leagues distant. Our latitude was now 49° 29' North, and our longitude 232°29' East. The appearance of the country differed much from that of the parts which we had seen; being full of high mountains, whose summits were covered with snow. But the valleys between them, and the grounds on the seacoast, high as well as low, were covered to a considerable breath with high, straight trees, that formed a beautiful prospect, as of one vast forest. The South East extreme of the land formed a low point, off which are many breakers, occasioned by sunken rocks. On this account it was called Point Breakers..."*

While he would never win any accolades for the originality of his nomenclature, Captain Cook was already recognized throughout European society as the greatest navigator that had ever lived. On his previous two voyages he had charted and explored the southern and eastern coasts of Australia, both islands of New Zealand, and much of the South Pacific, thus becoming the first captain to sail round the world in both directions. In 1775 he was awarded the Royal Society's Copley Medal, their highest award for intellectual achievement. Cook himself was a forthright man "whose ambition leads me not only farther than any man has been before, but as far as I think it is possible for man to go". Less famously, his voyages are also remember for spreading 'venereal complaints' throughout the Pacific, leaving a plague of illness and sterility amongst the native people in their wake, including, as it would turn out, the residents of this small cove.

Born to Scottish farm labourers, in class-conscious imperial England, Cook began life unlikely to distinguish himself. At seventeen he apprenticed as a grocery clerk, before quitting to sign on as a sailor in the tricky North Sea coal trade. Studying navigation and mathematics in his spare time, he advanced quickly, and within few years he was offered his own command. Instead he resigned and enlisted in the Royal Navy as a common seaman, anxious to sail in the war against France. Again, without family connections or influential contacts, he quickly rose by ability through the ranks and within ten years was in command of his own ship, distinguishing himself once again with his careful charting of the east coast of British North America. His acquaintance there with the famous naturalist Sir Joseph Banks, who was greatly impressed by Cook's meticulous navigational and cartographic skills, paved the way for his selection as captain on the first of the Royal Society's Pacific voyages.

The Royal Society was seeking more than far off coastlines when it first proposed Cook's third voyage in 1774, the same year the Spaniard Perez sailed secretly up the Northwest Coast. The greater prize was the elusive Northwest Passage, a route across the top of North America through Hudson Strait connecting the North Atlantic with the great sea of the west, the Pacific Ocean. Along with the pride of discovery was the temping prize of 40,000 pounds offered by the British Parliament.

Cook himself actually doubted the existence of the Northwest Passage, but agreed anyway to the voyage, seeking once again the chance to explore and discover new lands. Like the previous voyages, two vessels were again chosen. The lead ship was the *Endeavour*. Short and stubby, in Cook's eyes she was "of construction of the safest kind in which the officers may, with the least hazard venture on the strange coast."[41] She measured a mere 110 feet and weighted 461 tonnes, drawing just seventeen feet of water under her keel. Her full crew included twenty-two officers, seventy-one seamen, and twenty marines. The even smaller *Discovery* had eighty-one officers and men.

Just prior to Cook's departure, the first reports of Spanish voyages up the coast had just recently been published in British periodicals. Although the Royal Navy was now the preeminent power on the seas, the government was keen to avoid sparking an international incident so far from home. Cook was given strict orders not to touch upon any Spanish dominions unless by accident, or to disturb or give cause to offence to any Russian settlements further to the north. His orders were to reach the coast of North America at about 45 degrees latitude, and continue quickly north to 65 degrees to "explore such rivers and inlets as may appear to be of a considerable extent, and pointing towards Hudson's or Baffin's Bay."[42]

At age forty-seven, Cook set to sea one last time, leaving behind once again his wife and two young sons. As on the previous two voyages, the advancement of science, botany and biology were to play a major role on the voyage. Such directions were given as

---

[41] Barry Gough, Distant Dominions, p 25
[42] Pethick, First Approaches, p 60

much with an eye for future commerce, as the advancement of knowledge. Finally, there was the issue of empire. Cook was told:

> *"To take possession, in the name of the King of Great Britain, of convenient situations in such countries as you may discover, that have not already been discovered or visited by any other European power, and distribute among the inhabitants such things as will remain as traces and testimonies of your having been there; but if you find the countries so discovered are uninhabited, you are to take possession of them for His Majesty by setting up proper markers and inscriptions as first discovers and possessors."* [43]

As Cook's ship approached the coastline, the winds died and they were forced to drop anchor somewhere on the outside of Nootka Island. The official log of the trip, written by Captain James King after Cook's death, records the first encounter between the British and with the inhabitants of the Northwest Coast:

> *"We no sooner drew near the inlet than we found the coast to be inhabited; and at the place where we were first becalmed, three canoes came off to the ship. In one of these were two men, in another six, and in the third ten. Having come pretty near us, a person in one of the two last stood up, and made a long harangue, inviting us to land, as we guessed, by his gestures. At the same time, he kept strewing handfuls of feathers towards us; and some of his companions threw handfuls of red dust or powder in the same manner. The person who played the orator wore the skin of some animal, and held, in each hand, something which rattled as he kept shaking it. After tiring himself with his repeated exhortations, of which we did not*

---

[43] From First Approaches, P62

understand a word, he was quiet; and then others took it, by turns, to say something, though they acted their part neither so long, nor with so much vehemence as the other."

Eventually a breeze pushed the ships in closer to shore and more canoes came out, until they were surrounded by thirty-two canoes, whose occupants showed little surprise at the new visitors:

"Though our visitors [a surprising choice of words considering Cook was the one who had just sailed half way round the world] behaved very peaceably, and could not be suspected of any hostile intention, we could not prevail upon any of them to come on board. They shewed [sic] great readiness, however to part with anything they had, and took from us whatever we offered them in exchange; but were more desirous of iron, than of any other of our article of commerce; appearing perfectly acquainted with the use of that metal. Many of the canoes followed us to our anchoring place and a group of ten or a dozen remained alongside the Resolution *most part of the night."*

The next day the ships boats were put over the sides to search for a harbour up the inlets, but it was another night before they could tow the vessels south to a deep and sheltered anchorage. For the next twenty-six days, the *Resolution* and *Discovery* lay at anchor in newly named King George Sound (later named Nootka Sound) undergoing extensive repairs. Masts were replaced and the hull was caulked to prepare it for the voyage north. During that time they had plenty of contact with the villagers from Yuquot and their allies:

"A considerable number of the Natives visited us daily and we every now and then saw new faces. On there first coming they generally went through a singular ceremony; they would paddle with all their strength quite round both Ships, A chief or other principal person standing up with a Spear or some other Weapon in his hand and speaking or rather hollaoing all the time, sometimes this person would have his face covered with a mask. Either that of the human face or some animal, and sometimes instead of a weapon would hold in his hand a rattle. After making the Circuit of the ships they would come along side and begin to trade without further ceremony. Very often indeed they would first give a song in which all joined with a very agreeable harmony."[44]

While Cook's officers obviously recorded the events in terms that would cast themselves in the most favourable light back home, compared to many of their other encounters with the inhabitants of the Pacific, it would seem that relations did begin in a peaceful manner. More than two hundred years later, the Nuu-chah-nulth people still remember the arrival of Captain Cook in their oral histories. The following oral account from Mrs. Winifred David shows how they understood the visitors in their own terms:

"My husband wasn't all Clayoquot. One of his grandparents, his mother, was part Nootka and that's how she knew this story about when Captain Cook first landed in Nootka Sound. The Indians didn't know what on earth it was when his ship came into the harbour. They didn't know what on earth it was. So the chief, Chief Maquinna, he sent out his warriors. He had warriors you know. He sent them out in a couple of canoes to see what it was. So they went out to the ship and they thought it was a fish

---

[44] Captain Cook, the Journals of, p 541, Penguin Classics

come alive into people. They were taking a good look at those white people on the deck there. One white man had a real hooked nose, you know. And one of the men was saying to this other guy, 'See, see...he must have been a dog salmon, that guy, there, he's got a hooked nose.' The other guy was looking up at him and a man came out of the galley and he was a hunchback, and the other said, 'Yes! We're right, we're right. Those people must have been fish. They've come alive into people. Look at that one, he's a humpback. He's a humpback!' They call it ca pi, they're humpback fish.

"So they went ashore and they told the big chief: 'You know what we saw? They've got white skin. But we're pretty sure that those people on the floating thing there, that they must have been fish. But they've come here as people.' And they couldn't understand each other, you know. They didn't know what those white men were saying and they were talking Indian, too.

"So, the Chief told them to go out there again and see, you know, try to understand what those people wanted and what they were after. And they went out again and Captain Cook, he must have told his crew to give those Indians some biscuits, pilot biscuits, thick white pilot biscuits. So they gave them pilot biscuits and they started saying among themselves that they're friendly. Those people up there are friendly. We should be nice to them. And they started talking Indian and they told them to go around the Sound, you know. They started making signs and they were talking Indian an they were saying: 'Nu-tka-icim, nu-tka-icim' they were saying. That means, 'You go around the harbour.'

"So Captain Cook said, 'Oh, they're telling us the name of this place is Nootka.' That's how Nootka got its name. Because those Indians were saying 'Nu-tka-icim,

nu-tka-icim,' they were saying. They were telling them to go around the harbour. So ever since that it's been called Nootka. But the Indian name is altogether different Yeah, It's Yuquot that Indian Village. So it's called Nootka now and the whole of the West Coast [Vancouver Island], we're all Nootka Indians now."[45]

By Cook's journals, while the *Discovery* and *Resolution* lay at anchor at what Cook felt was a safe distance across the inlet from the village, a lively trade soon sprang up. The natives arrived the next day with several canoes full of fur and skins of every kind, including the thick sea otter pelts, and the real trade began. The skins were popular amongst the crew who knew they would be heading north to colder climates on the route home. Also offered were cedar bark garments, weapons, fish hooks, masks, and carved work, bags of ochre, beads, little ornaments of brass and iron shaped like horse-shoes and worn through the nose, and even chisel blades fixed to hands of wood (these were held at dear prices by the natives). In exchange the only items that the English brought specially for trade were glass beads, which were deemed worthless trifles by the hardheaded natives. What the Mowachaht wanted most was *Seekemaile* – iron or any good metal:

"Nothing would go down with our visitors but metal; and brass had, by this time, supplanted iron; being so eagerly sought after, that before we left this place, hardly a bit of it was left in the ships, except what belonged to our necessary instruments. Whole suits of clothes were stripped of every button; bureaus of their furniture and copper kettles, tin canisters, candlesticks, and the like, all went to wreck; so that our American friends here got a greater medley and variety of things from us, than any

---

[45] Captain Cook and the Spanish Explorers on the Coast, Nu-tka, p 54, Edited by Barbara S. Efrat and W. J. Langlois.

other nation whom we had visited in the course of the voyage."

At first Cook was impressed by the strictly honest terms under which trade was conducted. But the next day when some of the natives came on deck to trade his opinion quickly changed:

"We soon discovered, by this nearer intercourse, that they were as light-fingered as any of our friends in the islands we had visited in the course of the voyage. And they were far more dangerous thieves; for, possessing sharp instruments, they could cut a hook from a tackle, or any other piece of iron from a rope, the instant that our backs were turned. A large hook, weighing between twenty and thirty pounds, [used to retrieve the anchor] and other articles of iron, were lost in this manner. And, as to our boats, they stripped them of every bit of iron that was worth carrying away, though we had men left in them as a guard. They were dexterous enough in effecting their purposes; for one fellow would contrive to amuse the boat-keeper, at one end of the boat, while another was pulling out the ironwork at the other. If we missed a thing immediately after it had been stolen, we found little difficulty in detecting the thief, as they were ready enough to impeach one another. But the guilty person generally relinquished his prize with reluctance; and sometimes we found it necessary to have recourse to force."

Considering that by the time the two ships departed barely a scrap of metal remained on board, while the quarters of both officers and crew were filled to capacity with 1500 furs, rather disingenuously, it is strange that Cook never suspected that his own crew might have been the cause of some of the theft for their own gain. One particular set of items offered for trade did trouble

Cook and his men though, inviting a great deal of speculation, that would endure amongst non-natives for years to come. On a previous voyage some Maoris in New Zealand had eaten eleven of Cook's crew, so it was no surprise that when the natives offered human skulls and roasted hands they caused considerable concern onboard the small ships.

The ensuring cross-cultural exchange is a perfect example of the Cannibal Complex described by William Arens. Each side suspected the other of practicing cannibalism. Today it is hard to determine how much was truthful and how much was based on misunderstanding and miscommunication. When the Mowachaht offered body parts for trade, the crew actually bought three hands and one skull.

When Cook's official journals were published in London in 1784 to great excitement, they contained the following opinion: "But the most extraordinary of all the articles which they brought to the ships for sale, were human skulls, and the hands not yet stripped of the flesh, which they made our people plainly understand they had eaten; and indeed, some of them had evident marks that they had been upon the fire. We had but too much reason to suspect, from this circumstance that the horrid practice of feeding on their enemies is as prevalent here, as we had found it to be at New Zealand and other South Seas Islands."

An American wayfarer, a Connecticut Yankee named John Ledyard who was serving as a marine on one of Cook's ships recorded the encounter. It's worth noting that Leynard wrote his journals from memory six years after the voyage, with perhaps with more interest in book sales than historical truth, and published them just before Cook's official journals. There was of course money to be made in a good story:

> *"Like all uncivilized men, they are hospitable. The first boat that visited us in [Ship's] Cove brought us what no doubt they thought the greatest possible regalia, and*

offered it to us to eat; a human arm roasted. I have heard it remarked that human flesh is the most delicious. Therefore I tasted a bit. So did many others without swallowing the meat or the juices. But either my conscience or my taste rendered it very odious to me. We intimated to our host that what we had tasted was bad, and expressed as well as we could our disapprobation of eating it on account of its being part of man like ourselves. They seemed to be sensible by the contortions of our faces that our feelings were disgusted, and apparently paddled off with equal dissatisfaction and disappointment themselves. "[46]

Undoubtedly, after that gustatory demonstration by Cook's crew, the natives paddled off thinking that the sailors ate human meat, but that the hands they had offered were not fresh enough. There was no evidence that the natives actually ate flesh. What is possible is that they collected the body parts as trophies of war. A few days latter they returned with a small child, which many of the crew suspected was offered as food. The officers on the ship, including Lieutenant James King, were more circumspect and reserved judgement on whether or not the natives were cannibals, or just offering the child for sale as a slave:

> *"The man who brought the boy made motions of knocking the child on the head, which being observed by some of our gentlemen, they conceiv'd the fellow brought the boy to sell for food, & made motion to the man if they should eat the boy, which he nodded his assent to; but I was present & it is certain he only want'd a hatchet,*

---

[46] Jim MacDowell, Hamatsa, p 40, from James K. Munford, John Ledyard's Journal of Captain Cook's Last Voyage, 1963, p. 73, annotated from John Ledyard's Journal, 1783.

therefore it would be cruel to bring this as any proof of so horrid a charge as that of devouring their own species."[47]

That seemed to settle the matter back in England. For the next two centuries, this opinion was taken as proof of cannibalism by many, and those that followed Cook often found all the proof they needed. After he was killed in Hawaii, (some speculate as the result of his decreasing diplomacy and tolerance of natives on his third voyage) the publication of his journals fell to his official ghostwriters, Captain James King and Bishop Douglas. They combined Cook's journals with extracts from Kings own. King had begun the voyage as a lieutenant, but the death of Cook and then Clerke left him in charge at the journey's end. As it turns out, Cook's actual handwritten logs recorded an entirely different opinion that his supposed suspicions. Years later researchers discovered Captain Cook merely recorded that "even human skulls and hands" were offered for trade without speculating about the practice of cannibalism.

While the English were frank about the moral transgression they saw in the savages, they were a little less forthcoming about their own nefarious dealings. The ship's surgeon recorded a third sort of trade that was entirely omitted in the official publications:

"[We] had seen none of their young women tho' we had often given the men to understand how agreeable their company would be to us and how profitable to themselves, in consequence of which they about this time brought two or three girls to the ship.... Their fathers made the bargain and received their price of prostitution of the daughters which was commonly a Pewter plate well scoured for one night. When they found this was a profitable trade they brought more young women to the ships. [Thus] they found means at last to disburden our young gentry of their

---

[47] Beaglehole, 1967, 3:2:1414 (in Hamatsa, p42)

kitchen furniture, many of us leaving this arbour not being able to muster a plate to eat our salt beef from." [48]

But it was doubtful this account was with errors also. Later another officer wrote: "It was the prevailing opinion that the women brought on this occasion were not of their own tribe but belonged to some other they had overcome in battle." (This was undoubtedly true. A hundred years later Father Brabant would note that single women considered even touching a man's hand to be the height of immodesty, even during a marriage ceremony.) For their part the unfortunate women got the first new cases of syphilis and gonorrhoea on the West Coast. Although syphilis was actually a disease that first spread from native Americans to Europeans, it was not previously present on the West Coast. The native people did have some immunity too it though, due to a local disease later known as yaws, but it is suspected the arrival of syphilis still caused widespread sterility and hastened the coming population decline.

With the ships repaired, Cook took the next few days to explore the sound, and visited his new friends at Yuquot. He soon found that everything lay under some claim of ownership. Even the right to trade with the British was closely controlled by the locals. When a neighbouring tribe arrived to do business, Cook wrote:

> *"We found that several of our old friends were among them, who took upon them the entire management of the trade between us and them, very much to the advantage of the others. Having a few goats and two or three sheep left I went in a boat accompanied by Captain Clerke [of the Discovery] in another, to the Village at the west point of the Sound to get some grass for them, having seen some at that place."*

---

[48] Samwell, 1967 p 1095 (from Beaglehole)

"The Inhabitants of the village received us in the same friendly manner they had done before, and the Moment we landed I sent some to cut grass not thinking that the Natives would have the least objection, but it proved other ways for the Moment our people began to cut they stopped them and told them they must Makook [trade] for it, that is, first buy it. As soon as I heard of this I went to the place and found about a dozen men who all laid claim to some part of the grass which I purchased of them, as I thought I was at liberty to cut where ever I pleased, but here again I was mistaken, for the liberal manner I had paid the first pretended proprietor brought more upon me and there was not a blade of grass that had not a separate owner, so that I very soon emptied my pockets with purchasing, and when they found I had nothing more to give they let us cut where ever we pleased.

"Here I must observe that I have nowhere met with Indians who had such high notions of everything the country produced being their exclusive property as these; the very wood and water we took on board they at first wanted us to pay for... and frequently afterwards told us they had given us Wood and Water out of friendship."

Despite the differences, after the month-long stay, relations between the residents and visitors were still extremely cordial, such that the send-off was nearly touching. On the deck of the *Resolution* Cook participated in the first trans-Pacific potlatching of gifts:

"Our Friend the Indians attended upon us till we were almost out of the Sound, some on board the Ships and other in Canoes. [A] chief named [name missing – but possibly Maquinna] who had some time before attached himself to me was one of the last who left us, before he

299

went I made him a small present and in return he presented me with a Beaver skin of greater value [probably 'sea beaver', actually meaning sea otter], this occasioned me to make some additional to my present, on which he gave me the beaver skin cloak he had on, that I knew he set a value upon. And I was desirous he should be no suffer[er] by his friendship and generosity to me, I made him a present of a New Broad Sword with a brass hilt which made him as happy as a prince. He as also many others importuned us much to return to them again and by way of encouragement promised to lay in a good stock of skins for us, and I have not the least doubt they will."

To his lasting credit Cook recognized the inherent ownership of the land by the people who occupied it and never made a claim on it. That would be the task of those who would follow.

30. Chief Maquinna

A glance at the sky tells me a storm could be coming so I wander over to the fisher-folks tent to see if they have a marine radio. After lunch I study the route ahead. I realize that there is an eight-mile stretch of open coast missing between my chart of Nootka Sound and my next chart of Clayoquot Sound. Between Escalante and Estevan points lies a nasty stretch of reefs for which I have no guide. Worst of all I have no information on the headland that separates Nootka and Clayoquot. That's a bit of a worry. So I decide to stop by the camp of the fishers.

"Do you have any charts of the coastline down to Tofino?" I ask. Under the tarp the father is frying up chicken, "for a change," for diner in a pan that looked liked it arrived on Cook's voyage. As he replies he presents me with a warm beer from the general mess on their plank table. "Ah no. We just came out from Gold River. Never been down the coast that far actually. Maybe ask Jim up at the lighthouse. He's been the keeper their for twenty-three years. He's gotta have something."

I nod approval over my beer.

"Hey, do you want to stay for lunch? I'm not much of a housekeeper but you're welcome to some?"

Politely, I decline the invitation to dine, citing the imperative of finding a chart, and set off for the lighthouse. The weather radio on the kitchen table has just forecast that another low-pressure system will approach the coast sometime in the next few days. This means I won't get my badly needed rest day tomorrow before heading down the coast. I need to beat the storm or risk waiting here for several days to get round the next headland at Escalante and Perez Rocks. I'm running out of time to reach Tofino. It is less than a week before my flight home to Australia.

The steps up to the lighthouse are long and meticulously well maintained. Everywhere the paint is fresh and cut in precise lines of red or white or grey, making it seem like a three-dimensional chess set. Up by the lighthouse, I run into Jack, A big man with a potbelly who is one of the two lighthouse keepers. We fall into chatting about life on the rocky lookout. He has just taken the job 11 months ago. Satellite TV, he tells me, is very important. Other than work, he tries to garden and fish a bit to get some fresh food.

Eventually Ed appears, waking up late in the day for the nightshift. He's an old hippy whose been stationed at Nootka for twenty-three years. I ask him about charts of the area and he goes back into his house and rummages around and finds an old 1:75 000 scale chart that gives me a rough picture of the section missing from my own. But the scale is too large to be of real help. All I can glean from them is that there are two beaches I can may be able to land on before going around Escalante Point, but there is not enough detail to reveal how it easy might be. Just before Escalante Point is Perez Rocks. Ed tells me he's never been round, but during storms the waves that smash against them rise up like mountains that can be seen miles off.

Four sailors from the two sailboats now anchored in the cove also have arrived at the lighthouse seeking advice, so we study the charts and listen to the next day's weather forecast on the radio. There is a big low pressure crossing far to the north tomorrow and the north end of the island is forecast to get some severe winds. I'm sitting just south of that zone, but I'm pretty wary of the forecast all the same. Just to build my confidence Ed tells me about a group of kayakers and canoeists from a nearby wilderness leadership program that got washed ashore by a storm along this section of coast a few years back. A little concerned but still keen I try my best to memorize the features of the coastline and then take my leave.

Having nothing else to do, and happy to have chance to walk around and use my legs instead of my arms for a while, I wander up to the church, which sits on the high ground overlooking the water on both sides of the isthmus. From the outside it's like many others. Inside the front entrance are three beautiful stained glass windows, depicting the arrival of the Spanish and their missionaries on the coast. The windows were gifts from the Spanish government, but the pictures display that classic Euro-centrism with the noble savage receiving the blessing of the new white explorers. As I enter the main chapel I startle some young boys playing and they disappear out a door where the priest once might have entered.

The church was built in 1957 with the Spanish government paying for half, to mark their exploration of the coast. Since the 1970's though, the natives have controlled the church themselves and the last vestiges of the Papal legacy have been stripped from the inside. In 1990 the band removed the Catholic cross and pulpit and rearranged the pews into two rows facing each other. Today the front and back walls are bedecked with the traditional carvings of the Maquinna lineage, the ruling family of the band.

The Spanish also built the first rough church at Yuquot during their occupation of the village in 1789. A hundred years later, in the summer of 1889 Father Brabant built the second Catholic Church. At the time he learned something of the first:

> *"My first informant was an elderly man, one of those men of importance to be found in every tribe, whose chief pride seems to consist in watching all the important events of the day and assisting the chiefs with the counsel and judgement. I found my informant, Kragsota, on an early summer morning sitting in close conversation with his wife. As I passed by he hailed me and our conversation commenced.*
>
> *'Was there ever a priest at Nootka?'*
>
> *'Oh yes,' he said, 'at the time of the Spaniards, there were two priests, big stout men, and they both were bald-headed. My granduncle, who told me this, used to come around to Friendly Cove, and the white men would keep Sunday. There was the Sunday-house' – pointing to a spot about the centre of the present village – 'and they would go on their knees and cross themselves. At the turn of the winter solstice they had a great Sunday and they had two babies – is not that what you now call Christmas? Oh yes, there were priests here, and all the men and women would have bath on Saturday and be ready for Sunday. They learned songs – hymns – I know them yet.'*
>
> *And the old man began to sing, but the only words I could catch were: Mi-Dios [My God].* [49]

---

[49] Mission to Nootka, p10-11

The early Spanish missionaries never made a serious effort at Yuquot. They were Franciscan monks accustomed to the easier life on a profitable California missions where legions of native Americans laboured as virtual serfs in the agricultural enterprises of the order. Here at Yuquot there was no potential for such enterprises and the monks left with the rest of the Spanish, but not empty handed.

The Spanish believed rumours spread by Maquinna's rivals and enemies that the great chief sacrificed the children in secret rituals every full moon. Maquinna himself vehemently denied the allegation on several occasions, but it remained a convenient justification for fathers to buy slave children. The native villagers were only too happy to engage in the profitable trade. On one occasion, Father don Nicolas de Livera bought or 'saved' 22 slave children, believing that if they could be raised as Christians on the southern missions, one day they might return to their tribes as messengers of the true faith. There is of course no record of what happened to the youngsters. None are ever known too have returned. Most likely they lived out a wretched existence as forced labourers on the missions in Mexico or California.

While the Spanish were the dominant European force in the Americas for the first 250 years after Columbus arrived, they had little interest in advancing their empire on the distant West Coast. By 1771, only the Antarctic and the Northwest Coast of North America remained unexplored coastlines. The North Pacific was largely ignored until King Carlos III ascended to the throne. At the time the 'enlightenment' was transforming much of the rest of Europe with it scientific principals and Carlos wanted to include Spain by sponsoring scientific expeditions like the French and the English. At the same time reports of Russian fur traders moving down from the Bering Sea goaded Spain into action. So in the late 1760's the first navel base on the west coast of New Spain at San Blas was set up. Shipyards were soon busy building a fleet for the

Pacific coast. Then in 1774 Captain Juan Perez set sail on the most ambitious expedition yet to survey the Northwest Coast.

Perez's mission was largely reconnaissance. He was under strict orders from the Viceroy in New Spain to avoid detection by any other European, particularly Russians he might encounter. But if he found the land to be unoccupied he was to go ashore and take possession by the appropriate means:

> *"All places where possession is taken will be marked with a large wooden cross, making its pedestal from rocks and concealing in it a bottle or glass flask in which he will place a copy of the testimony of possession signed by him, the Chaplain and the two pilots. And in order that in the days to come this document may better be preserved and may serve as authentic testimony, the bottle will be sealed with pitch."*[50]

While their empire was now the largest the world had ever known, they had yet to ever land on Vancouver Island to which they already laid claim. Unlike the British, the Spanish recognized no native rights to landownership, primarily on the rational that they were not Christians. In fact the Spanish felt it was their obligation to save savages from their godless ways:

> *"The kindness of the King, who entrusted this government of New Spain to my charge, not only imposes on me the obligation of reserving these vast territories to him but also of endeavouring to enlarge them, as much as I am able, through new discoveries in unknown areas, so that their numerous Indian inhabitants, attracted to the kind, mellow and desired vassalage of His Majesty, may receive by means of the spiritual conquest the light of the gospel which will free them from the darkness of idolatry*

---

[50] From Pethick, *First Approaches*, p 38.

*in which they live, and will show them the road to eternal
salvation. These are the true motives that move the pious
royal heart of His Majesty in these undertakings. "*

As many captains would soon learn, sailing up the Northwest
Coast against the prevailing winds was a difficult undertaking.
Perez had difficulty making progress or approaching land, and
never managed to land anywhere to take possession. Like all
Spanish ships, scurvy and other diseases brought on by
malnutrition plagued his short voyage and he returned to port after
only a few short months with little information. A second
expedition in the same year did land on the coast much farther
north at 57 degrees in present day Alaska. A third expedition in
1779, the year after Cook was on the coast, reached the southern
extent of the Russian explorations at 59 degrees. Along the way
the Spanish established bases at Monterrey and San Francisco.
After claiming the entire coast and satisfied that no other nation
threatened their claim, in 1780 Spanish interest on the Northwest
Coast once again stopped.

Then in 1787 another expedition was sent north to check up on
the Russian advances in the last decade. On a lonely island near
Prince William Sound, they encountered a permanent colony of
Russian traders, one of six on the northern coast, some of whom
had been living there for several years. According to the local
commandant, men and supplies to occupy Nootka Sound were
already en route. But it wasn't the Spanish the Russians saw as
rivals; it was the English traders that were already active at Nootka
who concerned them.

Back at their homeport, Martinez, the Spanish captain, soon
received orders from the Viceroy in Mexico City to lead an
expedition to take possession of Nootka Sound (which the Spanish
called the Port of San Lorenzo). To complicate things further, two
American ships were known to be trading in the area. Sensing the
delicacy of the situation, the Viceroy wrote:

"If Russian or English vessels should arrive, you will receive their commanders with the politeness and the kind treatment which the existing peace demands; but you will show the just ground for our establishment at Nootka, the superior right which we have for continuing such establishments on the whole coast, and the measures which our superior government is taking to carry this out, such as sending by land expeditions of troops, colonist, and missionaries, to attract and convert the Indians to the religion and mild domination of our august sovereign. All this you ought to explain with prudent firmness, but without being led into harsh expressions which may give serious offence and cause a rupture, but if, in spite of the great effort, the foreigners should attempt to use force, you will repel it to the extent that they employ it, endeavouring to prevent as far as possible their intercourse and commerce with the natives."[51]

The British never saw it quite that way. The Papal Bull of 1493 that had divided the new world between the Catholic empires of Spain and Portugal meant little in the Protestant eyes. Martinez's crosses and buried bottles up in Alaska meant even less. In British terms, the strongest claims to 'empty' land were made by those who occupied and used it. While Cook had never claimed any section of the coast for Great Britain, the Spanish claim was also never recognized, and by 1789 English fur traders operating out of Canton where happy to take advantage of the situation. Thus in 1789, the four empires of Great Britain, Spain, Russian and the United States were all sailing for the Nootka Sound with the intention of staking a claim.

---

[51] Pethick, First Approaches, p 139.

Meanwhile at Nootka Sound, the leader of a fifth nation was making plans of his own. Chief Maquinna was the head of the Mowachah Confederacy made up of three groups from the outer coast and shores of Nootka Sound. Each clan had houses further up the inlets at Tahsis where they moved in the early fall to gather salmon, and at Yuquot, (meaning 'where winds blow', but known as Friendly Cove by the traders) where they spent the summers whaling and fishing for halibut far offshore. Maquinna was chief of the paramount group, which originally came from E'as on the outer coast. His was one of the tribes that claimed to actually have first received the rituals for hunting whales.

According to native traditions, the chief in the canoe that first paddled out to greet Captain Cook was Maquinna, also known as Chief Tsaxawasip. It was he that gave the first speech, offered his cedar hat, woven in the shape of a buck's head, for trade (for an axe) and invited the English ship to enter his sound. It was Maquinna who had prevented a rival group of Mulachaht from trading directly with the crew and claimed the British as his own property.

Eight years later when Captain Strange, the first fur trader arrived, it was once again a Chief Maquinna with whom negotiations began. (One historian has suggested Maquinna's son may have already succeeded him and taken his name by this point.) Many of Strange's crew were sick from scurvy by the time they reached the coast. For an adze and a saw Maquinna sold them a house at the north end of the village to use as an infirmary. One officer, Alexander Walker, spent time with Maquinna. He described him dirty and slovenly in appearance, but "a stout handsome young man, with a fine manly countenance, and being fond of our company, soon became our favourite." He was honest and shrewd and "the most intelligent person we met with."[52] Numerous drawings of the famous chief are recorded in the journals of early traders and explorers, which exist to this day.

---

[52] Gough, Distant Dominions, p 60, (from journal of Walker, July 14-19)

Above all, Maquinna was keenly aware of the strategic importance of the fur trade. Thus it was no surprise when John Meares arrived three years latter with a shipload of Chinese carpenters and blacksmiths that Maquinna welcomed him ashore as 'wacush, wasuch' or friends. Onboard Meares' ship, the *Captain Cook*, was Maquinna's younger brother Comekela, who had secretively but voluntarily sailed for Canton and Hawaii with Captain James Hanna two years before. At sea, he learned to become a competent seaman, and only one of several North Americans and Pacific Islanders onboard making a return journey home. As the two ships approached Nootka Sound, Comekela became excited about seeing his home. So wrote Meares: "Comekela, who for several days had been in a state of most anxious impatience, now enjoyed that inexpressible delight of once more beholding his native land,"

After an exchange of presents Meares asked Maquinna permission to build a house and factory in a small cove along the shore. Shortly after a two-storey dwelling with a defensive stockade was completed. At summer's end, the *North West America*, the first ship built on the West Coast was completed. In his own journals Meares later claimed that Maquinna not only sold him the land, but also accepted the English "as his lords and sovereigns." Four years later Maquinna would vehemently deny this, calling him *Aita-Aita* Meares, or 'Liar Meares'. In the meantime though, the two formed a productive alliance. Maquinna used his extensive trading network that reached across the Nimpkish Valley to the eastern side of the island, to bring large numbers of furs, which Meares happily bought. Meares supplied Maquinna with exclusive access to the trade goods that helped him further secure his growing hegemony.

At the end of the productive summer just as Meares was to depart, two American ships arrived at Nootka Sound, planning to spend the winter undertaking repairs. With some misgivings of the presence of rivals, but certain they would get few furs over the long winter, Meares sailed for Hawaii. As soon as he was out of the harbour, Maquinna brought out a new stock of furs to begin trading with 'Booton men'. In this way, Maquinna, along with his allies, Wickaninnish and Tatoosh were able to drive up the price of furs. Every season that the traders returned they found prices had nearly doubled and there was nothing they could do. Meanwhile back in Canton, an oversupply of furs had flooded the market and prices had fallen through the floor.

The next summer Meares's partner Colnet arrived on the *Argonaut* with 29 more Chinese craftsmen to start a commercial 'factory' at Friendly Cove. It was to be named Fort Pitt in order to curry favour with the Prime Minister William Pitt in London. It was also to be the start of a commercial trading empire they intended one day to stretch up and down the coast. But as Colnet entered the Friendly Cove, the unexpected presence of Spanish ships must have told him there was trouble ahead for the company's ambitious plans.

The show down between the Spanish and the British at Nootka Sound quickly became more than just a matter of furs and iron. The previous year the British had established a penal colony at Port Jackson, Australia, (later to become Sydney) and the Spanish rightfully suspected their claims on all of the Pacific Ocean and its shorelines were not being respected. For the British, the issue was not land, for they had no interest in claiming territory on the Northwest Coast, at least not yet. Their interest was commercial trade. As the main trading centre on the coast was Nootka Sound, Maquinna's doorstep suddenly became an area of prime international diplomacy and military brinkmanship.

When the Spanish Captain Martinez first arrived at Nootka Sound in the spring of 1789, he cautiously began to assert his authority. The two American ships were treated diplomatically, but when Colnet arrived, Martinez moved to arrest him Chief Callicum, Maquinna's ally, moved to protect his trading partner. Coming alongside the Spanish ship, he began what Martinez took as an insulting speech. Martinez raised a gun and fired, perhaps intending to kill him, or more likely to intimidate him. In any case, the gun misfired, and another sailor on the Spanish boat took aim and shot Callicum dead.

With his close ally dead, Maquinna feared the worst. Realizing that if his English allies were so easily arrested by the Spanish, he stood little chance himself, Maquinna and the rest of the village fled south first to Wickanninsh's village, and then latter to their traditional village site on the outside of the Nootka Sound called E'as. Martinez quickly moved ashore and began the construction of two forts to protect the entrance to the sound. Over the summer the arrest of several more captains, including one American boat, followed. But then at the end of the summer, as Martinez was preparing for his first winter in Fort Miguel, orders arrived from the Spanish viceroy in Mexico city to abandon the outpost. Martinez sailed south that winter crestfallen at having to abandon his efforts.

At the same time Meares, outraged at the destruction of his factory, the seizing of his Chinese workers (who disappeared south with Martinez, probably to become involuntary mission labourers) sailed for England. In London he was well connected. Immediately he began a vocal campaign to get Parliament to move against the Spanish. The popular press got hold of the story and soon a bill was passed in Parliament to boost the English navy. Meares claimed 600,000 pounds in damages from the Spanish. Eventually after much sabre rattling, a treaty was signed and two captains, George Vancouver and Quadra were dispatched by the countries to sail to Nootka and settle the necessary details.

Vancouver's voyage turned out to be more than just a diplomatic under taking. Arriving in Nootka Sound in 1792, he eventually became the first European to chart and circumnavigate Vancouver Island. His voyage of discovery, which carried many of the young sons of England's ruling class on her upper decks as junior officers including the irascible and insubordinate 'Pitt the

Younger,' the son of the prime minister, lasted four years, making it the longest human voyage of exploration to this day. It is a record that is likely to stand until the first human voyage to Mars. But at the end of it, Vancouver returned without a treaty, unable to come to agreeable terms with his Spanish counterpart.

Eventually in 1796 in Europe the Nootka Convention was finally signed. For the most part the Spanish caved into all the English demands, preferring peace in Europe to control of a distant coastline. Nootka Sound was declared a free port, irrespective of Indian claims, and the whole of the Pacific Ocean was opened to free commercial exploitation. The Spanish, with their empire crumbling all around them, would never again return to the Northwest Coast. The spoils remained to be divided between the British, Russians and the newcomers, the Americans.

Meanwhile at Nootka Sound, Maquinna and the rest of the Mowachaht had returned to rebuild their village at Yuquot. Despite the falling prices, traders were arriving with increasing frequently on the coast, and the furs were already becoming scarce. Armed with cannons and muskets, many of the captains took to using force rather than honest trading to get their furs. Trust between the Indians and the whites soon began to disappear. By the opening of the 1800s, the trading was no longer a route to easy fortunes. It was now a more desperate game.

Then in 1802, Maquinna made a move to assert his dominance once again. Maquinna had been enduring the indignities of the traders for several years now. On one particularly humiliating occasion Captain Strange had planted gunpowder under a chair he had invited him to sit on, badly burning his backside. Furthermore Martinez had shot Callicum for a trifle. When an American trader sold him a faulty musket and refused to replace it, Maquinna decided to make his move.

The offending trader was onboard the *Boston*, an American ship anchored near Friendly Cove. Maquinna directed his men to hide their knives beneath their clothes as they approached to trade.

Once onboard the slaughter began, and in a short time, all but two of the crew laid dead. Only Jewitt the blacksmith, and John Thompson the sail maker remained alive. Rather than kill the two men, Maquinna took them back to Yuquot to make use of their skills. Given no choice, the two Yankee sailors lived amongst the clans, learning all their ways, and became valued slaves. Jewitt in particular managed to attach himself to Maquinna, and soon began accompanying the chief on his trips around the sound.

The Americans waited patiently to be rescued but unfortunately for them the area was known to be bereft of furs and dangerous to trading ships. The prominence of Friendly Cove had passed and now few ships every passed that way. Finally two years after they were captured, Jewitt managed to get a rival chief to pass a message to the captain of a ship that had anchored in the sound. The captain, who had Maquinna on deck at the time, held him hostage until Jewitt was released, and soon after the two former slaves sailed to Canton and then on to Boston. Jewitt's journals, written in berry juice during his capture were later published. For a while he made a living in New England speaking to audiences of his experiences as a white slave amongst the savages of the West Coast.

For Maquinna, the results were more unfortunate. Once word got out that Friendly Cove was no longer so hospitable, for the next seventy-five years, few ships visited his quiet coast. Isolated and cut off from the valuable trading, the chief who had once commanded authority over much of the coast, soon lost his hold on power. Furthermore the dependence on white trade goods had caused them to neglect the traditions of the whale hunt, a once valuable source of food. In the two and half years that Jewitt lived at Yuquot, Maquinna struck and lost nine whales while only killing five. Never again would he claim the same authority on the coast

Back at Ray's place I catch him with a bit more time on his hands. It's a roughly built house, still with plywood on the floor, old couches and a woodstove for heat. There is a good smell of dinner coming from the kitchen. I pay him for the campsite for the night and we push the cats off the busted patio chairs. The place has a strong sense of historical indifference, more functional than neglected. It's a straightforward attitude where life is about place and belonging to it, not career or possessions. I can only envy him. We talk about the coast and the return of the sea otters and decline of the salmon. He reckons that the herring will return in about ten years with proper management. As he talks, I realize how he is this place, just the same as the wind, rain and waves. There is no separation in their being.

31. The Whaler's Shrine

I take my leave of Ray to have a walk down the only road on the reserve. It leads past an old graveyard, now overgrown but with plenty of new headstones. Further along it passes the shore of a small lake. The sun has come out and after two weeks of salt water I'm excited about bathing in a freshwater lake. I strip down on the gravel shore and wade out and plunge in enthusiastically, hitting the muddy bottom and stirring up a cloud of silt and darkness.

I want to swim out to the deeper parts of the lake but I feel extremely ill at ease bathing here, despite the obvious signs of frequent use by others. So instead, after a quick dip, I sit down on the gravel to dry off in a small patch of sunlight and look out at the island in the middle of the lake. It's a forlorn looking place with stunted trees and an unwelcoming feeling, much like the otherworldly forest I had seen on the Brooks Peninsula, but more solitary. The sun creeps through the treetops to the west in long slivers that lie like knife blades across the water in the late afternoon. Despite my moves as it shifts, I can't get warm. After a while I feel a deep chill setting into my bones.

Years ago, George Hunt had come to this place to remove one of the most powerful ritual 'artefacts' every collected on the West Coast. Filip Jacobsen, the younger brother of Adrian who had worked with him to bring the Bella Coola troupe to Berlin, was still living on the coast down in Clayoquot Sound. He was working part-time as a collector, and in 1897 he sent a large collection of 'Nootka artefacts' to Boas, who was now working as a curator at the American Museum of Natural History in New York. The collection intrigued Boas, who had long believed that Nootka culture was largely derivative of Kwakiutl. In the masks and information, Boas could now see the Nootka culture was more unique than he previously believed. Anxious to learn more, he wrote immediately to Hunt, who along with his wife had just visited Boas in New York:

> *April 11, 1903*
> *Mr George Hunt,*
> *Alert Bay, Fort Rupert, B.C.*
>
> *My Dear George, -*
> *I suppose you have reached home by this time, and I trust that you found your family well and prospering.*
> *I write to ask you to go, as soon as you have obtained all the little specimens of which you have on the list, and that are required for our Kwakiutl collection, to the Nootka. I have $500 for this purpose. The special of your trip must be to locate the whaler's house and to get good material illustrating the customs regarding the whalers, which you have so often described to me; but besides this, you must try to make a good collection illustrating the life of the Nootka. As you will remember, we have no good Nootka masks, and we do not know what any of the masks mean; and a great many things used in ordinary every-day life which differ from those of the Kwakiutl are also*

needed. I know that the Nootka have a great many customs regarding the ex nta [sic]. We have nothing relating to these. There must also be many large painted boards, carved figures, etc., to be had along the West Coast. I can pay the freight here, so the full amount of $5000 will be available for your work. You must, of course, get your material considerablely south from the Koskimo, so that you are sure to get the pure Nootka, and not customs that are mixed up with Kwakiutl customs. Do not fail to send with every specimen very full information written out in English. Out of the money that we have set aside for this work, you must pay your travelling expenses and pay yourself at the rate of $75 per month from the time when you start from Fort Rupert until your return.

I trust that you are feeling perfectly well now, and that you will have only pleasant memories of your stay in New York, which I, for one, enjoyed very much. Mrs. Boas sends her kindest regard to you and to your whole family. I hope your photographic apparatus is working well. I am enclosing a check for $500 on the Canadian Bank of Commerce of Victoria, B.C.

Yours very truly,
Franz Boas [signed][53]

Hunt, at this point had never seen the 'whalers house' but for two years had been tempting Boas with rumours of it's existence. He was very concerned that Dr. Newcombe, his main rival on the coast, intended to buy it for the Chicago Museum. Were it not for Hunt's insistence on searching for the shrine, its existence may have passed virtually unknown outside of the Mowachaht culture

---

[53] In The Yuquot Whalers Shrine, Aldona Jonaitis, p 152, from Original letters in the Dept of Anthropology Archeves, American Museum of Natural History and Franz Boas Papers, American Philosophical Society, Philadelphia

on the coast. Only two records of the shines existence ever surfaced in the writing of the early explorers. One day while supervising some work, an officer named Walker on Cook's voyage came across a "temple in the middle of the woods" (It's worth noting that Walker lost his original journal, but later rewrote it from memory more than thirty years later. It was not published though until 1982.) Of the chance discovery he wrote:

> "*Some of our People, who were cutting down Trees behind the Village, discovered what they took to be a burying place, but which upon examination was found to be intended for some religious ceremonies. Some of the Natives at this time were along with us, but as soon as they saw one of our Gentlemen and me, going towards the temple, they appeared to be afraid and ran away. We followed them, and gave them some Presents to induce them to return, but could not prevail. We insisted on someone accompanying us and at last we called Mokquilla [Maquinna], who readily did what we desired. Those who formerly had appeared so backward, now followed us of their own accord, but none of them entered the holy place along with us but Mokquilla.*
>
> *He told us of the House of Enekeetseen [masks], where he practiced those ceremonies, which we had seen him perform at his own House. He called it "Mocappamme." This Temple is in the middle of the Woods, and is overgrown with Shrubs and Weeds—everything about it is slovenly. It is surrounded by a slight railing, which includes a space of five or six Yards square. Within the railing, at the North and South Ends, are two wooden representations of a Crow [probably ravens or thunderbirds. The later are closely associated with whaling] elevated on long slender poles, that are joined by a Straw or Grass rope. From the lead which Mokquilla*

*took on all these occasions, he appeared to be at the head
of their Ecclesiastical Establishment.[54]*

As for the shrine in the woods that Walker had seen, it wasn't
mentioned again until 1817. Camile de Roquefeuil, onboard the
French ship *Le Bordelais* recorded seeing either a different shine,
or one that had since changed considerably in the thirty years since
Walker described it:

> *"The Indians call by the name of tche-ha the shed that
> serves as the burying place of only the great chiefs of
> Nootka. At the entrance of the shed there are five rows of
> rudely carved wooden statues extending to the other
> extremity, where there is a kind of cabinet decorated, like
> the whales, with human skulls. Several of these statues
> have the sexual parts of man and even have natural hair. A
> gallery of human bones marks the limits of the shed.
> Opposite the entrance there are eight large whales made
> of wood placed in a line, with symmetrically arranged
> skulls on the back of each. On a lake near the tech-ha is a
> canoe usually strewn with feathers. The chiefs are interred
> by burying their bodies eight feet deep under the shed;
> after a certain time their corpses are unearthed and their
> heads removed. The skull is placed on the back of a whale,
> in memory of the deceased's harpooning skills. Finally,
> they erect his statue as a monument to his honour and to
> indicate that no other may be buried under the statue. The
> chiefs alone have the right to enter the cemetery, and
> Macouina [Maquinna] has killed those whom he knows to
> have been there. He goes their often in the night or in the*

---

[54] In The Yuquot Whalers Shrine, Aldona Jonaitis, p 22 From Walker,
Alexander, 1982, An Account of a Voyage to the North West Coast of
American in 1785 & 1786. Ed Robin Fisher and J.M Bumstead,
University of Washington Press.

early morning, before anyone is awake in the village, to salute the souls of his ancestors and in order to implore the sun, as he does to his god, to make him lucky in the other world." [55]

No mention of the shrine was made again for another ninety years until the letters between Hunt and Boas. Then it appears it was moved, from behind the village to the more remote island on the lake, but this is mere speculation. Hunt meanwhile probably learned about it from a Mowachaht woman of high birth who had married into the Fort Rupert Kwakiutl. But just to see it would require several months of careful work on Hunt's part. Eight months after he sent the $500 check, Boas had yet to hear back from Hunt:

Dec 28, 1903
Mr George Hunt,
P.O. Alert Bay,
Fort Rupert, B.C.

My dear George,-
    I am getting rather anxious to hear from you. I have had only one letter from you from Nootka, in which you told me about the good progress of your work. I trust that everything has been going on satisfactorily, and that you will have succeeded in obtaining some material and some figures referring to the whale ceremonial.
    I am just about to send off to the printer the third part of your translations, which I expect will be printed on the course of the coming year.

---

[55]   The Whalers Shrine, p 23, from Roquefeuil, Camile de, English trans.: Voyage Around the World Between the Years 1816-1819. London, 182 sir Richard Phillips and Co..

With kindest regards to yourself and to your whole family, and with the best wishes of the season.

  Yours very sincerely,

 Franz Boas [signed]

Hunt wrote back, professing to have written three times, and sent 318 pages of stories and box of Mowachaht collections and details of his continuing efforts:

> *"I am trying to get a grizzly Bear Mask and Hoxohkw Hemsewe [Kwakiutl] from here But we Have none here, and now I have to go to the ts!awadaenox tribe to get some of the masks that you wanted and then when I get them I will send them altogether with the Bills. I have Brought a Nootka Indian home with me to tell me some stories Here for it was he who told me the stories on the west coast and I Had to Pay his Passage to this Plase. I came Home on the 28th of last month and found my wife Very sick with Diarrhoea for she was nothing but skin and Bone. And now she is little Better now. That is all at Present will you Be kind Enough to Remember me and my wife to Mrs Boas and to your Dear Children. good Bye to you*
>
>   *Yours very truly*
>   *Geo Hunt*

In the material Hunt sent he enclosed the first photograph of the shrine taken during his first visit to Yuquot. In a later letter he described the difficulty he had just to obtain permission to see the closely guarded shrine:

> *Nootka*
> *Friendly Cove*
> *9 June 1904*
> *My Dear Dr. Franz Boas*

Last winter when the chief found out that I wanted to find the oemts'a or Whaler's Praying House he asked me if I was pexala [a shaman] I said yes. Then they Brought a sick man to me to Heleka or to get the sickness out of him for they say that I could not go to see the Whaler's Praying House onless I was pexala. Wel I told them to Bring the sick man to me after medle nigh, then I will show him that I was pexala. So they did. And I was Lucky to get the man Wel. And as soon as he was made wel. I was aloud to go But not known By Every Body only the Head Chief and his speaker, and that is How I was taken to this sea otter washing ground also [another smaller shine] I will let you know more about the Prayer in the next mail

goad bye to you sir
Geo Hunt

With the photo in his hands, Boas soon realized what Hunt had been telling him all along. Hidden in the woods just behind the village for hundreds of years remained one of the most unique North American anthropological artefacts every to come under his gaze. If he could get it before his rivals in Chicago, it would be the jewel in the crown of the Northwest Coast Indian Hall and the American Museum, and possibly one of the most outstanding finds in North American anthropological history. Boas wrote back even more urgently to Hunt:

Jan 23, 1904
Mr George Hunt
Alert Bay, Fort Rupert, B.C.
and Care Mrs S. A Spencer [Hunt's sister]
288 Yates Street, Victoria, B.C.

My dear George.-

I have just obtained final authority to make an attempt to purchase the whaling-house of which you sent me a photograph. You will of course understand that we place great confidence in you in trusting you with so large a sum for the purchase of an object the price of which is entirely indefinite; and I have the confidence that you will do all that is in your power to get the house with all its contents as cheaply as possible. My suggestion would be to take about $500 in silver to Nootka, and to tempt the owner of the house by very slowly adding to small offer of perhaps $100 or $150, and if he does not want to come around, even to go so far as to apparently break off all negotiations. I am certain that if you go about it in the right way, you can get it for less that $500. I want you at the same time to take just as many photographs of the house as you can get, so that we may be able to set the whole thing here again just as it was on the spot. If you can get it, it is our plan to build a whole house just like the one in which the carvings are, in one of our halls, and to put trees and vines and bushed made of wax around it, so as to make the whole thing look just as it looks now….

If it is quite impossible to get the house for $500, I will authorize you to pay as much higher as may be necessary, up to the limit of $800. I hate however, to give so much money for the specimen, and I hope you withstand $500 in silver. In case you should be compelled to pay out more than $800, you must get the purser of the boat to telegraph to me from Victoria, so that I can telegraph back to you what to do. I should want to have a telegram anyway, telling me how the negotiations stand…. Please attend to the matter as soon as possible

Yours very truly,
Franz Boas [signed]

The idea that Boas in New York could teach Hunt anything about negotiating with the natives of the coast is quiet laughable. Hunt was after all the son of a Hudson's Bay trader and member of one of Alaska's dominant trading clans. All Boas could do now was wait, and write more letters. The third of four went like this;

> *May 11, 1904*
> *Mr. George Hunt,*
> *Fort Rupert,*
> *P.O. Alert Bay, B.C.*
> *Dear George:-*
>
> *I am disappointed at not having heard from you before this. I see from my bank statement that you cashed the check for $800 on the 10th of March, and I think there would have been time to have received at least a receipt for this amount from you. I trust everything is going well, and that your endeavour to get the whaler's house will be successful. Please let me hear from you at once.*
>
> *Yours very truly,*
> *Franz Boas [signed]*

Two weeks later Hunt did write, only to say that the steamer he had caught had broken and he had to return home and wait sometime before he was able to go again to Nootka. Finally, when he did arrive all the chiefs were off on sealing schooners, where they got good wages for their harpoon skills. Finally one month later, Hunt sent the letter Boas was anxious to receive.

> *"Nootka*
> *Friendly Cove*
> *June 22 1904*
> *My Dear Dr. F Boas*
>
> *I write you these few lines to let you know that I have bought the whaler washing House at Last on the 20th*

of this month. There were two chiefs that Brought the trouble about it, for one of them said that his forfather made it then the other said that he Had Right to it they Began to threaten to Have a Row over it, and one Day I called them together and Brought them to friendly terms and at Last they told me to Put the $500.00 Dallers out and as I Did they told me to Dived it in Equel 250.00 doller Each so they took it. And the older man Had to sign the Bill. and they Made me Promes to leave the House alon ontill all the People go the Bearing sea and to New Westminster. then they will ship it on the steamer. So I told them that I was going to get one man to see that Every thing will Be Put on Bord the steamer and I am Promised By them that they will work to Bring it out in the night time an if the steamers comes on the night time they will Put it on Bord of here. also you will see by the Bill what collection I made her. Now I will sent all the storie of the House to you from fort Rupert and the Prayers of it. Now this morning I was told that there was another....

And so George Hunt managed to eventually buy the Whalers Shrine. Not mentioned in his letter is that Hunt had to also give the two chiefs ten Hamatsa songs, which he owned himself as a ritual initiate. On subsequent visits to Yuquot, other villagers would offer to sell him other shines and washing houses, but never again would he see an equal specimen. After a lifetime of collecting, Hunt himself described the shrine as "the Best thing I Ever Bought from the Indians". Eventually it was sent in two separate shipments. Nine anxious months of waiting and repeated inquires in letters from Boas followed before it arrived in New York. Two months later, Boa ran into problems with the museum administration and resigned to take up a teaching position at Columbia University. The shrine itself did not excite the same attention in his replacement. All its pieces, documents and photos went into a vault in the museum basement, where they were laid to rest in the dark, virtually entombed for the next eighty-five years.

***

I decide to take a walk along the outside beach, which is open to the full strength of the afternoon sun. A couple families are playing with their kids in the sun. For a little while I chat with one of the women. Ray is her grandfather. Every summer she and her sisters bring their families out from the reserve at Gold River for a few months. They stay in the empty rectory at the back of the Church. As we sit and talk on the steep gravel beach, a grey whale comes into the bay. We watch the spout draw nearer and nearer until it is just a few yards from shore. Then the huge creature begins rolling in the surf, washing up against the pebble beach in water only five or ten feet deep. For a moment I think it must be injured as it flops around, it's flippers and flukes flapping against the air.

"No," says the woman, who shows no surprise, "it's just rubbing the barnacles off its thick skin. They come here all the time to do that." Again and again the huge creature allows itself to wash up against the shore. I can't help wondering if this was part of the magic of the shrine.

The Whaler's Shrine that finally arrived in New York in 1905 consisted of eighty-eight anthropomorphic figures, four carved whales, sixteen skulls and the simple shed structure of the house itself. The human-like figures have a range of expressions, from smiling, to singing, to orating, to grimacing. All have extraordinarily captivating eyes according to those who have seen them. From the differences in size, wood, and style of carving, they appear to be the work of several carvers over a long period of time. The oldest resemble masks collected by Cook, with a distinctive pre-contact style, and are badly decayed. The newest and most numerous resemble masks collected by Jacobson and were likely made not long before Hunt purchased the shrine. Hunt also recorded two other stories that contain alternate origin oral histories connected with the shrine.

While Hunt and Boas had managed to acquire the physical shrine, and some stories connected with the origin and rituals of whaling, it was several years before Hunt managed to learn an origin story for the shrine itself. A Kyuquot-Mowachaht woman named Sarha (perhaps Hunt's misspelling of Sarah) was the person who dared tell him, after she moved away from her people to marry a Fort Rupert chief. According to her oral account, the shrine had been the property of the Ts!a'xwasap lineage, (the second name of the same Maquinna lineage), for eleven generations. (Like many heredity titles, it is not passed strictly from father to son. But if the figure of eleven generation that Hunt recorded with the story is accurate, that would make the shrine at least 220 years old when Hunt recorded the story of it, meaning the shrine might date from about 1700, predating the arrival of the Europeans by at least eighty years.) In Sarha's story, a childless Maquinna welcomes his grandson from a northern village:

> *"[The child], Henademes was born a hermaphrodite and raised in the ways of a woman with an apron and long hair. He had straps around his ankles and would not allow the young men to come near him when they wished to lie down with the girls. Instead Henademes called a pretty young virgin to lie down with him, and as she slept, he raped her. Ashamed, she returned to her house, but said nothing. So he called another young virgin to lie with him, and as she slept, he raped her. But she rose from his bed angry, and said she would reveal what kind of person Henademes was. He begged her in vain not to, but at daylight she went to her father and told him of the rape.*
>
> *"The father of Henademes was shamed by his son and decided to hold a dance. He instructed the song leaders to make songs, the words of two verses to be the words of a*

woman's song, and the words of the next two verses to words of a song of a man. The tribe was invited and all came to the house. Henademes appeared and began the dance dressed as a woman. As soon as the words changed he took off his whole dress and was naked. All the tribes saw his penis. Now he became a man. His father gave him the name Dawinaasem and sent him to live with his grandfather, Ts!a'xwasap (Maquinna) at Yuquot.

"Ts!a'xwasap was happy to receive the boy because he himself had no sons. So he took him at once to his purifying house at a lake behind the houses. At the time there was nothing inside the normal house but the skulls of four humans and hemlock branches. Ts!a'xwasap turned over the purifying house to his grandson. Next Dawinaasem asked his grandfather for a wife. Ts!a'xwasap brought him noble princesses of the chiefs. But he rejected each one in turn out of fickle jealously. Finally he embraced the daughter of a common man when she showed she was not ashamed to defecate in front of him. Examining her excrement he found four round hard pieces like stones. He picked them up in his hand and took them to his purifying house.

"That night he dreamt that of four men that told him he would find four whales on the beach in the morning. In the morning they arose and went into the seawater at the inside beach of the village, and then up to the other on the outer seaside of the village. Then he saw four whales lying dead on the beach. Now Dawinaasem sang his sacred song. All the men arose and went to see why he was singing. Then Dawinaasem gave a feast of the four whales to his tribe. Now his name was Ts!a'xwasap, the former name of his grandfather.

"Ts!a'xwasap wished to add to what he had put in his purifying house. When evening came he started and went

into every house of the Mowachaht and he just stood in the house, he never spoke and went out. Not one of the men dared to ask him why he was doing this. Then he went back to his house and lay down with his wife. When it was late at night he arose and went into the other houses and stole ten cradles in all of which lay, newly born by their mothers, boys. Then he carried them back into the woods and went to his purifying house and placed upright the cradles around the inside of his purifying house. Then three of the children cried. Immediately Ts!a'xwasap said, 'That is what I wish, that you may cry, supernatural ones, for the whales when they come drifting ashore when they are dead.' Then he went home to his house and lay down with his wife.

"As soon as the day came Ts!a'xwasap arose and went into the water in the sea on the inside beach of the village. When he had finished he went up the beach and went near to the other beach on the outside coast of the village. There he saw three whales lying dead on the beach. He sang his sacred song and the Mowachaht all awoke and went to look. Then Ts!a'xwasap feasted again his tribe.

"Now the ten lost babies were looked for by their fathers. As soon as all the men gave up looking for them they said that the wolves had devoured the children. They never guessed that Ts!a'xwasap had stolen them. He did not allow a single man to go near the purifying house after this for he told his tribe that if anyone should go near 'to look at my purifying house, then I shall throw sickness into him so that he will die, for I shall not have any pity, even if my father should go I should kill him.'

"Now the Mowachaht were really afraid of Ts!a'xwasap after this. Not a single man dared to go to the lake. Now Ts!a'xwasap was searching for graves and he took the skulls of some men who had been dead a long

time and he put them into his purifying house. When one hundred skulls and two corpses had been put in he stopped for a little while. Then on the floor at the rear of the house on the right hand side he laid down forty skulls, close together with the top of the head up. He also laid forty on the left side. Then took much moss and put it on the skulls as bedding. Then he split cedar wood, fourteen pieces, and took a skull and put it on top of each and arranged them around the sides and entrances of the house. These were the watchmen against those who are secular who might come near the house. Then he found a grave and took ten whole bodies of the people, really dry bodies, and he put them upright, in the house facing the door. It occurred to him to go again to steal some newborn children. When it was late at night he went into all the houses and stole many children in the cradles and stood them around the inside of the purifying house. Then he went and lay down with his wife.

"As soon as daylight came Ts!a'xwasap heard his tribe talking to one another that there were no more cradles on the floor and no children newly born by their mothers. Again all the men ran about in vain and also the women searching for their children. But not one of them dared to go near the lake. Then all the men gave up searching for them. They never charged the disappearance to Ts!a'xwasap. Now he felt happy, for the cradles in which one hundred and twenty children were standing close together and twelve corpses went all around the purifying house.

"Now Ts!a'xwasap said that he dreamed he was asked by the wolf to do this and he asked his wife to go and lie down in the purifying house. She did not dare to disobey the order of her husband. As soon as they arrived there, Ts!a'xwasap asked his wife to lie down on the left side of

the house and he lay down on the right, each on forty skulls. As soon as the morning came Ts!a'xwasap awakened his wife and they went to bathe in the lake When they had done so he said to his wife, 'O woman! Now you have seen our purifying house, don't talk to my tribe about what was seen by you inside of it when we go home to our house.' Then his wife replied, 'What would be the result if I should go and talk about it? You know I do not talk with them although they are my relatives and your relatives.'

"Now Ts!a'xwasap dreamed of the wolf who came and asked him to rub his body with hemlock of four branches and also his wife, in the evening and in the morning when first daylight came, and that they should go every fourth day and stay in the purifying house. Now the whales always came and lay dead on the beach. Ts!a'xwasap became really a chief of the Mowachaht for he continued giving feasts of the whales. Therefore he was called a good chief by his tribe and they did not allow him to go back to his father's side at his former village.

"Now Ts!a'xwasap had a son. As soon as he was strong enough he gave over to him his purifying house and the name Ts!a'xwasap. Then the new Ts!a'xwasap had a son, and as soon as he was also old enough he gave over to him the purifying house and his name Ts!a'xwasap. Now all the cradles and the corpses were rotted, so the new Ts!a'xwasap just took cedar wood and carved it, imitating the children and the corpses. As soon as this work was done he took up the cradles with the children in them and twelve corpses and put them down outside of the purifying house and took the carved children and twelve carved men and stood them in their place. He did not touch the skulls. It is said that Ts!a'xwasap is eight

generations beginning from the Ts!a'xwasap who changed the carved cedar wood for corpses. That is the end."[56]

***

That evening I try to make the most of the social opportunities in camp. After dinner I wander over to the fisher-family's tarp for a slab of salmon fried up in the yet unwashed cast iron pan. We talk about the fishing over a beer, but the alcohol quickly catches up with me. Shortly after sunset I can barely stay awake. I excuse myself and gratefully head off to bed.

***

In the morning I awake just before dawn to the sound of wind howling in the trees. Without checking outside, I turn over and fall back to sleep. It's light when I wake up the next time and when I poke my head out of the tent at first I think the sky is thick with clouds, until in the half light I catch a tone of deep blue and realize that it's a clear sky, distorted by the setting of the moon. I pull on some clothes and wander up to the lighthouse helipad. Looking south, I can see a moderate northerly wind blowing, perfect to push me quickly down the coast. With yesterday's forecast that a storm is to arrive sometime in the next day or two, the decision to go is an easy one to make. I pack up my camp and catch one last forecast from the fisher-family's VHF radio. There's a gale warning for the northern half of the island today, but just strong winds for the south. Even without a chart, I know there are landing sites every four or five miles along the route. I feel game to take my chances. I've got just four days of food left though, just enough to make it all the way home. I trust my own judgement that the timing is right.

---

[56]   My own paraphrasing of the original version in Franz Boas, the Religion of the Kwakiult Indians, 1930, p 262-269.

As I pack my boat at the water's edge Ray appears. I ask him about fresh water. He points down a dirt track and says I'll find a spring further along. I grab my water bags and head down the track. Along the way I come across an old totem pole lying on its back in the grass. A velvety layer of moss is starting to creep onto the edge of its features. I can recognize the main clan crests, Raven with his straight beak, Eagle with a hooked one, Bear with his big teeth and ears, Wolf with his snout, even Frog with folded legs and White Man, carved with big round eyes and the triangular hat of the early explorers.

Back at the house I find Ray warming up in the sun on his porch with the cats, and I ask him about the pole. Enthusiastically he tells me back in 1919 it was carved by ten of the old-time carvers, making it the oldest totem pole on still on the coast. It was a gift for the Governor-General of Canada, Lord Willingdon, who was on an official tour of the coast aboard the new CPR steamer *Princess Norah*. In front of a large gathering of local fishermen, cannery workers and the crew of the ship, Napoleon Maquinna presented the 30-foot pole to the vice-regal "Skookum Chief".

After gratefully accepting the gift, Lord Willingdon found himself in a bit of pickle. By that time the official policy of the Department of Indian Affairs discouraged removal of totem poles from village sites, so he could hardly take it with him. So instead he announced that it should stay in the village. But Lord Willington was also made aware that gift was given in the potlatch tradition. So he asked Napoleon Maquinna, what sort of gift he would like in return. Like his namesake ancestors, Maquinna had an eye for the main chance, and quickly indicated he would be happy to have a 'drag saw' (a chainsaw), a fairly expensive item at the time. True to his word, Lord Willingdon made sure one was delivered a few weeks later when the CPR steamship *Princess Maquinna* passed through Nootka Sound.

The village at Yuquot went on to develop an outstanding reputation as a small engine repair shop and the pole was a popular attraction at Yuquot for many years. It was one of only a handful that remained on the coast, until it finally fell naturally from old age just a few years ago. The provincial museum soon made requests to take it down to Victoria for preservation, like they managed to do with the one up at Ehashasiaht in Esperanza Inlet. But the Mowachaht objected. They didn't want to turn it into an artefact on display, a hostage of the culture that had nearly destroyed them. When I ask Ray what they plan to do with it, he says, "Just leave it, like in the old ways," meaning to lie as it fell after living its natural life, to rot red and turn to soil, the spirits of the carvings returning to rest in the midden.

"What about Whaler's Shrine" I ask him.

"We'll get that back someday too," says Ray, "It's ours. It's coming home."

In 1989 it was brought out of storage and fully erected in Northwest Coast Indian Hall in the American Museum of Anthropology for the first time, as Boas intended. By this time though, the Northwest Coast Hall was now used just as a storage room at the American Museum. The special showing was for Chief Ambrose Maquinna and Chief Mike Maquinna who had travelled to New York to see it and begin the lengthy process to repatriate it.

32. Hesquiat hanging

I charge out of Yuquot, and out the wide mouth of Nootka Sound, turning due south away from the open Pacific toward some rocks where the waves are breaking far offshore, which I must go around. For the first five miles I stay well off, and when I pass the ubiquitous Cliff Point I'm still more than a half mile out.

There are sea otters everywhere, rolling on their backs in the sun. Then suddenly I spot a cloud of spray rising on the water ahead. Whales! Their backs arch in the distance. As I paddle on I soon find myself surrounded by a least six grey whales, all rising and diving to feed on the bottom below. The slow moving creatures are roughly the length of a cruising sailboat, all dark and shiny and covered in barnacles. They have almost no dorsal fin, but their giant flukes are as broad as my paddle. They seem everywhere at once and I'm soon wondering if one is going to surface beneath me. When one does blow a couple boat lengths away, I jump two inches off my seat.

I don't linger long. Although it's very unlikely they will bother me, I fear if I rest too quietly on the surface they might have a hard time avoiding me when they surface. I also have some real concerns about the weather. The sky directly west out at sea is still clear, but to the north behind me is a dark line of clouds pushing up against the mountains. And far in the distance on the southwest horizon I can see a bank of fog.

The two sailboats that were anchored in the cove overnight have both also decided to make a run south ahead of the approaching low. Both are reaching far out to sea on the northwest wind. They have the luxury of tacking out to sea on the rising wind and clearing all the hazards along the shore in one giant triangulation. The swift green boat pulls away quickly toward the horizon while the lumbering white one takes a closer course to the shore. At Sharp Point I'm a bit concerned about the winds forecast later in the day, so I make the unsavoury decision to continue paddling and piss my wetsuit rather than paddle the half-mile to shore and delay my progress with a landing.

Past Escalante my charts run out. I do my best to recall the location of the three-bailout beaches and the route through the inside of Perez Rocks. I'm moving quickly with the wind and small swell behind me, almost ideal conditions, except for the tide flooding against me. Along the coast the land is flat and after Escalante the mountains seem almost to disappear altogether by the time I reach Perez Rocks.

I'm expecting the worst as I arrive at the Perez Rocks, but instead it is relatively calm. A small aluminum skiff with a man and women aboard pass me in the channel. They look pretty surprised to see anyone here, but they don't stop to talk. I wonder where they are going. Perhaps to an isolated squat up the coast, or to the lighthouse, whose only shore access is at a bay half a mile behind me.

After negotiating the reefs and thick beds of kelp I spot a small beach on a back of a tiny grass and log covered islet and stop for a break. I've already paddled ten miles before lunch. On the shore there is a gentle breaking surf. As I step out of my boat I surprise a family of seals who take to the water. After a stretch, I strip off my wetsuit to rinse it out, and laugh at the decision not to go ashore earlier on. The sky is still clear and it seems that the predicted poor weather is holding off. Now that I can see the lighthouse at Estevan Point I relax, knowing I'm most of the way round. With the familiar mountains of Clayoquot Sound now in sight I take a leisurely lunch on the small sandy atoll. I spend the rest of my lunch break watching the seals watching me from the shelter of the surrounding reef.

The predicted high winds don't seem to be coming and I feel relaxed as I set off. The shallow bottom breaks far off shore so I keep far off. Just before the lighthouse I finally leave the uncharted gap and cross on to the edge of the seventh chart I have used on this trip. I spot a shortcut though an inside channel and I shoot through some small breakers to calmer seas on the inside. On the shore is the lonely Estevan lighthouse. I consider landing but the shore is rocky and inhospitable except for a beach two miles back. Instead I press ahead, eagerly watching the mountains and islands I know so well come into view; first Colnet, then Lone Cone and then Vargas. Just by their familiar shapes I know I'm getting close to home. Ahead of the approaching storm clouds, the white tubby sailboat is also turning in towards shore. It enters Hesquiat Harbour just ahead of me. I'm amazed that on such a fine sailing day, we are making the same distance down the coast. A hundred and thirty years ago, other mariners were less happy to be so close to these shores.

***

On March 13th, 1869 The *British Colonist* newspaper in Victoria ran the headline "Dreadful Marine Disaster on the West Coast – an English Bark and All hands lost Near Nootka Sound." Based entirely on rumour and innuendo, it threw the entire town into a state of agitation and nearly inspired a vigilante attack on the native village here in Hesquiat Harbour. In the end, two Indians were hanged, the first formal executions by the British of natives on the west coast.

The front-page story ran:

> *"By the arrival of the schooner* Surprise, *Captain Christianson, from the West Coast of this Island, we receive intelligence of the loss of an English bark, supposed to be the* John Bright, *with all on board near Nootka Sound. Capt. Christianson thinks the bark was lost about the 8th or 9th of February, during a heavy gale which lasted two days. When first seen by the Captain, the wreck was lying on a rocky beach, some three miles [sic] South of Nootka Sound, and not far from an Indian village. She was lying on her beam-ends, the sea making a clean sweep over her, the foremast alone remaining intact.*[57]

Of the twenty-two missing passengers on the *John Bright*, the *British Colonist* wrote "All have undeniably found either a watery grave, or have fallen by the hands of West Coast natives."

The young sealing skipper, John Christianson had come across the *John Bright* awash on the rocks off Matlahaw Point, opposite right where I am paddling now. After a quick reconnaissance of the shore for survivors he found the badly disfigured body of a woman, stripped of her clothing and most of her skin, high on the shore. From the natives he purchased three rings and an accounts book that bore the ship's name. He quickly sailed for Victoria with news of the shipwreck and suspicions of a massacre up the coast. Privately he informed the colony's Governor Fredrick Seymour of his personal suspicions of foul play and urged that a warship be dispatched to investigate. Governor Seymour was initially very reluctant to heed Christianson's advice since he suspected he was lying. His long career in colonial administration had taken him to Tasmania, Antigua, Nevis, and the Bay Islands of Honduras and had taught him that coastal traders were an unscrupulous lot, always eager to call for gunships to support their interests.

Still, there was alarm in the town. Five years earlier in Clayoquot Sound, the trading schooner *Kingfisher* had been

---

[57] British Colonist, March 13, 1869

attacked and pillaged by some Ahousahts led by a chief named Chapchah. The investigation and retribution had been a dismal failure for the previous governor. Fifteen natives had been killed, several villages shelled, countless homes and canoes destroyed in a long summer of reprisals. But the Admiralty had failed to capture the main suspect, leaving British authority on the coast in tatters. Meanwhile Chapchah's reputation as the chief who had defied the King George men on the great war vessels made him a hero on the coast.

This was a concern to Christianson. He made his living taking the Clayoquot hunters out sealing every year off the coast. Without the rule of law, his safety was far from secure, and he was not going to keep quiet. Undeterred by the governor's scepticism, Christianson returned to the wreck site a month later and found several more bodies, some without heads, that he took for freshly dead. Soon his suspicions of foul play began creeping into the press reports. On April 23, the *British Colonist* ran with a new story:

> *"Six more bodies of the* Bark John Bright*'s people found with their heads cut off? They were without doubt murdered by the Indians.... Capt. Christianson's belief is that these men were alive when he first discovered the wreck and that they were secreted in the bush from the Indians; that one by one they came from their hiding places down to the beach to procure food to relieve their misery, and were ruthlessly slaughtered by the savages."*

The same day a letter penned by Christianson appeared in the paper calling for action from the government. The press and the public took up his call. The governor's inaction was sharply criticized in newspaper editorials:

> *"We are exposed to the attacks of savages, who are allowed to rob and murder white men trading up coast, with impunity.... The Indians are boasting far and wide that they can commit depredations with perfect security.... The blood of the murdered victims calls for vengeance."* [58]

A plan for vengeance soon followed. On April 30, the paper reported:

> *"We have been informed that our duty as white men is perfectly understood by some of our fellow citizens, such that a no. of 50 are prepared with military rifles and six-shooters to go up to the scene of the murders and wipe out the whole tribe of murderers..."* [59]

Forced to act to maintain order, the next day the governor announced the HMS *Sparrowhawk*, would sail shortly to the Hesquiat village to investigate the wreck. Onboard as the only interpreter was Christianson. In Clayoquot Sound they stopped to pick up a local chief and friend of Christianson, Chief Ghwyer, whose tribe was a traditional enemy of the Hesquiat people. The ship anchored at Hesquiat and the company of marines was put ashore to search the village. The detachment then proceeded along the shore to exhume the bodies from the makeshift graves. By this time they had been dead for nearly three months. In all eleven rotting corpses were pulled from the earth. It fell to the ship's surgeon, Dr Peter Comrie to conduct the autopsies.

Dr. Comrie concluded that there was no medical evidence to indicate that the bodies had been decapitated. Marks from blades would have still been obvious on the bones if this had been the case. But some native witnesses testified that two of the dead had been shot after reaching the shore alive. When the villagers refused to produce the accused, the captain had the marines set fire to two

---

[58] British Colonist, April 26, 1869
[59] British Colonist, April 30, 1869

houses and ordered the ship's cannons to destroy a large canoe. In the end the *Sparrowhawk* steamed back to Victoria with two male prisoners and five witnesses.

Along with the lack of physical evidence, at the trial, there were numerous transgressions of the normal proceedings. Christianson was sworn in as the interpreter, but he himself did not speak Nuu-chah-nulth, the language of the accused. Instead his trading ally, Chief Ghwyer, an enemy of the Hesquiat, was chosen to translate the native language into Chinook, the trading language of the coast. Christianson would then translate the Chinook into English for the judge. Several of the Hesquiat witnesses claimed to have seen the accused shoot two survivors who managed to reach the beach alive. The first of the accused, Chief Katkeena, pleaded guilty. The second, John Anayitzaschist, emphatically pleaded innocence in the shooting of a female passenger. Despite the questionable circumstantial evidence, twenty Victorian jurors found him guilty. Both Anayitzaschist and Katkeena were sentence to death.

In order to set an example, it was decided that the two men would be hung on the beach near the site of the wreck. A month later the *Sparrowhawk* once again streamed up the coast. On the deck was the Catholic Reverend Charles John Seghers, not yet a bishop and on his first visit up the coast, who had been so eager to work among the Indians of the coast. As the ship pulled away from the dock he baptized the condemned men. The next day as the ship approached Hesquiat, it struck the same reef that had condemned the *John Bright*. Fortunately for those aboard, the seas were calm, and they managed to reverse the steam engines and get back underway with only minor leaks.

The next morning the carpenters, under the protection of the marines, were sent ashore to erect the gallows near Matlahaw Point. At midday several canoes filled with Hesquiat villagers approached the ship. Allowed to come to the side of the ship, John Anayitzaschist said a tearful goodbye to his brother and asked him to take care of his wife and children. Katkeena remained reserved. The next morning four boats were lowered over the side and the police, the high sheriff, the Royal Marines, Father Seghers, the ship's captain and officers, and the two condemned men all went ashore.

The Hesquiat villagers gathered by the scaffolding. The condemned, along with Father Seghers climbed the steps in front of the gathered crowd. In his last words Anayitzaschist, still maintaining his innocence, denounced the chief of the tribe. The black hoods were placed over their heads, then the two nooses. Then without warning, the latch was sprung. Anayitzaschist died instantly, but Katkeena chocked and squirmed until the executioner managed to jam his foot down on the knot. An hour later the bodies were taken down, put in coffins, and turned over to the Hesquiat. Before noon, the *HMS Sparrowhawk* was steaming south once again.

Some citizens in Victoria did question if justice had been done, or if the condemned were merely convenient scapegoats for the crime. There were numerous procedural errors in the trial, particularly the dual roll of Christianson as both a key witness and interpreter. But popular opinion and the influential *British Colonist* stood by the action in its editorials. In the minds of the colonists, it was never a question of justice, or the right to a fair trial, just brutal vengeance:

> *"No sane man who has read the evidence can doubt that the hands of these savages were stained with the blood of the poor, helpless survivors from the wreck of the bark ... With savages we must act in a manner intelligible to them; it is absurd to suppose that our views of equality and justice can apply to people ignorant of the commonest sense of humanity. [There will] be time enough to treat them as we do ourselves, when we have educated them to realize the difference between harshness and mercy."*[60]

***

As I paddle past Matlahaw Point the waves breaking on a series of reefs that curl round into Hesquiat's shallow harbour. The wind that has been at my back all day is now just a light breeze, which clocks round the point with me, staying on my back until I pass the tiny native village of five houses just inside the wide mouth of the bay. Most of the houses are tucked in the woods behind a lush wall of berry bushes. There is just one boat tied up at the concrete breakwater, and the only sign of people is one man standing alone on his veranda looking out at the water. The shallow entrance of Hesquiat Harbour by the old village was notoriously dangerous in rough seas. Now only one family remains here. Most of the rest of the houses, and the church that the Catholics struggled to establish, have all fallen into the ground. The sailboat I thought I saw turning in here has actually gone on further to the next entrance of Hot Springs Cove.

After the long day I can't wait to make camp, but not within sight of the village. My shoulders are tired and my grip is sore. It has been my longest day of paddling on the trip, and the muscles in my chest are beginning to spasm. Around the next point I see a wide beach. The first spot I land is too rocky to pitch a tent, so reluctantly I push off again. Twenty minutes later I collapse on the warm sand at the back of the bay. It is my longest day of paddling yet – eighteen miles, almost the same distance I covered the first week.

When I recover, I take a quick swim in the warm water and walk to stretch my legs. I find some tracks on the beach, perhaps wolf or dogs from the village (which would be half wolf) and some fresh bear-shit by my camp, purple from eating berries that grow plentifully along the edge of the forest. At least it won't be hungry.

One of the things I love about Clayoquot is that there is so much warm sand to dig your feet into at night. It's such a welcoming sight to see the mountains of Clayoquot in the distance. After all these days of travelling I'm just on the edge of home. Across the harbour a powerboat drones in the distance. Geese fly south in a V formation high in the sky. I've got three nights left out, and tomorrow I'll be in at the hot springs for a long soak. I feel like the trip is almost complete.

As the sunsets, my mood lifts. A big beautiful full moon rises orange in the sky across the harbour. There is a delicious sound of miniature breakers peeling quietly on the round boulders of the beach. The night sky is the clearest of the trip. I decide to sleep out, without a fire or tarp. With the hard paddling of the trip now behind me, it is possible for me to start thinking beyond this trip again and my thoughts turn back to my home in Australia and the woman who is waiting for me. And then there is the ring, still in the gold box in my yellow bag.

I've been spending a fair amount of time on this trip thinking of Rosie. I'm anxious to see her, as much because I miss her as because I fear losing her. But I know she is going to want me to travel less in the future. It's a reasonable request, but one that conflicts with the work I have chosen for my life. I bought the ring because I wanted Rosie to have something when I am away. I wonder if it can be enough.

A heavy dew soon settles on my bag and I fall asleep watching the moon rising higher in the sky.

33. Father Brabant

Five years after the hanging on the beach, Seghers returned to Hesquiat, this time as the Bishop of Vancouver Island, accompanied by Father Brabant, on their second mission trip down the coast. By their own accounts they had received excellent welcomes in the villages along the coast. Heading south from Nootka Sound, Brabant recorded their arrival in Hesquiat this way:

> *"September 25 [1874]. – Next morning we left Muchalat in one of their canoes, with the chief and eleven of his young men, en route for Hesquiat. When off Perez*

Rock we met a Hesquiat canoe crowded with young men, who were on the lookout for our expected arrival. As soon as they recognized us, they put about, intending to precede us and warn the tribe. However, our Muchalat crew took to their paddles, and a regular race between the canoes took place. There was no wind, and the sea ran mountains high. We had not met such a heavy swell in all our travels. Although in company with the Hesquiats, we would lose sight of them for several minutes to see them again rise on the crest of the heavy waves, whilst we were, as it were, in the abyss of the ocean. It was a really grand piece of sailing we had on that day from Perez Rock. We at last lost sight of the Hesquiats in the fog, but we could hear them fire off their guns ahead of us as a signal to the tribe to be ready. We found the Chief's house, where we stayed for four days, cleanly swept out, and mats laid all over the floor. The Indians were full of joy to see us.

"We began our work at once; taught the Lord's Prayer, Hail Mary, Creed, Ten Commandments and Seven Sacraments, all of which the Indians learned with much zeal.... We said Mass every morning at 5, at which time all the Indians were present, and during which they recited the Holy Rosary. We here noticed every morning – and, in fact, whenever we assembled the Indians – such zeal and fever that old men unable to walk were carried on the back of the young men to the Chief's house, and some of them came on hands and feet.... Here it struck the Bishop that this tribe would be a good place to start a Mission, being the most central and the Indians of the best good-will. He mentioned the matter to the Chief, asking him to assemble the other Chiefs of the tribe and propose to them the matter in question. This having been done, we were informed, in the presence of the whole tribe, that land

would be given for Mission buildings and other purposes.... ["61]

Thus in the spring of 1875, Bishop Seghers directed Father Brabant to take charge of the West Coast Indians. On the 6th of May, Brabant sailed out of Victoria once again, this time with two young heifers, and a young bull, a Newfoundland dog and a small crew of carpenters. A few days later they reached Hesquiat. Since Chief Matlahaw was absent in Victoria, Captain Brown overruled the Hesquiats' objections to any location and construction of the mission building shortly began.

Lumber for the mission was gathered from a shipwreck of the barque *Edwin* that had washed ashore nearby the previous December enroute to Australia with a load of milled wood. This time for the rescue of the sailors, Chief Matlahaw received a silver medal from the Dominion government and a substantial cash reward from the United States. Some of the Hesquiat had salvaged some of the wood for their own houses, as part of their traditional laws of salvage. But Brabant had made his own claim to the wood, saying Captain Warren had bought the salvage rights from the ship's owners, and "after some trouble and reasoning they were prevailed upon to let us have the use of it." Perhaps this was the first indication the Hesquiat had that the priest had not just come to teach more of his rituals and rhymes.

By July, a Catholic mass to celebrate the Feast of the Most Precious Blood was said in the simple new church, attended by the entire village and a visiting delegation of Muchalats. The next day the last of Brabant's helpers returned to Victoria and the father was left alone to teach the word of God amongst the savages, but still unable to speak a word of Nuu-chah-nulth. As so he began his mission. His first trip north was to Nootka and Kyuquot, where he was badly received because of animosity toward his Clayoquot and Hesquiat guides. The memories of the recent war were still fresh in

---

[61]   Mission to Nootka p29

their minds. "My Indians, suspecting danger, slept with knives in their hands," he wrote. [62] Soon after he received a letter from Bishops Seghers calling him to Victoria for two weeks.

When Brabant returned to Hesquiat his real troubles began:

> *"Upon landing I was told that an Indian woman, "a doctoress," had died during my absence, after a few days' sickness. Next I heard that a large number of Nootka Indians were sick and several had died. The report arrived that the sickness was smallpox. The whole tribe was wild with excitement that they would come to Hesquiat and kill as many of the tribe as had died of the disease! I spurned the threat and persuaded the Indians not to be uneasy.*
>
> *"On the eighteenth of October the wife of Matlahaw died rather suddenly at Hesquiat. As I suspected that everything was not right, I assembled the Indians on the hill, and told those who were living in the Chief's house to move. Also, if there was anybody else unwell, to come and give me information. Upon arriving home, I was met by Charley, whose mother had died during my absence. He reported that his father was sick. I went to his house and found the old man very sick, evidently with smallpox. He was lying in one corner of the room and in the other corner was his sister, an elderly woman, also in the last stages of the fatal disease. I baptized both of them, saw them well provided with food and water and went home convinced that a very trying time was before me.*
>
> *"I was not disappointed, for next morning the first news I heard was that both were dead and that others had been taken sick. As soon as Mass was over, a large number of Indians came to my house and I made preparations to have the dead buried. I went and dug two graves, but when the time for the funeral had arrived no*

---

one would help me take away the corpses. I reasoned and entreated my visitors to give me a hand, but all to no purpose. At last, after several hours of talking, a Cape Flattery Indian, living with his Hesquiat wife, volunteered. Others followed his example, and I mustered a force of ten to the burying of the dead. Never was such a funeral seen by mortal man! First I had to give medicine to every one of them. As I had none, I boiled water, broke some biscuits in it, sweetened the whole with sugar, and insisted that this would be the very best preservative in the world against smallpox.

"Then began the march. I led the procession, then came the ten in a line, with their faces blackened and covered with Indian charms. They were shouting and jumping, and when we came to the house where the dead were, not one dared to come in and assist me. But the Cape Flattery Indian again gave an example of bravery. He was accompanied by Charley's father-in-law and Charley himself. The coffin was a small canoe, to which was attached about forty feet of rope. We took up the old man first. He presented a ghastly sight as the blood and bloody matter covered his face and streamed out of his mouth. The woman was covered with two new black blankets and had evidently died first. Her brother had rendered to his dead sister the pious duty of clothing the corpse. She was put into the same canoe, and then orders were given to take hold of the lines. Everyone wanted to take the very end, but after some confusion the canoe was pulled out of the house. I acted the steersman for a good distance into the bush. After securely covering the original coffin with Indian planks, we all returned to my house. Before entering, the Indians all rushed into the river praying and shouting. Having thrown away their blankets, which were their only covering, they next came

in, everyone of them as naked as the moment he had been born. Some thoughtful woman, after some time, came with a supply of blankets and the spectacle became rather more decent and respectable.

"Next day I went to see the Chief's daughter who was very low with smallpox. She was a courageous woman and did not give up till she was quite blind and her head as black and as thick as a large iron pot. She was baptized and seemed to be in the best disposition. Her own father and another old Indian helped me to bury her. The sight of the corpse was simply horrible, and as we left the shanty in which she died swarms of flies surrounded us all. At this time, Matlahaw, the Hesquiat Chief, his father Townissim, Omerak and Charley had obtained permission to sleep in the Indian room of my house. Upon according this privilege, Matlahaw promised and gave me all the strip of land between the river and the beach.

"I passed most of my time in vaccinating the Indians and in trying to cheer them up, for the fear and discouragement in some cases were altogether alarming. Matlahaw and Charley were hardly alive. Hence they would sit for hours together, telling me of the importance of their lives and insisting upon my using all possible means to preserve them from the disease. Charley had been vaccinated successfully in Victoria. Although I tried it twice on Matlahaw, the vaccine had no effect. [Brabant does not say specifically if he actually had a supply of the actual smallpox vaccine or was still using a placebo of sugar and crackers.] This seemed to increase his fear. He now became morose and avoided the company of his friends. In fact he was not to be seen in the daytime for several days. He used to be up before daylight and two or three mornings, as I got up, upon looking through my

window, I noticed him sitting alongside of his father, apparently engaged with him in very secret conversation.

"On the twenty seventh of October he shot some blue jays in my potato patch. The rest of the time he stood outside, watching my movements, and from time to time exchanging a few words with the Indians who were constantly about my house. Towards evening the report that an Indian woman was very sick was received. I went to see her, but noticed that her case was not very serious yet. However, next morning the first thing I did upon getting up was to go and see the old woman, who was, if anything rather better than the day before. After I had returned to my house and was about to go and ring the bell for Mass, Matlahaw came into my house and asked me for the loan of my gun. Upon handing it to him, I said it was unloaded. He simply remarked that he had powder and shot in his shanty, which was made of a few Indian planks and which with my permission he had constructed behind my little barn.

"All the Indians of the tribe, save the old woman who had smallpox and Matlahaw and his father, were at Mass. The old man was missed at once. Afterwards it was found out that he had crossed the bay with his little grandchild and gone up Sydney Inlet, where his wife had gone before him. There she and her female slave died of smallpox. The old Chief, in a fit of passion, took a stone and with it killed the husband and one old slave. When the Mass was over, and just as I was finishing my breakfast, Charley came into my room and said, "Lookout, Leplet, Matlahaw is sick. You had better take your gun from him." I made one or two inquiries, and after saying a few words jokingly, to give heart and courage to the messenger, who looked alarmingly excited or downhearted, I went out, my pipe in my mouth, to see the would-be patient.

"When I arrived inside of his shanty, I noticed in the middle a small fire, before which he was squatting down. He had on his Chief's hat and also the coat presented by the Superintendent of Indian Affairs. Behind him, against the wall, stood my double-barrelled gun and an Indian musket. I asked what the matter was, when, smilingly, he looked up, and pulling the skin of his leg, answered, "Memaloose - smallpox." I assured him, saying that I would give him medicine and that by evening he would be all right, Again he looked up, his face being very pale and the sinews of his cheeks trembling, and pulling at the skin of his throat he repeated, "memaloose". Once more I repeated that I would give him medicine and that he would be well before evening.

"Then I asked him to hand me my gun, which he took without getting up. Then pointing it towards me he explained, as I understood, that one of the barrels was not loaded. The fact of the muzzle of the gun being pointed straight to my face and noticing caps on both nipples and the cocks pulled up caused me instinctively to turn away my head, when lo! the explosion took place and blood spurted from my hand. The smoke was so thick that I could not see the would-be murderer. Thinking the whole affair to be an accident, after calmly remarking that I was shot in the hand, I walked down to the little river where I bowed down to bathe my wounds in the stream. Matlahaw shot again. This time he hit me in the right shoulder and all over my back.

"I now knew the man wanted to kill me and I ran off to my house, where I found no one. Then I ran to the rancherie and was met by nearly all the men of the tribe to whom I told what had happened. Some of them pretended that the Mowachats had done the shooting. After stating again and again that it was Matlahaw they became

convinced that he indeed was the guilty party. After a few moments a film came over my eyes and thinking that I would not survive, I knelt down and said my acts of faith, hope, charity and contrition. Then I got up, went to my house and wrote on a piece of paper the name of the man who had shot me, put the paper in my bureau, locked it and put the key into my pocket. By this time the noise and alarm outside of my house was deafening. The loyal men of the tribe were there with axes and guns to kill their Chief. But he had run away into the bush and had not been seen after the shooting, save by an old woman.

"Meanwhile I had been divested by some savages of my coat and underclothing. The Indians, upon noticing the blood, lost courage and one after the other walked out of the room, announcing to their friends that I was dying. This was also MY opinion, although I felt no pain whatever, either in the hand or the back. I lay down and ordered cold dressing to be placed over my wounds. I noticed very little of what was going on, thinking that the best thing I could do was to pray and prepare myself to die.

"Early the next day, October 29, two canoes, fully manned, left Hesquiat. The first went to Hot Springs Cove, where the sister of Matlahaw was residing with her Indian husband. The Indians, excited over the doings of her brother had decided to bring her home. In due time the canoe came back and the girl was landed on the beach before my house. She knew not what was in store for her. She knew not that as she was left there alone, crying, the Indians were plotting her death in expiation of what her brother had done to me. Such, however, was the case. When the plan was well prepared an elderly man came rushing into my house where I lay on my bed. He wanted my opinion, as the Indians were going to kill her. As the

savage spoke his hair stood on end, froth was on his lips and his members trembled with excitement. I gave orders to have the young woman removed to a place of safety and to have her taken proper care of. I appointed one of the chiefs, a relative of hers, to act as her guardian during this time of unusual excitement.

"The other canoe came back next day. She had gone to Clayoquot where a man, Fred Thornberg, had charge of a small trading post. This man was living with an Indian woman. When the Indians with the message called at his place, he met them with a Marlin rifle and would not allow them inside until he was fully convinced that his visitors were Hesquiat Indians. As his neighbours, that is the Indians of Clayoquot and Clayoquot Sound, were not to be trusted, he advised the Hesquiats to avail themselves of the darkness of the night to return to their homes. He sent a number of yards of calico (with his compliments and condolences) to be used by the Indians as a shroud for my 'corpse.'

"On November 1, Monday at noon, a deputation of Indians excitedly entered my house and told me that they were going to send a canoe with the news of my state to Victoria, and report to the Bishop and the police. I told them quietly to please themselves, but, as they were determined to leave at once, I gave them a paper on which I had written a few words every morning.

"Meanwhile my wounds became more and more inflamed. The Indians were up with me day and night, constantly pouring cold water over my injured hand. The wound in my back and side gave me great pain because I had to lie on them and they could not be reached by cold water dressings. As the hours and days advanced the swelling increased and inflammation was rapidly gaining. I was trembling with cold, although the Indians kept up a

good fire. At last, on Tuesday, the 9th, just as it was getting dark, an Indian ran into my house out of breath and shouted that a man of war was entering the harbour.

"*I cannot describe my feelings and those of the poor Indians who were in my room and acted as nurses. Half an hour later, Dr. Walkem, who had volunteered to come to my assistance, rushed into my room. After examining my hand he expressed the opinion that it could not be saved and that I would have to submit to amputation. By that time Bishop Seghers, God bless him, had also come in. I can see him now, a picture of sadness. With tears in his eyes he told me how happy he felt to find me alive ... I could hardly utter a word. My strength was gone. I had not tasted food or drink for several days.*

"*The Bishop went into my bedroom, opened a bottle of port wine and gave me a dose of the medicine, as he called it, in the presence of the natives and lo! my strength and courage came back at once. I told them of the details of my situation since I had seen him a month before in Victoria. The doctor of the Navy, Dr. Redfern, after thoroughly examining my wounds, declared that nothing could be done at present. I would have to go to the hospital in Victoria, and he urged upon me the propriety of taking some food. He then cooked a meal. Although everything was prepared in an artistic shape, I could not take more than one or two mouthfuls.*

"*Next morning Captain Harris of the H.M.S. Rocket came on shore and proposed to have the would-be murderer arrested. In fact he stated that it was part of his object in coming to Hesquiat. But just then an Indian came into my house with the news of new cases of smallpox, and expressed his uneasiness and that of his Indian friends to be left alone with the dread disease in the village. Happily, Captain Harris did not understand the* *messenger. So we urged upon him the necessity of returning to Victoria, as the doctors insisted that my wounds would have to be attended to without further delay. Besides, I told him, the man who had shot me had run away into the bush. He had not been seen since and that he might be ten or twenty miles away in the mountains. An arrangement was then made with the principle men of the tribe that they were to take Matlahaw to Victoria in case he could be arrested. The Provincial Police would pay them for their trouble the sum of $100, and a supply of provisions.*

"Thereupon arrangements were made to have me conveyed on board of the man-of-war. Eight men placed me on a cot, took me down to the beach between two lines of Indians, whilst one of the chiefs made a speech regretting what had occurred and bespeaking the speedy return of "their priest". When we arrived at the vessel, the cot was slung from the spanker-boom and an awning was stretched over the whole. I was made to feel as comfortable as possible under the circumstances."[63]

Brabant spent five months in Victoria recovering. Matlahaw had not been captured. A few days after Brabant had been taken to Victoria, the chief's body was found slumped against a tree not far from the village. A few days later, the tribe arrested Matlahaw's father Townissim, still regarded as a chief, and took him to Victoria. There he was held for six months in jail as witness to the shooting.

Brabant did not lose his hand or his desire to return to the mission. When he returned to the village, he also came back with a plan to take control of the village away from the chiefs. His first action, after cleaning the bloodstains from the floor of his cabin was to appoint three native men as Indian constables. At High

---

[63] Mission to Nootka, p 38-45.

Mass that Easter Sunday, he gave each of them a coat and pants, "to distinguish them from other savages." [64] In this way he replaced the traditional power structure in the village and set himself for a direct confrontation with village leaders. Brabant then placed the raising of Matlahaw's son, the future chief, in the hand of his three constables.

A month later when Townissim returned to the village, he began organizing against the priest. At the same time Brabant began speaking out again the "Indian superstitions". Shortly after the arrival of a drift whale in the harbour gave Brabant a chance to learn something of the villagers' own religious rituals, but as a devout Christian, he paid them little credit:

> *"A few months ago an old Indian Chief, called Koninnah and known all along the coast, died in Hesquiat. This man enjoyed the reputation of bringing dead whales, almost at will, to the shores of the Hesquiat. Even now he gets credit for the whale that floated on shore yesterday. For the Indians say that their chiefs do not forget their friends and subjects when they reach the other world.... This man I am told, had here in the bush a small house made of cedar planks. To this house he would retire from time to time to visit his charms, and go through his devotions, prayers and incantations. His charms mostly consisted of human skeletons, especially those of ancient Chiefs and famous hunters. To these skeletons he would speak as if they were alive and order them to give him a whale. Each of the skeletons had their turn. In addressing himself to them he would give due credit to those of their number who, he had reason to suspect, had been granting his request.*
>
> *"It is narrated that Koninnah one day was boasting of causing a dead whale to strand in Hesquiat Harbour. As it*

---

happened, the flesh was tough and the oil not sweet. The Indians found fault with their supposed good luck so Koninnah told them that he would get another one of them of better quality: a couple of days later his prediction was verified."

Brabant saw no comparison between such rituals and the Catholic tradition of praying for favours at the tombs of saints, or the blessing of the Mission of the Sacred Heart by the Bishop and placing of it under the protection of St. Anthonine, or even his own recently answered prayer to the Virgin Mary for a recovery after his shooting. Instead he wrote, "The Indians tell their yarns with such conviction of truth that it is almost painful to have to contradict them."[65] He redoubled his efforts to wipe out the "superstitions." In particular he began to rail against the traditional restrictions on the preparation of salmon, while gradually enforcing his own cultural norms on the village:

"I made a rule in church that all the people, men women and children, must a least wear a shirt. No one will be admitted to my house except if he wears a shirt under his blanket. After this I showed them the absurdity of some of their superstitions.

As it is the salmon season, the old people are as usual preaching to the tribe the propriety of conforming with the old established regulations, lest this great article of food should leave the neighbourhoods and not come back again. For instance, salmon should not be cut open with a knife. They should not be boiled in an iron pot and not given as food to dogs or cats. The bones muse be carefully collected and thrown into the sea. Under no consideration must salmon be given to any white man, including the priest, least he prepare it in lard or in a frying pan. It

---

[65] Mission to Nootka, p 50.

should not be taken into the house in baskets, but carried into the house carefully one in each hand. These and other details will show what an amount of absurdities are in these peoples' minds. It is almost humiliating to have to say that this and like matters formed the subject of my sermon today. It created quite a revolution in the camp and had the effect of my presence here becoming a cause of alarm, and a matter of regret on the part of the men and women in the village." [66]

Rather than realize he was forcing the collapse of an ancient culture, steeped in deep ritual relations with the land and the sea, with considerable zeal he sought in everyway possible to facilitate its destruction. Shortly after Brabant decided to go fishing himself and catch a large salmon, with the intention of violating every ritual he could uncover.

"Upon landing, I called the dog and put the salmon into a fine, large basket, which was against the rules. The brute took the basket and preceded me home. Of course no Indian would attempt to molest the large, faithful animal. Quite a number of men and chiefs assembled in my house and protested against my using a knife or frying pan. I took no notice, and proceeded with my work. My aim was to show them that their superstitions were absurd and to try by all and every means to get them to give them up." [67]

He also took on a belief that a supernatural spirit inhabited a cave on a nearby mountain and would kill anyone that approached it. "It struck me that if I could not prove this to be a fraud, I could not hope to uproot the rest of their superstitions. Hence I resolved to visit the mountain, and show them that they had been deceived

---

[66] Mission to Nootka, p 60.
[67] Mission to Nootka, p 64.

by their forefathers."[68] After offering up the Holy Sacrifice of the Mass, he and Father Nicolaye, a fellow priest of much less determination and fortitude that had recently arrived to spend the winter at the mission, set off up the mountain behind the village. After spending a day and a night searching the mountain for the cave, the two priests returned with their Indian guides:

> *"We arrived at the mission about dusk. Our Mission flag was hoisted at the stern of our canoe as a sign of victory of the Cross over pagan superstitions. Upon our landing no Indians could be seen outside of the houses. Only one man came to meet us ... the first remark which he made was to the effect that now he was convinced that the beliefs and legends were pure superstitions."[69]*

As the winter progressed, after the solstice, and Christmas, the young men of the village began the annual observation of 'Osemitch', the ritual practice of bathing to prepare for a hunt. Brabant observed them closely but made no direct efforts to intervene, perhaps sensing his position in the village had become rather tenuous. Then in early January, the village received news that a popular Chief Nitaska had died:

> *"January 11. - Nitaska's death is a great event in this region. The tribe are mourning and general gloom hangs over the village. The dead man was evidently a great favourite and very much liked. As for us, we consider his death almost as blessing for our work. The man's influence was to great and he was inclined to work against us as regards the conversions of the people."[70]*

---

[68] Mission to Nootka, p 61.
[69] Mission to Nootka, p 63
[70] Mission to Nootka, p 68.

By the end of March, much of his work to convert them was coming undone:

> *March 20 - ... Since the 5th of the month, the Indians had been unable to go fishing and had very little food in their houses [because of poor weather that prevented them from fishing]. They were actually starving and their little children have been crying for food. You can see the misery on the faces of both old and young. The oldest people assert that with their memory they have never been in such a state of distress. Today the weather being fine, an abundance of herring and salmon were brought into the camp. As regards the spiritual state of the tribe, it is worse than ever. They blame me for the absence of food. They laugh at the doctrine which I teach. I gain nothing by making the sign of the cross. I am the Chigha, the devil. "[71]*

Shortly afterwards, short of rations, and loosing ground to the pagans the Reverend Father Nicolaye departed, "sick at heart of the discouraging state of affairs here." Once again Brabant was alone. Unimpressed, Bishop Seghers sent Nicolaye back to the Hesquiat, and instructed Brabant to build a second mission at Barkley Sound for Nicolaye to take over. While Brabant was away building the new mission, Nicolaye struggled with the work of conversions in Hesquiat, wrote Brabrant:

> *"He continued to preach Sunday after Sunday against the Indians' superstitions, and the medicine men. He told them none could expect to be baptized except if they would not first abandon their practices. In a moment of fervour forty men and women resolved to comply with the conditions. Before ten days had elapsed ten of the number had transgressed the rules. In a few days more, sickness*

---

[71]   Mission to Nootka., P70

*having broken out in the settlement, recourse was freely
had to the medicine men and women. In short, when he left
for his new mission only seven had remained faithful. The
old people are most determined to frustrate our plans. Two
of them, Eskowit and Eagakom, have declared that they
will kill the priest in case their sons die.* "[72]

The following winter was also a hard winter and by March, the
village was starving again.

*"March 1 – Since the middle of January [when a drift
whale provided a few weeks of feasting] there has been a
great scarcity of food. Owing to the easterly gales, which
commenced last October and which have not been
interrupted by fair weather except for a few days about
New Years, no one had been able to go fishing.... The old
people are desperate and most abusive against anyone
who transgresses the old customs. Quite a few of the young
people do not mind them"* [73]

The following winter, Seghers, now an archbishop, paid a visit
to Brabant. Disappointed that after five years little progress with
conversions was being made, the archbishop decided to take
matters into his own hands:

*"January 26 – 1879 ... Upon arriving, the Archbishop
told me that he had come to baptize my Indians. I replied
that none were fit to receive the sacrament. He insisted. In
order to avoid all further controversies I confined myself
to the cooking. After a couple of days he commenced to see
that it was premature to speak of baptism to most of the
people. He thought, however, that it was wrong to be over-*

---

[72] Mission to Nootka, p 73.
[73] Mission to Nootka, p 74.

exacting, both as to knowledge and conduct. Today ten people, six men and four women, received the sacrament of regeneration at the hands of the new Archbishop of Oregon. All the Indians were present and the long ceremonies of the Ritual were followed."[74]

But the efforts were in vain:

"February 9 – I have just returned from Victoria where I have made my usual purchases for the next twelve months. Nothing unusual has occurred these last three or four months. Upon my return home I learned that several of the Indians baptized by the Archbishop have returned again to the pagan practices – only three or four have remained faithful. As I had foreseen this, it did not upset me much. In fact I had told his Grace that such would be the case. As the Indians also mistrusted these would-be Christians it caused very little scandal.

They are now, however, watching with concern the conduct of one who is supposed to be sincere about his Christianity. The fact is his wife has just given birth to a little boy. Everyone watches the couple to see whether they will have recourse to the Indian medicine man or woman. Never within the memory of even the oldest people was a child born and not at once taken charge of by one or more sorcerers.... Upon the birth of an infant several of them rush to the place. They all take hold of the newly born, sing, squeeze its little belly, pretend to cast out the evil one and often exhaust the little one to death.

July 21 – The father of the child is a determined, good man. He has an amount of trouble with his relatives who all want him to take the child to the doctors. The infant is weak and gives doubtful signs of a long existence. This

---

[74] Mission to Nootka p 79.

gives them chance to find fault with him all the more. But he does not mind their suggestions or interference. In my own mind, I can see the consequences if the infant should die." [75]

Brabant decided that the best course of action was to discredit the sorcerers directly. The similarities between the new sorcerer in the village and the central figure of his own doctrine seem to escape him:

"December 3 -- The greatest obstacle to the conversion of the Indians is the idea that they will have to give up the sorcerers.... Very few men are sorcerers, but the number of women is very large ... The starting point is either a dream or a so-called vision, or discovery of something unusual in his wanderings on the beach.... We have one here now, the first since I have been stationed here. He is a young, sickly fellow of silent, morose disposition. He is the last person that I would have suspected of being inclined this way.... They say that he pulled a snake out of his abdomen and that he will walk on the salt water as if it were terra firma. They also say he walks on the branches of trees to their extremity, and thus passes from one tree to another. As I always strive to draw good out of evil, so I tried to in the present case. Nothing like facing the enemy. It may be hard at first, but it is the only way to convince of the future.

While Brabant and his first local convert, a Hesquiat he baptized Michael, moved to discredit the shaman of the village, the elders of the village decided to challenge the ban on Sunday work Brabant had attempted to impose on the village. By now he had far exceeded his original instructions that while he was to serve as an

---

[75] Mission to Nootka, p 81-82.

arbiter and guide for the Indians in their civil lives, while actual authority was to remain with the chief of the tribe. Increasingly Brabant was exercising his authority by coercive means.

"April 20 [1880] -- ...Early this March the Indians became very dissatisfied and troublesome. The old people were finding fault and exciting the others at every chance. They now made up their minds that they would work on Sundays and ignore the established rules. First, they came to ask permission to go out fishing. As they pleaded scarcity of provisions, the weather having been very bad, I allowed them to go out one Sunday, and again on the following. On the third Sunday, there being and abundance of food in the village, they went out without leave. When the bell was rung for High Mass, they all came on shore and attended Mass. I warned them and insinuated that the transgressors of our Sunday law would be punished. I could not punish them all, but the one who started the others would be the sufferer. After Mass a messenger came to tell me that all the men of the tribe were preparing to pull out their canoes.

Upon looking out I saw about thirty canoes in a line and on a certain signal being given, they all pulled out together. This was very clever on their part. I could not punish any single starter. However, I walked down to the beach and noticed that not only the men but even most of the women were bent on desecrating the Sunday. Only two or three of the Indian Policemen had remained faithful. With their assistance I took away a number of nets, said a few words to the leaders, and walked back to the Mission. On my way a scuffle took place between the police and some of the worst of the lot. This I stopped without delay and with any harm being done save the tearing of a few shirts and the pulling out of a handful or two of hair.

When I got home I tried to take the matter coolly. But how could I? Here it was nearly six years. And only one convert and two or three decent fellows, although heathens. The Apostles fared still worse, and the missionaries in China and elsewhere have no better times. Nothing like persevering and fighting the matter through.[76]

To his credit Brabant was not deceived about his successes and when the new bishop arrived for a visit Brabant did not hide the reality of his failing efforts.

"[He] expected to receive the great reception ... But my Indians, with the exception of one family are still pagans. I thought it would look like hypocrisy to make them turn out and act as Christians."[77]

The following winter he observed the Klookwana, the important wolf ceremony of the Nuu-chah-nulth. While many missionaries at the time were campaigning for the ban on the potlatch, surprisingly Brabant believed it did no harm to his work. He wrote:

"I can see nothing to find fault with at the present time. When I see the masquerades, cavalcades, historic processions, dramas, and other entertainments of our white populations abandoned and given up forever, it will be time enough to tell the Indians that they must give up their festivities."[78]

The next ceremony was to take place in the church though:

---

[76] Mission to Nootka, p 84-85.
[77] Mission to Nootka, p 86.
[78] Mission to Nootka, p 88.

"March 29, 1882. – A young Indian most unexpectedly called at my house, a few days ago, and asked to be married. This was quite a new thing. Never before had anybody applied to me for matrimonial services. ... First I administered baptism. Then I brought them to the altar and everything went on well until I told them to join hands. This was almost too much. Single women are never to touch a young man's hand – it is an act of immodesty – and how could she do so in conspectu omnium, *for quite a crowd were in the church? After some coaxing and persuasion, she at last put out the tip of her finger from under her blanket. The bridegroom, now rejoicing in the Christian name of John, grasped hold of it and the ceremony proceeded without any further difficulties."*[79]

But the parents objected to the innovation of marriage in a church. Traditionally it had been an opportunity of much ceremony and exchanging of gifts. The bride's family, feeling jilted of the legitimate bride price, refused to recognize the legitimacy of the marriage. A row proceeded and Brabant used the opportunity to advance his position in the village:

"The following Sunday I preached on matrimony, explaining its sacredness. Next, I called their attention to the fact that their old marriages almost amounted to selling their daughters as one would sell a canoe or a horse --- just as of old the chiefs sold their slaves. This I had told them more than once, but it had no effect. However I know that the young men were favourable to the Christian marriage [since they did not have to exchange a bride-price]. As they occupied one side of the church, all the women occupying seats on the other, I turned to the men. I told them to stand so that I would have

---

[79] Mission to Nootka, p 91.

all those who were yet single married in the church. If the girls did not comply, I would take the matter up and go with the men to look for wives in other tribes. This seems to have had the desired effect. Several women, about to be married, fearing that they would be jilted, sent word through their parents that they were not of the number who had objected to the Christian marriage. "[81]

By this time sealing ships had begun calling at Hesquiat to hire the men as harpoonists for the fur seal hunt. The trade was profitable on both sides, although considerably more risky for the natives. The ships would head north to the sealing grounds in the Bering Sea, where the canoes would be put over the side each day for the men to go off and hunt. Many were lost at sea in their canoes when a fog or storm overtook them. Once two men who failed to returned to their ship managed to reach the Aleutian Islands of Alaska. Local natives sent them to a nearby trading post and from there they caught a steamer to San Francisco where they were turned over to the British consul, who returned them to Victoria. When they finally showed up in Hesquiat they were greeted as heroes.

Sea otter pelts, although rare (less than ten per year for the village) were also worth thirty to ninety dollar each, a small fortune that put cash in their hands. Many of the younger men began to purchase clothing from the trading ships that came to call. Sensing another chance. Brabant made a new rule – that no man may come into his house without pants on. He wrote: "This was hard on them. "They had always considered this covering of the their lower limbs superfluous – a real bother. But I was inexorable. Pants on or remain outside."[80]

That October another ship was wrecked on treacherous reefs near the outer coast village of Homais. After hurrying to the scene,

---

[80] Mission to Nootka, p 93.

Brabant presided over the recovery of the bodies and their burial. After reporting the loss of the bark *Malleville*, Brabant forwarded some jewellery and personal items collected by the villagers. A year later the American government forwarded a reward of two hundred dollars and a gold medal for Chief Aime. Feeling secure now in his position in the village, that winter Brabant moved once again to destroy the influence of the shamans;

> *December. – The Indians have commenced some of their winter festivals and the Chief being engaged in a Klookwana, a young woman fell into trances and began to prepare to become a medicine woman. As my position with the majority of the people was becoming solid, and as I could reckon upon being sustained in anything I would undertake for their good, I decided to interfere. Since the medicine men and women all sat around this candidate for new honours, I sent a posse of strong men to scatter them with menaces and threats. All the impostors immediately left the house and the young woman took to the bush. It is now settled that for the future consulting and employing medicine men and women can no longer be tolerated in the neighbourhood. Thus the greatest obstacle to the conversion of the Hesquiats is forever removed.*"[81]

But with the traditional healers discredited Brabant soon found himself involved in his own healing shames, much like his smallpox vaccine:

> *September 14. ... Since the abolition of the medicine men and women free recourse is had to me for medicines and medical treatment. Day and night calls are made of remedies for the old and young. They want medicines for any and every complaint and there is no end to it. Strong*

---

[81] Mission to Nootka, p 99.

burning medicines are preferred. In fact, mild remedies are discarded. Since last year I have applied a square yard of blistering and mustard plasters to the aching limbs and bodies of my parishioners. I hope this habit of calling for help for even the most trivial ailments will soon cease. If not, I have a hard and busy time before me.

For a while things appeared to be going Brabant's way:

1885, November. – Since the beginning of last year the religious status of the tribe has greatly changed. Many adults have been baptized and received into the Church. All the marriages are now contracted in the Church and it is only a matter of time to have all the young people gather in the bosom of the Church. At last perseverance and prayer have carried the day. Deo Gratias! [82]

But that winter turned out to be another dangerous one for Brabant, as he lived in fear of a second attempt on his life:

"I now have a paper on my desk stating that, if I do not turn up and that my body is found with evidence of having being murdered, traces of it can be found on the lower limbs of the man who committed the deed. I have, since the beginning of this trouble, carried a revolver with the object of wounding in the lower limbs the man who committed the assault. Then nobody but the guilty party may be hauled up." [83]

The source of the father's concern was the family of a young Hesquait man named Wewiks, who had just returned from serving six months in jail for breaking into the store of a trader. In prison

---

[82] Mission to Nootka, p 100-101.
[83] Mission to Nootka, p 102.

he contracted consumption (tuberculosis) and died shortly after getting home, but before he did, the family threatened revenge on the priest

But it wasn't Brabant who was murdered, but his dear friend Archbishop Seghers. The next winter while doing mission work in Alaska, Seghers was killed by a paranoid priest who believed that the archbishop was planning to kill him. Then the same summer the measles plague arrived on the coast. Thousands of natives working in the hop fields of Puget Sound died in the camps around the fields. Others fled, bringing the sickness to the villages, and many who did recover, weakened by the disease, died afterwards from tuberculosis. Particularly hard hit were the children. Brabant counted 40 dead that summer in Hesquiat alone.

By this time, after twenty years at Hesquiat, Brabant was now aided in his mission with another nearby Catholic father in Clayoquot. With the dominant position of the Catholic doctrine now secure in Hesquiat and much of the rest of the coast, the church now had a new concern though:

1895. -- Our Indians over all the coast are well-disposed. This being the known seems to have excited the Presbyterian and Methodist denominations. Their efforts to invade the coast are very pronounced. A monthly steamer now visits the coast, as the government has established a Scandinavian settlement at Cape Scott at the northern end of the Island, and bound itself to carry the mails and provisions once a month. With these facilities of travel and the peaceful behaviour of the natives all along the coast, the zeal of the Protestant ministers has grown to the extent that they now have established themselves at different points on the coast. When a man's life was in danger and when the only means of travelling was an Indian canoe, when the mails reached us only once or twice a year...we were welcome to do alone the work of

> *converting the natives. Now with the present facilities and the absence of danger, the ministers come in sight to give trouble and pervert our Indian children."*[84]

As a solution, Brabant proposed to the bishop that an industrial school for boys and girls be built. In the meantime a Presbyterian school teacher, now established at nearby Ahousaht in Clayoquot Sound became an irritation to Brabant, "and the poor little children so anxious to learn to read and write will be perverted without noticing it."[85] Finally in 1899, the new Bishop Christie sent instructions for Brabant to start building the school. Brabant quickly pre-empted land in Clayoquot Sound, close to Tofino and hired a crew. Finally in October of 1899 the first Indian Residential School on the west coast of the island was ready to open.

---

[84] Mission to Nootka p 112.
[85] Mission to Nootka p 113.

34. Final passage

When I wake the weather has turned and in the early light of the morning I can see that rain is on its way. I pack up quickly, eager to make it to Hot Springs Cove before a storm pins me down on this unprotected beach. By the time I launch the opposite side of the harbour three miles away is hidden behind a curtain of drizzle. I take a compass bearing off my chart to set my course into the white fabric, and make a note to keep the fishing boat that anchored after dark last night on my left as I cross.

Less than halfway across all signs of land behind me disappear and I'm completely surrounded by the grey mist. I have only my compass and my chart once again to guide me. A light wind begins to whip my face with rain. I keep on course as best I can, and eventually the far shore comes into view. It is largely featureless and difficult to place on my chart. Hopefully I've stayed on course. Once I'm within a hundred yards of the shoreline I turn south towards the mouth of the harbour and start looking for recognizable land features to fix my exact position on the chart. Although I tried to make a cross straight across in the fog, it is obvious that the wind has drifted me farther back in the harbour than I predicted.

Eventually I spot a long beach leading to a rocky point that coincides with an obvious point on my chart. Now I know where I am. As long as I can keep the shore visible on my left I should be fine. Although the gentle beach quickly turns to jagged cliffs ahead, much like the outside of the Brooks Peninsula, there are no boomers along the route ahead marked on my chart to worry about. The water is quite deep the whole way along though, so the biggest hazards are the confused patterns of the rebounding waves coming back off the cliffs to my left.

Not too unexpectedly a gale seems to be setting in. From the way it is building, slowly and steadily, without gusting winds or sudden heavy rain, I figure it is a large warm front, which makes it less of a worry. Although there is a good chance it will keep strengthening for the rest of the day, it is likely to keep building in this predictable manner. I'd be more concerned if it looked like a gusty cold front was setting in. Looking at my chart it's about eight miles down the unsheltered coast to the mouth of the harbour. The shore I am following is actually a peninsula and the entrance to Hot Springs Cove lies just around the point at the end, in another long narrow inlet. To my left is a line of jagged cliffs and the occasional reef close to shore, but the sea bottom here drops suddenly and there are only a few very unprotected gravel beaches.

Landing in this gale is not really an option anywhere. My only two choices are to push forward toward the mouth of the harbour and the open sea or retreat.

For a moment I ask myself if I should turn back. It would be an easy matter to wait out the gale at the beach I just passed. It might take a few hours, or all day. But for now conditions don't seem that bad, and a day in camp waiting out this gale sounds like no fun at all. Thinking mainly of the hot springs that await me, I make a quick decision to push on as long as progress is possible. If it gets too much I can always turn back and run with the wind and waves behind me back into the safety of the harbour.

For a while I make good progress, and I keep myself about a half-mile offshore to avoid the rebounding waves. Despite the headwind and the increasing swell and chop coming in from the open ocean directly ahead, I can see I'm making progress as the shoreline slips by at a steady rate. But as the storm worsens, the visibility drops and I'm forced to run closer along the shore just to keep it in sight. As I paddle I keep watching the beaches for possible landing sites, but in the heavy swell the line of reefs and rocks along shore make them all look exceptionally unsavoury. On the chart it looks possible to land at one small cove marked as an Indian Reserve, but it already looks too dangerous to approach close enough to check.

Despite the conditions I feel fairly calm. Somewhere along the way on this trip, these sorts of conditions, which once scared me enough to send me running with my tail between my legs, have now become comfortably within my limits. There is none of the anxiety I once felt at the beginning of this trip.

Then up ahead I hear a motor, and within a few seconds a small boat appears out of the wall of mist and rain, almost surfing down the swell into the harbour. Under the small canopy I can see four faces disappearing with all but the top of the boat in the troughs between the waves. Their wide eyes betray their surprise to see a lone kayaker out in this gale. I am just as surprised to see them. I would not head on this water in such an unseaworthy boat. I unlock my grip from the paddle long enough to given them my best attempt at a casual wave. From the backseat a man with a big smile waves back. I presume they are heading to the reserve at Hesquiat. There is nowhere else out here to go.

As I near the mouth of the harbour the swells continue to build. The troughs of the waves are now as long as my boat. It obvious too that the tide is falling, actually running out against the storm. This makes the waves steeper as I near the shallow banks at the mouth of the harbour. My boat starts smashing down as I crest the top of each wave, and I'm nearly able to surf down their backsides into the deepening troughs. I have to devote so much attention to reading the water ahead that keeping track of my position on the chart has become a nearly impossible task. Soon enough I tell myself I'll be at the point and then it will just be a short but tough paddle round into the shelter of the Hot Springs Cove.

But in typical warm front style, the gale steadily worsens, approaching storm conditions. In the driving rain I push on for another hour, stopping only once for a five-minute break. I have to balance carefully and only long enough to drink some water and swallow a couple granola bars. Then in the distance I hear the droning of a large engine and my eyes search the water for signs of another boat. As the distant hum quickly becomes a load buzz almost dead ahead, a constriction grips my chest. If it's a high-speed zodiac, the kind the whale watchers and the coast guard use, running under radar, my little kayak would be totally invisible on their screen. In the deep troughs of these waves, it would be easy for a fast boat to be on top of me before either of us knew what was happening. I can feel my grip aching on the paddle shaft as my eyes desperately scan the water ahead.

Then a hundred feet up, almost directly above my head, a floatplane pops out of the mist. It is flying about hundred feet above the water, under the clouds and lower than the tops of the trees along the shore. It buzzes past in an instant and I soon hear it circle at Hesquiat, abort it's landing and turn back round behind me. A couple minutes later as it passes overhead again, the pilot tips his wings and I can see his face looking right down at me. Bloody idiots flying in this weather, I say to myself, before realizing the hypocrisy of the accusation.

After another hour of hard paddling, and watching my progress slow to a crawl, the coastline has become severe and barren, but far in the distance it ends. This means I'm approaching the mouth of the harbour. I know that the conditions going round the point will be even worse than along this shore because of the heavy currents coming out of Sydney Inlet on the far side of Hot Springs Peninsula. I'm not looking forward to this.

But on my chart there is a possible second option, a passage that runs into Hot Springs Cove like a secret backdoor. An arrow-straight tectonic fissure cuts directly through the tip of the peninsula. In fact the point ahead is actually a small island, cut off from the main peninsula by this shallow tidal channel that cleaves the rock.

From my cockpit I search the shoreline for the narrow entrance, and at first I think I see it between some rocks ahead. But when I approach I can see that it is nothing more than a dangerous dead end. I point my bow straight into the wind and the waves and rest my paddle as I closely examine my chart. It's a nervy exercise in balance. As soon as I look down at the chart I lose the horizon and my balance is thrown off. But after a series of quick glances up and down, I manage to read enough to see that the passage actually is further ahead. The questions remain: will I be able to see my way through the boomers, and will the tide be high enough to paddle right through?

Finally the real passage appears on my left. According to the chart it should be a perfect straight shot through. But now that I can see the entrance, my heart sinks. It is guarded by what kayakers call a rock garden, a collection of house-sized rocks and hidden boomers. The huge swell running through is sending waves smashing off the sharp rocks in all directions, pushing water about the entrance into a huge pillow of white foam. Exhausted from three hours of hard paddling, and not wanting to confront what could be worst conditions around the point, I sit at the entrance, trying to make sense of the churning mess.

At first, just the idea of entering the channel seems foolhardy. The white foam is pure chaos and even a hundred yard off my tiny boat is pushed around like a little stick in the rebounding waves. Heavily loaded, my manuverability in this sort of situation is pretty poor. But the longer I sit there just watching, the more order I begin to see in the swirling chaos. Predictable patterns of how the waves wash off the rocks start to reveal themselves to my eyes. Tentatively I begin negotiating my way forward, closing the distance to the first rock. Looking down the passage now, I can see for much of its length it's not much wider than the length of my boat.

I keep slowly edging forward, getting more cocky and confident as I close the distance. Just the challenge of trying keeps drawing me in. Now I am between the first of the rocks that guard the entrance and my kayak is washing back and forth in the surge of each wave. With each surge of swell, my little boat lifts up and down, forward and back in a roundabout ride over which I have almost no control. But it's predictable. As I look ahead I think I can see how the sets work. From here it is just fifty yards to the narrow slot that guards the entrance to the calm water in the sheltered passage behind. I'm just not sure if I can make it in through the maelstrom in between.

After five minutes of playing chicken with my own nerves, I convince myself I've got the timing of the surge patterns figured out. I watch the waves sets roll in behind me, and just after one final big one, I pull the last of my energy from my body and dig in for a final sprint. It's the hardest fifty yards of the trip, but I've never felt more confident in my kayak. I pull hard and a few seconds later I finally pass into the sanctuary of the lagoon, I can't feel anything but the adrenaline my body has emptied into my veins.

35. Hot Springs Cove

In the shelter of the trees that flank the narrow shallow channel, the water is dead still and clear. I pull my boat out on a small beach, stretch my cramped legs and eat a cold lunch standing in the rain. This is actually my return home I realize. Earlier this summer on the trip with Graham and Lori up to Hot Springs we had paddled up to this end of the channel to look out at the sea beyond. It had been a similar sort of day and none of us had any interest in heading out into the sort of conditions that I have just left behind. At the time, that was also the farthest north I had ever paddled on the coast.

Now on this southbound journey I have finally returned to Clayoquot Sound. The exploration has ended. From here on, my trip would be one of returning, rather than discovery and I welcome the change. This is the point where what I know meets what I have learned. From here south to Tofino I'll be in waters I consider some sort of home.

***

Father Brabant remained at the Hesquiat mission until he retired in 1908 to Victoria, where he died four years later. His replacement,

Father Moser was nowhere near his equal in determination. Within a few years Moser abandoned the mission at Hesquiat to live at the Christie school near Tofino. Soon after church's influence at Hesquiat began to decline. Two more priests tried and failed to maintain the Mission of the Sacred Heart, but never again would the village people be under Catholic control. By 1920 Moser was no longer even welcome at Hesquiat when he came past to call.

Then in 1922 school attendance was made compulsory for native children by the federal government. It was the result of the white government's belief that the only way to properly destroy native culture was to bring the children under total church and state control. The residential school system was designed as the next solution to the Indian resistance to assimilation. Their official mandate from the federal government was described by one bureaucrat as: "To obtain entire possession of all Indian children after they attain the age of seven or eight and keep them at schools."[86]

The various churches in the province divided up the country in little fiefdoms and began an indoctrination program to halt the generational transmission of native culture from parent to child. The Catholics had the west coast from Tofino north to the Brooks Peninsula, while the Anglicans had Fort Rupert and the rest of the Kwakiutl territory. To the south the Protestants had from Barkley Sound right to Victoria, including a very large school at Port Alberni.

But the church no longer had much influence in the outer villages making enforcing the new laws a difficult problem. Since Father Moser was no longer welcome, the local police began accompanying him on patrols to the coastal villages. Together, the representatives of the church and the state threatened native parents that unless their children came to board at the school from the age of seven until the age of fifteen, they would be forcibly removed, and in many cases adopted out, never to return. In all

---

[86] Stolen from our embrace, unattributed, p 50.

roughly 5,000 Nuu-chah-nulth children, about a third of the school age population, were taken from the reserves to be re-educated and assimilated into white society at the schools. While most ended up at one of the three schools in the immediate area, some Nuu-chah-nulth children were sent to all of the eight schools spread throughout B.C.

The primary purpose of the schools was assimilation, not education. Discipline, religion and manual labour were the corner stones of the institutions. When children arrived at the school, which were generally large, imposing intuitional buildings unlike any they had lived in before, a program to wipe all connections to their culture began. The first day the children were stripped naked by the nuns and priests. Heads were shaven and all their clothes and possessions were confiscated. Even new leather shoes and wool 'oxford' suits, which many of the fishermen could afford for their children, were confiscated, never to be seen again. In their place each child was issued heavy canvas pants and shirts. Across the front was a large number in black that, along with their new Christian name, would be the starting point of their new identity. Everything was done to sever the children's connection to their families and their culture, while replacing it with what the missionaries and the federal agents believed to be a superior culture.

Native languages, the mother tongue of the children and in most cases the only language they spoke, was either severally discouraged or banned outright in the schools, as was simply talking to brothers, sisters or close relatives. Family ties were a particular thorn in the side for the program and the priests and nuns did everything they could to break the will of the young children as soon as they arrived. They enforced order with strapping, often across the students' bare backsides in front of classmates to ensure proper humiliation. Often punishments were administered indiscriminately to entire classes. Constant mental and sexual humiliation in the classroom was almost the norm. In one case

Nuns punished girls by having them stand at the front of the class with their skirts raised to expose their genitals. Having the students drop their pants and forcing the rest of the class to slap their bare backsides was another common punishment designed to inflict maximum humiliation. The determination of the missionaries to break the back of the native culture knew few limits.

Meanwhile contact with outside family was limited to summer visits for the rest of their childhood, except in the rare circumstance when both parent and child could read and write well enough to communicate by mail. The restrictions to speaking English only and limited contact ensured that as the children grew older they would find it more and more difficult to communicate with their own people, particularly the elders of the village who were the storage vaults of traditional knowledge. The process of cultural shaming also sought to ensure that the students would express no interest in traditional native ways.

At night the students were housed in dormitories, up to 25 to a room. The windows were barred or had heavy screens and often the doors were locked from the outside at night by the priests. The diet was strictly non-native foods and lacking in nutrition - mushy porridge for breakfast six days a week, and domestic meats at the dinners. Native foods such as smoked salmon were prevented from reaching the kids when they arrived in care packages. During the 1950s at the school in Port Alberni, the rations were so poor that scurvy broke out amongst the students and the board of health had to intervene. Suspicions were raised that their proper rations were actually being diverted by the principle to feed his prized purebred bulls.

During the normal day the students spent a few hours in class every morning and spent the rest of the day doing manual labour to support the mission. The boys gardened or took care of livestock, while girls worked in the kitchen or washed laundry. For those who were able to adapt, and not attract the unnecessary attention of the nuns and priests, the experience was a survivable one. Despite the odds against it, some did learn to read and write, but most 'graduated' at the age of 15 with little more that the crudest of educations. Even if they did well though, successful students were prevented from continuing on past the age of fifteen in the early years of the program. It wasn't considered appropriate for an Indian to learn too much or go further in school.

For many others though, those unwilling to bend to the church's control, the residential school experience was one of pure terror. The priests were unrestrained in their use of physical, mental, emotional and sexual abuse to control and brainwash the children. Few students escaped having their normal social development scarred by the experience. Many children fled the harsh discipline enforced at the school, escaping by canoes to paddle back to their homes. Once the police tracked them down, they would be returned to the priests, who beat them, shaved their heads, and locked them up in the school 'jail' on restricted rations. One priest at the Port Alberni residential school used to take repeated offenders to the barn basement, tie them to a bull ring, and whip the bare backs of the boys until they bled. Stories still circulate in the community of how other students were brought in to mop up the blood from the floor and the walls afterward, an action designed to spread further fear amongst the classes. The principal whipped one Comox boy so savagely that his eventual fate is still remembered and discussed today. The body was later found dead, just off the property. The priests blamed the death on the boy's attempt to escape. No one was ever charged, but there are many who still finger the priest.

In the 1992, a study organized by the Nuu-chah-nulth Tribal Council prompted a flood of stories about the abuse. And so the people of the West Coast came to have a new ugly set of oral histories. In many cases the stories are brutal, filled with anger and despair. One former student, Danny Watts, described how he was lured by a priest into a room to be raped:

"Of course he began by praying to the Lord. Then he proceeded to take my pants off, and then his own pants and he would have an erection and he'd lay behind me. And simulate sex, and have a climax. It was bad enough that this man was doing this to an eleven-year-old boy. What made it worse was he used to make me kneel and ask for forgiveness. We'd do this bullshit about, oh lord we've sinned, and please forgive us. What did I do? I was just a young boy being manipulated by this old man."

"You always had to be careful. On a Sunday afternoon, you stayed as far away from the buildings as possible, so that you wouldn't be picked for this. I would clean the inside of that pigpen to such a state that I would sit inside of it and just sort of contemplate. Then I wouldn't have to be part of what was going on at the school. [It was] violence to your soul to have this Christianity shit pushed down your throat day in and day out, to have to pray before you eat and pray before you go to bed. And pray after some guy is trying to shove his prick up your ass." [87]

The priest was Arthur Plint, who soon became the West Coast's most notorious pedophile. At his trial, Judge John Hogarth stated, "As far as the victims of the accused in the matter are concerned the Indian Residential School system was nothing but a form of institutionalized pedophilia and the accused, as far as they are concerned, being children at the time, was a sexual terrorist."[88] Many of his victims, probably the full number will never be known, committed suicide, some shortly after the trial. Plint was sentenced to merely eleven years in jail. The United Church battled lawsuits for cash settlements in court. Danny Watts went on to become one of the leading Indian rights activist to ever emerge amongst the Nuu-chah-nulth. From the 1960's onward he has

---

[87] Indian Residential Schools – the Nuu-chah-nulth experience.
[88] Indian Residential Schools – the Nuu-chah-nulth experience.

played a leading role in land claims negotiations and provincial aboriginal politics.

Girls under the care of nuns did not escape abuse. By the time Emily Rice left the Kuper Island residential school off Vancouver Island's east coast, commonly referred to as Alcatraz by the 'inmates', she had been raped by three priests and one nun. On one occasion when Rice resisted Sister Margaret Mary's advances, "She took a big stick with bark on it, rammed it inside my vagina. She told me to say I'd fallen on the stick and that she was just trying to get it out." Rice crawled into the infirmary the next day and told the lie, under fear of more abuse. But it was no use. As soon as she returned to the dorm a few days latter, the nun returned and it continued. Later in life Rice twice underwent reconstructive surgery of her vagina and suffered permanent hearing loss from the attacks."[89] Stories like these are common amongst survivors of the schools.

Finally in 1973, after widespread protests the government realized that the missionaries needed to be brought under some control. The Indian Residential school system was dismantled and native children were brought into the public school system. Primary schools were set up on the villages and the system of forced removal was dropped, as was all religious control. But today high schools remained largely in white communities, requiring many native children to move away from home if they want to finish school. Native graduation rates remained desperately low, while suicide rates continued to climb.

While the worst levels of church and state control are now in the past, back on the reserves the communities still had the legacy of abuse to deal with. After the last generation of native kids was returned home from the residential schools, like the previous five generations, they were angry, abused strangers, without experience in normal sexual relations, parenting, or even peaceful social relations. As aliens in their own community, strangers in their own

[89] Stolen from our embrace, p 49.

families' houses, the one-time victims now turned on their own communities. By 1995, the rate of incarceration for aboriginals was four times higher than that for non-aboriginals. One third of aboriginal men in jail were in for violent sexual assault.

Then in early 1990s white society began to recognize that they had some responsibility to bear. Pressure from aboriginal groups forced the investigation into the abuse at the mission schools. Around the province several abusers, like Plint, went on trial. A healing movement built on the native tradition of oral sharing began to grow, helping the communities to deal with the churches' legacy. The Catholic Church turned the former Christie school site into a drug and alcohol treatment centre for native families, but the federal government still refused to take any responsibility for any of its policies. If genocide is defined as a deliberate attempt to destroy a race or a culture, both church and state still have a lot to answer for.

***

Down the channel and out into the familiar waters of Hot Springs Cove, I let the wind, now at my back, push me toward the government wharf. On the western shore is the small native village also called Hot Springs, made up of roughly twenty houses. All are nearly identical two-storey government issue reserve houses, the sort you would see from here to Newfoundland. They sit clustered on the small slope, an aberrant patch of civilization chain-sawed out of the woods. There is no obvious midden here, or even a nice beach to land a canoe. Instead there are couple of wharves and a floating fuel dock for fishing boats. Almost directly across the inlet on the opposite shore is the smaller government wharf. A few zodiac whale-watching boats with their long red pontoons, are tied up, along with some fishing boats. Nearby is a big old wooden boat with classic west coast lines, now converted into a floating hotel.

It's strange to be in such a busy spot. I feel a bit excited about seeing other people, but at the same time I don't really want to chat. This trip has wrung out my brain, particularly the paddle I just finished. I don't feel at ease yet discussing with strangers what I've been through. Something has shifted inside me since I was last here, like a realignment of my own tectonic plates. While it was a simple thing that I wanted to do – to confront the limits of my abilities entirely on my own – I have yet to make sense of what success means. Parts of who I am are disconnected, and I have not had time to put myself back together as one. I feel stopped in time, liminal, inchoate, and fragile in this state.

I slip between the tall pilings of the government wharf, and land my kayak on the rocky beach. Despite all the boats, there is no one around. The hot springs are a popular destination for kayakers and for once I am very thankful I am not going to attract any more attention. I get out to stretch my legs, pull my boat on the shore and tie it to a tree, and set off down the familiar trail to find a campsite.

As I stroll through the tiny campsite, it's hard not to feel cramped, knowing so many people will be now sharing my space. I'm not happy with the idea of pitching my tent next to half a dozen others. Once I pick a site I walk back to my boat, and paddle it down to a closer landing site and start hauling up my gear. An hour later I've pitched my tent, carefully positioning the tarp over it to keep off the rain.

I try to make a second lunch, this time a hot one, in the open air cooking shelter but all I've got left in my food bags are just the most unappetizing dregs of three weeks of rations – stale bannock, peanut butter, jam, and a few stray nuts. Fortunately there is a little café just at the end of the pier, so I make my way over for a coffee and sandwich. All the comforts of civilization don't come without a price though. For only the second night on the trip, I'll have to pay a camp fee, but I don't begrudge it. After lunch, which is late enough in the day to be early diner I drop my campsite fee into the drop box and head down the boardwalk to the hot springs for a soak.

After two and half weeks of paddling in the rain and sleeping on the ground, it is easy for the afternoon to slip by soaking in the springs. When the sun starts to set it seems a pity to leave so soon, so I stay on longer. In the end I don't leave the hot springs until well after dark. Once again I have neglected to bring a flashlight. After so much attentiveness and sustained effort to reach here safely, it seems something is throwing me off balance. For the second time this summer I have to stumble back along a mile of rough boardwalk in the dark. Once again I'm lucky to make it back with stumbling off the boardwalk into the forest.

Back at the campsite a light rain is falling and the cooking shelter at the campsite is crowded with the half dozen other campers who I earlier saw at the springs. Some young German and Swiss travellers have formed an impromptu collective and are cooking up a potluck dinner on their camp stoves. They have come to Tofino for the whales and the kayaking and the rainforest and have caught the Hot Springs band water taxi, the *Spirit of Matlahaw* up here to camp for a night.

There is also a couple from Toronto who have kayaked up. He's a journalist like me, writing and photographing an adventure story about his paddle up from Tofino for the travel section of the big city's newspaper. Wasn't it just amazing to be so far from everything, he asks me as he shows me his blisters? I nod in agreement. After a scrounge through my food bags, I ask if he has any recipe ideas for peanut butter, rice and cabbage, but he claims to only know how to reheat freeze-dried camp food.

While I had never lived here for more than six months at time, somehow my summers of guiding here have left me with a sense that this will always be some sort of home for me. It's a sense of knowing that seems to spring from my connection to the land and my intimacy with it. It's a feeling I have yet to have in my new home in Sydney

Mike Laanela

36. Tofino bound

The next morning I'm up early to head up the trail to the springs to soak. It's only a little past six when I slip into the empty pools. Everyone else seems to be on nine-to-five time, I muse. Not much in the world has changed since I've been away. I have the springs all to myself for a few hours, until the first boatload of tourists arrives just after nine. Back at the campsite I have a long chat with the talkative wharfinger who collects the fees. He's an older guy named Dave. He tells me a fellow named Bernard runs a sort of restaurant out of his house on the reserve. I've heard of it before but never been, so early in the afternoon I paddle across in my kayak.

The reserve is unlike any other on the coast. Stuck on a hillside, rather than stretched along a beach, two rough gravel roads form a terrace pattern with the houses. This was actually once in Ahousaht territory, but in the 1920's the Hesquiat band migrated here as the men began to acquire fishing boats.

Bernard's house is supposed to be easy to find in the small village but I soon lose my way. As I wander along one of the streets I spot a small store on the ground floor of one of the houses. Video rentals, junk food and small selection of groceries are packed tight on the shelves. I grab a few things and take them to the till. A heavy-set Caucasian man is sitting on a stool behind the counter.

"Kayaking?" he says, looking at my cloths.

"Yeah, nice to finally get to the hot springs,"

"Up from Tofino?"

"No, down Quatsino. Seventeen days."

"On your own?"

"Yeah."

We chat for a while longer about my trip. I ask him about the reserve and how he came to live here. He tells me he married a local woman. They have kids now. I wonder how the winters would be here when the storms regularly prevent all but the sturdiest of boats from heading out. He says its tough on the kids, they get bored, get into trouble, or just veg out. Too many end up smoking pot and playing video games all day. Anybody's kid would. Summertime is good though, they can get outside if they want to, and there are outdoor recreation programs like Rediscovery that take them kayaking and camping to try to put them back in touch with their native heritage. Things are improving, but the challenge of healing faced by the community is so huge it seems almost insurmountable at times. This is the reality of life on remote reserves across much Canada now. A private circle of healing that increasingly looks inward. Native culture is still living through a difficult transformation.

With directions, I am soon able to find Bernard's place, a plain looking two-storey house with a large veranda for outdoor dining. The front door is open and I look inside. A native man and a Caucasian man are sitting on the couch in front of the TV.

"Hey, hi, come in, please," says the man. "I'm Bernard, Welcome."

"I heard you serve salmon burgers," I begin.

"Oh yes, sure we do. Have a seat on the couch. That's Brian there. Introduce yourself. I've got to get back to the kitchen."

I sit down in front of the TV, and Brian switches it off. He's doing survey work on wildlife for a government contractor. He's been staying with Bernard, who also rents rooms, for a few weeks now.

"Yeah the salmon burger are good," he says. He's just finishing his lunch. We talk for a while about the politics of Clayoquot Sound. Since 1984 when the Nuu-chah-nulth Tribal Council declared Meares Island native land, and gained a court injunction to block logging in the island just off Tofino, the politics around here have been highly confrontational. It seems ironic that the island they claimed is named after one of the first Europeans to negotiate to purchase it from them, almost exactly two hundred years later.

After a while Bernard returns with a salmon burger on a plate of fries. The big pink slab of fish dwarfs the Kaiser bun.

"My uncle brought this in the other day," he says of the fish.

***

When I get back to the other side a few hours later, Dave, the wharfinger invites me over for dinner, on the promise that I tell some stories of the paddle down. I consider heading to the hot springs for another soak, but instead I lie down to nap in my tent. I don't have to do anything today, and I have no intention of trying.

I show up at Dave's houseboat promptly at seven in my least stinking clothes. He fixes me straight up with a strong scotch and soda from the mini-fridge. The ice cubes are a particularly nice touch. Dinner is chicken baked in the oven. By midnight I am pissed to the gills. In the darkness and once again without my flashlight I climb over the edge of the boat and walk back up the steps to the pier. It's a clear night, but the round moon has already set and the trail is nearly pitch black as I stagger the length of the wharf and start up the boardwalk to the camp. At the fork in the path, I turn off left toward the campsite, but the boardwalk does not.

Next thing I know I stumble to the ground in the blackness and feel a snap in my ankle. A sharp pain snatches away my breath. Then every foul word I ever learned spills out of my mouth in a muffled scream.

It takes about ten minutes for me to get my head together, which is made all the more difficult by my state of complete inebriation. My right ankle is throbbing. There is no way it will take any weight whatsoever. Crawling down the muddy path to my tent seems like a lousy option so I decide to head back to Dave's, where I know there is ice for my ankle and a spare bunk on the galley. I roll myself up on my good leg and hop back to the railing at the end of the pier. A few minutes later I reach Dave's boat. The lights are out. So I knock on the window. Dave appears on the back deck.

"What the hell?" he says.

"You got any ice left, I twisted my ankle."

***

The next morning when I wake, Dave makes coffee while I unwrap the tensor bandage. My ankle is the size and colour of a Florida grapefruit. It doesn't look like I'll be paddling to Tofino in the next few days. This presents a problem, because my schedule is pretty tight. My flight is booked for the end of the week, and my parents will in town in two days to meet me.

After spending a few hours on Dave's couch drinking coffee, I make the call on his radio to the water taxi over in Hot Springs Village. I'm catching a ride the rest of the way home. I'll really miss the paddle back to Tofino from here, but it is one I've done countless times before. For me now, the real trip ended yesterday when I reached the sanctuary of Hot Springs Cove. With my ankle like it is, loading, launching and carrying my kayak doesn't look like a worthwhile experience. I'm now ready to be at the end of this journey.

Afterward I thank Dave for the help and hop back to my camp to take it down. By three o'clock I managed to hop and paddle all my gear to a pile on the wharf. I open my last can of tuna on the broad planks and spread it across some remnant rye crisps. The sesame seeds have a nice nutty flavour that compliments the fish. I shake the last crumbs from my food bags into the ocean. There is nothing left. Sometime after three, I see the boat pull away from the village wharf and cross the harbour for the government wharf. I stand up and put away a few odd bits of gear. A few minutes later my kayak is lifted onto the roof of the boat. A few straps tie it down. I pass my gear to the young crewman who stacks it on the back deck, then stagger aboard. The captain recognizes me from few weeks before. He greets me as I enter the cabin.

"Another trip" he says.

"Yeah," I say, "Down from Quatsino." I'm getting happier to say it. He says nothing, but arches his eyebrows, then asks about my ankle. He is expecting something more dramatic than what I tell him and chuckles at the end of my embarrassing tale. We talk for a while as he takes the boat out. Once out of the cove he powers up and turns up the inside passage behind the island heading for Tofino. Over his life he has seen changes he tells me. He's lived all his life here, like his father and grandfather and their fathers before. He's seen the wilderness transformed from wild to industrial to tourist playground. The stories of his people are the oldest of all the stories here.

At the northern end of the channel I point to some bluffs, a cliff face about a mile away. I ask him about the painted outline of a Thunderbird about the size of a man, in the middle of the sheer rock face. We can't see it from here.

He looks at me, surprised. "Not many people even know that's there," he says. He looks over in the direction of the bluffs far off to our left for while and asks me how I know about it. I tell him I used to guide kayak trip up here and how I still love the stories that bring the land and sea to life.

"My grandfather used to talk all about that stuff. I wish I'd listened to him more," he says thoughtfully.

Then I remember the ring in my bag and my thoughts turn to what awaits me back at my new home. I take my hat off and look at the heron feather still tucked in the seam. It's now battered and bent. Our journey on the sea is behind us now. Pulling it carefully from the seam, I walk to the back of the boat and drop it into the sea that is rushing away from me.

I say goodbye to my coast. This is its story I have told.

Bibliography

The Adventures and Suffering of John Jewitt, captive of Chief Maquinna, Jewitt, Annotated and illustrated by Hilary Stewart, Douglas and McIntyre, Vancouver 1997.

Apostle of Alaska, Life of the Most Reverend Charles John Seghers, a Translation of Maurice De Baets' "Vie de Monsiegneur Seghers", By Sister Mary Mildred, S.S.A., 1943, St Anthony Guild Press.

Charles John Seghers, Priest and Bishop in the Pacific Northwest, 1839-1886: A Biography, by Gerard G. Steckler, S.J., Thomas Aquinas Collage, Santa Paula, California

Almost a Hero, the Voyages of John Meares, R.N., to China, Hawaii and the Northwest Coast, by J Richard Nokes, Washington State University Press, 1998.

Islands of Truth, the Imperial Fashioning of Vancouver Island, By Daniel W Clayton, UBC Press, Vancouver, 2000

The Journals of Captain Cook, Prepared from the original manuscripts by J.C. Beaglehole for the Hakluyt Society, 1955-67, Selected and Edited by Philip Edwards, Penguin Classics, 1999.

West Coast Marine Hazards Manual – a guide to local forecasts and conditions, Environment Canada.

The Indian History of British Columbia – The impact of the White Man, Wilson Duff (1997), Royal Museum of British Columbia.

First Approaches to the Northwest Coast, Derek Pethick (1976) Douglas and McIntyre Ltd.

Vancouver Islands West Coast 1762-1962, George Nicholson, Self-published (seventh printing) 1965.

The Nootka Connection – Europe and the Northwest Coast 1790-1795, Derek Pethick (1980), Douglas and MacIntyre.

Cedar, Hilary Stewart (1984) Douglas and MacIntyre Ltd.

Contact and Conflict – Indian-European Relations in British Columbia, 1774-1890, Robin Fisher, 1992.

Captain Cook and the Spanish Explorers on the Coast – Nutka, Ed. B Efrat (1978) Sound Heritage Series.

Mission to Nootka 1874-1900, Father Augustin Brabrant, Edited by Charles Lillard, (1977), Grey Publishing.

The West Coast Nootka People, E. Y. Arima (1983), British Columbia Provincial Museum special publication No.6.

Notocias de Nutka – An account of Nootka Sound in 1792, by Jose Mariano Mozino, translated by Iris Engstand, 1970, Douglas and MacIntyre.

Since the time of the Transformers. Alan D. McMillian, Ed. UBC Press (1999)

Hamatsa – The Enigma of Cannibalism on the Pacific Northwest Coast, Jim McDowell, Rondale Press (1997)

Franz Boas, the early years 1858-1906, Douglas Cole (1999) Douglas and MacIntyre.

Cougar Annie's Garden, Margaret Horsfield (2001), Salal Publishing.

Kwakiutl Ethnography, Franz Boas, Ed Helen Codere, University of Chicago Press (1966).

Captured Heritage – The scramble for NWC Artifacts, Douglas Cole (1985), Douglas and MacIntyre.

The Social Organization and the Secret Societies of the Kwakiutl Indians, Franz Boas, Based on personal observations and notes made by George Hunt, (Reprinted 1970).

Kwakiutl Art – Audrey Hawthorn (1967), Douglas and MacIntyre.

The Yuquot Whalers Shrine. Aldona Jonaitis and Richard Inglis. University of Washington Press. (1999).

The coming of the Spirit of Pestilence – Introduced infectious diseases and population decline among NWC Indians, 1774-1874, Robert t Boyd (1999), UDC Proce

Gunboat Frontier – British Maritime Authority and the Northwest Coast Indians, 1846-1890. Barry M Gough (1984), UBC Press.

Distant Dominion – Barry M Gough (1980), UBC Press.

Kwakwaka'wakw Settlements, 1775-1920 – A Geographical Analysis and Gazetteer. Robert Galois (1993), UBC Press.

Kwakiutl Legends - as told to Pamela Whitaker by Chief James Wallas, (1981) Hancock House.

The Way of the Masks, Claude Levi Strauss, (1979), Douglas and MacIntyre

Brooks Peninsula – An Ice Age Refugium on Vancouver Island, Occasional Paper #5, BC Ministry of Environment, Land and Parks. (1997)

An Iron Hand upon the Land – the law against the Potlatch on the Northwest Coast, Douglas Cole and Ira Chaikin (1990), Douglas and MacIntyre.

Alaskan Voyage 1881-1883 – An expedition to the northwest coast of America, Johan Adrian Jacobson, translated by Erna Gunther (1977), Chicago University Press.

Seeing the Ocean though the trees, A conservation-based development strategy for Clayoquot Sound, Ecotrust Canada, Vancouver, 1997.

Author Mike Laanela has been a sea kayak guide, a treeplanter, photographer and travel writer. He is currently a reporter and editor for CBC News online, based in Vancouver, B.C. This is his first book.

Made in the USA
Las Vegas, NV
09 March 2023

68800619R00239